Laureate of Peace

Shakespearian Studies
also
The Christian Renaissance
Atlantic Crossing
The Burning Oracle
Chariot of Wrath
The Starlit Dome
The Dynasty of Stowe
Hiroshima
Christ and Nietzsche
Lord Byron: Christian Virtues
Byron's Dramatic Prose

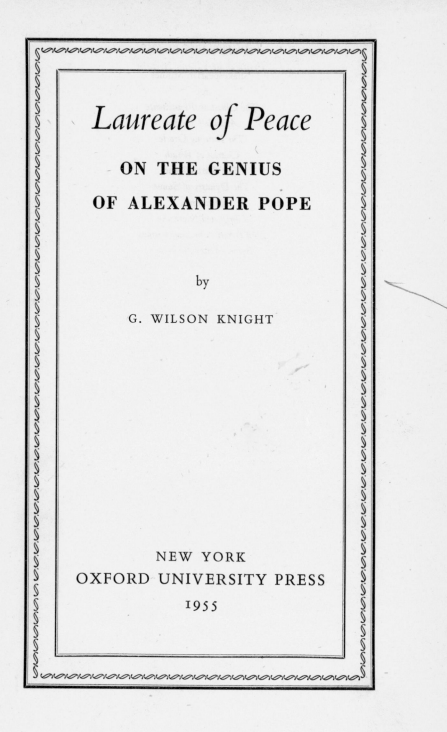

Laureate of Peace

ON THE GENIUS
OF ALEXANDER POPE

by

G. WILSON KNIGHT

NEW YORK
OXFORD UNIVERSITY PRESS
1955

First published in 1955
Printed in Great Britain
by Butler & Tanner Ltd
Frome and London

CONTENTS

48405

PREFACE

ON the presentation of this study—the first, so far as I know, to be devoted to the total contents, as opposed to the style in isolation, of Pope's poetic work—a few preliminary notes may prove helpful.

The book is composed of five sections, all but one of which are new. The opening is in the nature of a general survey intended to make a rough stage-setting for what follows.[1] This is followed by 'The Vital Flame', which appeared first in *The Burning Oracle* in 1939 and has been for long out of print. It has been given a surface revision, mainly a smoothing of syntax, and I have incorporated three or four new quotations, but nothing has been added to the thought. Since its first publication, this essay has helped to reorientate the contemporary understanding of Pope's poetry, particularly (as I note on pp. 48, 51 and 171–2 below with references to Professor Maynard Mack's important and standard edition[2]) in respect to the *Essay on Man*. Such defences are forced on me by the nature of the opposition which my methods of interpretative analysis are still, after twenty-five years, receiving in England. An attempt is made to clarify the issue in my third section, a study of the unjustly neglected *Temple of Fame*, in the course of which I have occasion to discuss the mutually interpretative functions of the arts of space and time in direct relation to my own technique of spatial interpretation.

The fourth section is given to Byron's praise of Pope. Of this I knew nothing when I composed 'The Vital Flame' some sixteen years ago, and, when I came across it during my Byronic studies, I was indeed gratified to find that my own understanding of Pope had been so closely paralleled by Byron. If I was mad in respecting

---

[1] I rather think that my characterizing (on pp. 7–9) of literary periods in terms of certain favoured mechanisms may owe something to a conversation with Professor Lewis Horrox some twenty years ago.

[2] I take this opportunity to pay my tribute to the excellence of the *Twickenham* edition, now nearing completion under the general editorship of John Butt.

Pope's 'message', in which he himself so ardently believed, I was mad in excellent company; and even those who most rigorously oppose my refusal to limit my studies to discussions of biography, sources, technique and the manipulation of language, will, I hope, agree that the triangle made of Pope's reiterated claims, Byron's ringing acceptations, and my own interpretations of both Pope and Byron is, to say the least, a self-consistent and harmonious entity. But to many readers it will, I hope, be rather more than that.

My final section discusses Pope's poetic thought in relation to our own time. It has for long been my practice, both as a university lecturer and as a writer, to insist at every turn that what we call great literature is only great to us in so far as it radiates living meanings, today; and it has always appeared to me both strange and sad that the treatment of literature as rooting backwards into sources and causes should in every age be academically honourable, while any attempt to establish contact with its forward pointings is considered the preserve only of amateurs and cranks. This contact can be greatly assisted by stage-production, or public reading: my own understanding of Pope was first awakened by listening to Professor D. Nichol Smith's reading of certain passages, during his lectures, at Oxford, in 1922.

Great poetry speaks to us with a living voice. When in the summer of 1950 my brother and I wanted words for a bronze tablet to be placed by a memorial tree to our mother in the Garden of Remembrance at Lawnswood, our choice fell on a couplet from the *Essay on Man*:

> *Safe in the hand of one disposing Pow'r,*
> *Or in the natal, or the mortal hour.*

That Pope should have provided the words we wanted is, perhaps, worth the recording; and it may also be worth recording that it seemed, to us at least, natural enough that such a need should be met by words of Pope.

It is a pleasant duty to acknowledge the courtesy of Messrs. John Lane the Bodley Head Ltd. and of Mr. John Cowper Powys in allowing me to use an extended quotation from Mr. Powys' *Rabelais*.

My line references to Pope and Shakespeare follow, respectively, the *Globe* and the *Oxford* texts.

G. W. K.

I

DICTION AND DOCTRINE

I. DICTION AND DOCTRINE

AT the start of the eighteenth century a new way of life was being established in England. The fruits of the Revolution were maturing. Under Queen Anne party politics were getting, if at first rather unsteadily, into their stride, as a safeguard against bloodier methods; new classes were rising rapidly to education, power, and prestige; there was peace and renewal after distraction and unrest. The age of Anne recaptured, in its own fashion, something of that assurance, and more than something of the harmony, of the age of Elizabeth I. Its poet was Pope: 'Be mine the blessings of a peaceful reign.' [1]

Dante, Shakespeare and Pope all reflect a unified and harmonious life-view; but Milton does not. The medieval synthesis assists Dante's creation of a circular system within which, like the figures on Keats' urn, the various turmoils of human existence could be placed. The problems handled by Shakespeare were, if not greater, certainly more involved. Dante used neither epic nor drama; neither physical nor spiritual conflict assumed even a provisional autonomy; all was settled, labelled, and in its place, and action at a discount. At a period of balance after civil turmoil and national victory, Shakespeare's work shows a subtle interplay of militaristic and spiritual conflict; the main emphasis falling on the spiritual, at most, except for *Henry V*, on civic or civil, conflict; and the expression is accordingly drama. There is not the controlling serenity of Dante, and yet, considering the great forces, medieval and Renaissance, at play, the resulting harmony is remarkable. The triumph is more a triumph of insight into the central stuff of man than a triumph for 'order' or 'tradition', though order and tradition are part of the final synthesis.[2]

[1] *Windsor Forest*, 366.
[2] For a discussion of the dangers to Shakespearian study of any too exclusive a

3

In Shakespeare the individual man's aspiring quest is variously contrasted with, overrules, or is subdued to, concepts and visions of harmony; tempests interweave with music, the music is wrenched out of, one with, the tempests; man himself becomes cosmic.

With Marlowe and Milton, in *Dr. Faustus*, in *Paradise Lost*, humanism is set against religion; the humanism is damned and yet damnation cannot silence its challenge. These works are great as symptoms of a dislocation, but their artistic integrity suffers: their technique is disrupted by the conflict it should resolve. The Elizabethan balance was, at the best, precarious. With the growing multiplication of divergent thought-streams and religious sects, together with the upstarting of dynastic nationalisms, in France pre-eminently, emphasis fell next on heroic action. Milton's great poem, half-epic, half-dramatic, feels the whole cosmos in self-conflict, and, as his iron technique clamps down on a hell of frustrated energies, the result is less harmony than torture; and the unresolved opposition of *Paradise Regained* does little to close the gap.

Cromwell's attempt at a theocracy overleaping the established ordinances of church and state led naturally to a military dictatorship; and that, by revulsion, forced a swerve back to the human; to the King; to the classical values. But, after the Restoration, the court, no less than Cromwell's dictatorship, reflected a part only of the nation. It remained parasitic, the organic relationships of the Shakespearian period being gone. In this hot-house atmosphere we find Dryden with consummate skill trying to make order from chaos.[1] Of innately Chaucerian affinities, he was, in general, a writer of clarity and common sense, and a firm supporter, though with little personal fire, of authority in state and church, leaving as his best record *Absalom and Achitophel*, with its satire on religious zeal and moral of submission to the throne. Dryden tends to put man in his place as firmly as any medievalist, while rating high, as the medievalist did not, the classic virtues, and hankering after heroism. At the Restoration drama had become pure, if sometimes rather impure, entertainment, without any such inward pressures and tensions as

concentration on the 'order' concept, see my 'Prefatory Note', with its 'Chart of Shakespeare's Dramatic Universe', to the 1953 re-issue of *The Shakespearian Tempest*.

[1] Dryden's poetry has been well handled in our time, pre-eminently by Mark van Doren's study (New York, 1920; London, 1931); by T. S. Eliot in his *Selected Essays* (1932); and by Bonamy Dobrée's *Restoration Tragedy* (1929).

you find in Shakespeare, Marlowe or Corneille; and this left Dryden free, without claiming more for man than his due, to *play* at heroics. He, or his audience, were half aware that the heroic ideal was a necessity, that the comprehensive system of Christendom was, in fact, dissolved, and that the Renaissance could not be written off as a blunder. The humanistic values of love and honour held compelling force over the mind, but it was less easy to place their resultant extravagances. Dryden's heroic plays record the attempt to give them a provisional placing in terms of entertainment.[1]

What Dryden lacked was a personal core to his life's work. It has, it is true, a key, in his search for order and authority, but those are mental concepts, and the core of a great poet's work cannot be merely conceptual; it will exist in the realm of symbolism, or reflect some great power of religion or nature; it will not be the product of human reason. Dryden does not attempt the extraordinary assimilations and harmonizations of Shakespeare; he does not plunge into the impossible task which Milton found beyond even his almost superhuman poetic strength; instead, he deploys his rich Chaucerian common sense over a mental world where religion is religion, science science, nature nature, man a creature of entertaining ambitions, and the king on his throne.

Pope's work, though profiting by the general tidying up that stands so firmly to Dryden's credit, has that pulsing heart for lack of which Dryden's remains a little cold; it is a single, organic, whole, as surely as Dante's or Shakespeare's; and it shows a wondrous harmony. How was that done?

First, we can say that it was done by selection. His concentration is focused on man, body and soul, felt in direct, even intimate, relation to nature, society, and the cosmos. With him the medieval is, if not exactly forgotten, certainly not stressed, nor is there any central reliance on Christian myth or dogma. Though himself a catholic by upbringing, his poetry is Christian in spirit rather than in form. His own satiric verse he sees as a 'sacred weapon', directed by 'Heaven', to be handled with reverence, inspired by a 'priestless muse', and opening 'eternity'.[2] Traditional religion is, it is true, nobly handled in

---

[1] And even, perhaps, *humour*. I am thinking of certain striking thoughts advanced by Douglas Jefferson in *The Significance of Dryden's Heroic Plays* in the Proceedings of the Leeds Philosophical Society, 1940, v, iii, 125–39, and *Aspects of Dryden's Imagery, Essays in Criticism*, Jan., 1954.

[2] *Satires, Epilogue*, II, 212–35.

the *Messiah* eclogue and *Eloisa to Abelard*, the last witnessing a profundity of religious feeling, but significantly deriving its extraordinary dramatic power from the opposition of natural impulse and transcendental authority. The *Essay on Man* builds its statement from a mass of pagan and Christian lore permeated throughout by the poet's own psychological and religious sensibilities, with as its heart and hinge a human doctrine of sublimation that forecasts the teaching of *Thus Spake Zarathustra*. We may say that his poetic universe flowers from a soil of classical-Renaissance humanism, though it is a matter rather of imaginative appeal than of learning or scholarship. Greece and Rome were guiding stars to him, and the heroic values are throughout emphatic. But there is no reliance on themes of war or social conflict; he is our only great poet since Shakespeare who has not left us a drama. His poetic universe is, moreover, peopled by delicate spirits and angelic hierarchies. More, it offers, as we shall see (pp. 46, 71-6, 179-80), a religious insight attuned to that of the Gospels and finally sharpened into a militant ethic recalling St. Paul; so that there is, as it were, *a New Testament structure about his life's work, as a whole* (p. 156 below). He is a poet of peace; his stage is mainly destitute of action, and epic themes, except for his translation of Homer, are only present through the medium of humour or burlesque. And yet, somehow, the heroic, the Renaissance, values are not only preserved, but emphatic; and in this successful marriage of New Testament and Renaissance lies the extraordinary importance of the accomplishment of his poetry and the secret of its unique composure.

Whether or not he can be called a 'deist' depends on our understanding of the term. If to write:

> Safe in the hand of one disposing Pow'r,
> Or in the natal, or the mortal hour,
>
> (*Essay on Man*, I, 287)

is to be a deist, the term can pass; otherwise, it cannot.[1] From the heterogeneous mass of philosophies and theologies that leave the seventeenth century an unweeded garden of riotous growth, he selects, prunes, and fertilizes. But it is a creative selection; he has felt the deep necessities, the real lines of force, and labours to give them

---

[1] I am thinking of the poetry. Writing from the more biographical standpoint, Bonamy Dobrée says: 'He was, in fact, as near as does not matter, a Deist' (*Alexander Pope*, 1951, II, 29).

encouragement and discipline. The vast field of speculation is narrowed down, as with heat-rays through a lens, to one burning spot. Therefore, though various philosophers, including St. Paul, may be contributory, he claims to be dominated by none;[1] he is neither in any *limited* sense Christian, nor is he anti-Christian; neither properly Whig nor Tory; he is as happy discussing philosophy with Bolingbroke as in visiting Cobham's patriots at Stowe. No labels apply, and yet his work is simple, lucid and coherent. In Pope, as in Shakespeare, what is best and most significant in his age, not in its thought merely, but in its life, becomes incandescent. But he is not, any more than Shakespeare, to be interpreted in the light of his—or any other —age; he is himself the light. He speaks for his age not only as a poet, but as a prophet; he makes his age, the little community of Augustan England, or London, prophetic; and prophetic not only for England, but for the world.

Pope's statement may be glancingly illuminated by a brief reference to various shifting figures of the poetic imagination. The characterizing medium of medieval literature was allegory, in which persons, animals or flowers were made to express something other, with little rights on their own; or, if they had such rights, as in Chaucer's maturity, they existed on the plane of simple realism, where things are just what they claim to be and no more, the art of the novel foreshadowed. In allegory a surface is deliberately arranged for us to see through it to a more important reality: nature may be slighted, and its laws neglected.[2] In Dante's *Divina Commedia* the human drama is ordered according to a scheme, and subordinated, with or without allegory, to meaning more important than the persons. In Shakespeare man has more rights and is, as in Pope, central, though hierarchies of natural, cosmic, and divine significance are included. A vast mass of lore, belief and observation is, far more tightly than in Spenser, crammed together, and the cramming itself witnesses to a realization of nature, man and the divine as a 'knot intrinsicate'. The separate elements are not used merely to reflect, or in any way serve, each other, nor for comparison alone; they are all but identified. At the limit, we have the human story, as in *King Lear*, becoming a universal contest; man, as in *Antony and Cleopatra*, is divinely transfigured and given, at a high moment, cosmic stature;

---

[1] *Horace, Ep.* I, i, 23–34.
[2] These remarks are necessarily constricted. Anyone anxious for an exact understanding of medieval allegory will turn to C. S. Lewis' *The Allegory of Love* (1936).

and his final victory becomes in *Pericles* 'the music of the spheres'. The poetry is always asserting identities, and its characteristic medium is accordingly metaphor.

Shakespeare's language is often as far from commonsense as James Joyce's. To a rational inspection it may seem to be telling a great truth, perhaps the greatest of all truths, in terms of a myriad lies. Its molten breaking down of all cultural distinctions, with nevertheless a supervening organic cohesion and a reference at every point to human affairs, is probably more mysterious than one normally supposes. It could only have happened then, and in that place; when language was in the melting-pot and where two ages met, under Elizabeth and James, in England.

Naturally enough, the contributing elements flew apart; and next we have the *striving* for the unity, as in the epic of Milton, with its titanic actions and iron will towards a synthesis never properly captured. And if we want a characterizing device, we may point to Milton's use of extended and arbitrary simile. He is, however, half in Shakespeare's world, since he develops his similes so far from their purpose that they become poems on their own, the little asides holding, for a while, as much right as the action they are supposed to serve. They are not, strictly speaking, similes at all, since the quality of likeness is not really of their essence, nor germane to the artistic purpose, which might be called atmospheric rather than elucidatory. They are really too good for what they claim to be doing, and we may be left with a grand sense of disjunction. For a more perfect use of simile as such, we must go to Dryden. We have observed how, in his task of ordering what had become an indeterminate and heterogeneous mass of thoughts and values, Dryden included pretty nearly everything whilst deeply impregnating with belief very little, if any, of it. He keeps things firmly distinguished. He can use allegory for his purpose and turn a Shakespearian metaphor; there is little he cannot do; but his finest skill is seen in his similes. His use is rational and practical. Inspect any of the similes in *All for Love* and you will find that they are far more obviously helpful than Shakespeare's clustering impressions or the Miltonic elaboration: they really do illustrate and illuminate, fitting like a glove. Their exquisite suitability derives from Dryden's critical sense of things as, normally, unlike: he has selected them with care. In Shakespeare and Milton comparisons complicate; they disturb and distend our understanding, jerk us into new modes of experience. With Dryden, they simplify and clarify,

8

and, their work done, can be forgotten: there are no metaphysical implications. As for the famous 'conceits' of the 'metaphysicals' themselves, these appear somehow to be enjoying all the problems raised by both types of simile, whilst playing one off against the other.

And what, now, of Pope? He certainly builds on the good work of Dryden in simplifying what was in danger of overcomplication; he shares his respect for order and precision, and follows him in use of the couplet. But his field is at once less wide and more intense. He controls an, at first sight, anyway, smaller world, and yet one which reveals depth on depth of meaning. His focal centre is man; not man dramatically interlocked with a great mesh of natural and cosmic energies, as in Shakespeare; nor man and his universe torn by the 'mighty opposites' of conscience and culture, as in Milton; nor man viewed variously according to the subject, political, religious or literary, as in Dryden; but Man who in himself must achieve the synthesis or harmonization which religious and political schemes are always claiming to achieve for him, and with no great warlike or other action to assist his self-escape. Pope does not at first appear to survey all the intellectual and emotional ground covered by those others, but he covers exactly as much of it as is proper for man's task, as he saw it, of personal, civic, and religious regeneration. All the rest may, indeed, be supposed to be included, housed, in man; in individual men and women, as persons and personalities, felt as a number of most vital entities, or wholes; though these, with the society which it is their business to compose, are also felt in closest contact with those other natural and religious hierarchies which make that greater whole, the universe. Now since for all practical purposes, and Pope is very practical, the proper place for the realities shadowed by religion and philosophy is to be felt primarily within the human personality, the characterizing literary medium is, naturally enough, 'personification'.

We must avoid, for our immediate purpose, any too rigid understanding of the term. Its most obvious connotation suggests that kind of personifying of human qualities we find in the Olympian deities of Greece and Rome; and we may recall not only the great powers of ancient myth exerted on the poetry of the Augustans, but also how the noblemen of Pope's day like Lord Cobham at Stowe, whose seat Pope celebrated in one of his *Moral Essays*, loved to fill their halls and grounds with classic statuary and temples. Though they never with him became so heavy as they did later in the poetry of Gray and Collins, Pope's earlier work is sprinkled with what might be called the literary derivatives of classical mythology; that is, abstract or spiritual qualities felt as personal entities, as in

> *Black Melancholy sits, and round her throws*
> *A death-like silence, and a dead repose.*
>
> (*Eloisa to Abelard*, 165)

From this we may pass to a general use of capitalized abstract words that assume a protagonist importance, even though there be little personifying, as such:

> *All Nature is but Art, unknown to thee;*
> *All Chance, Direction which thou canst not see . . .*
>
> (*Essay on Man*, I, 289)

We meet a number of lesser abstractions, neatly used, which house emotions and values of age-old, often classic,[1] lineage, with sometimes a direct pointing to the ancients as exemplars of heroism and virtue. The valuation is, however, enlightened by a distinction of true from false heroisms that may be said to flower from Christian teaching. In *The Temple of Fame*, a poem packed with persons of classic renown, imperial war-makers get no praise:

> *'Ambitious fools!' (the Queen reply'd, and frown'd)*
> *'Be all your acts in dark oblivion drown'd;*
> *There sleep forgot, with mighty tyrants gone,*
> *Your statues moulder'd, and your names unknown!'*
> *A sudden cloud straight snatch'd them from my sight,*
> *And each majestic phantom sunk in night.*
>
> (350)

Pope's ease of statement derives in part from his reliance on a variety of acknowledged acceptances.[2] Fame is personified to correspond to a value Pope and his readers recognize as of high worth; 'frown'd' gathers force from a general respect to figures of authority; the threat of 'oblivion' subscribes to 'fame' as a central good; 'tyrants' avoids a difficult distinction by use of a label weighed in the balances and not

---

[1] For an account of the classical and Renaissance hinterland of Pope's diction see Geoffrey Tillotson, *On the Poetry of Pope* (1938), 'Language'.

[2] The general or communal qualities of eighteenth-century diction are discussed in J. R. Sutherland's *A Preface to Eighteenth Century Poetry* (1948).

found wanting throughout centuries of use; and 'statues' itself witnesses to the agreed desirability of having a statue, if at all possible. The statement's general valuation is easy enough to accept; but observe how the points made against false heroism are made in heroic, not in religious or even semi-religious, terms. When those are rejected who thought to build renown on slavery or usurpation,

> *Or who their glory's dire foundation lay'd*
> *On Sov'reigns ruin'd, or on friends betray'd,*
>
> (408)

the lines speak in terms of generally accepted values of loyalty to king, country, or friend. Such a word as 'sovereigns' exists not merely as a label; it wears an aura of traditional reverence, is itself a field of semi-spiritual radiations.

But the glamour is never a false glamour, never an idolatry. The words are tested for their life, for their living and creative force, and any not ringing true will not be used. Or again, we may say that age-old and all but rigid words are rendered fluid, infused with new vitality for a subtle and highly enlightened purpose, as when the warrior imperialists are denied the fame which, one must admit, history has in fact allowed them. What Pope is doing may be best pictured in a line of his own:

> *Then Marble, soften'd into life, grew warm.*
> (Horace, Ep. II, i, 147)

'Marble' is an example of a concrete noun carrying a wealth of associations concerned with the Mediterranean, with architecture, with statuary. But see how this line itself dramatizes for us the process by which a first solid acceptance is made into something of human warmth. So always in Pope the word or thought of heroic pedigree is 'soften'd into life', made part of a contemporary and vital, more deeply Christian, message. Pope loves his words, his art:

> *This subtle Thief of life, this paltry Time,*
> *What will it leave me if it snatch my rhyme?*
> (Horace, Ep. II, ii, 76)

The personification of Time is exquisitely set beside that other, non-temporal, possession, 'rhyme', felt with a personal, a parental or a lover's, emotion.

We may be thought to have extended the term 'personification' beyond reasonable limits; but the very extension is germane to our enquiry. Pope's words are well-chosen entities, they exist almost as little *personalities*; and this comes from their holding traditional and communal, though mainly aristocratic, associations. They are to be contrasted with the ignition-quality of metaphor; and yet, again, they are not snatched cold from the outer void of mental speculation or divine aspiration; they are warm, like a rich necklace warm from human contact. They are not clichés. A cliché is a word or phrase worn dull by vulgar use; these are words worn bright by noble use. They are valuable with the value we attach to an heirloom, or some old volume once in famous hands. In Pope's hands these words of pedigree come newly alive; if they did not, there would be no honour in their use. Both nouns and verbs have, as words, a simple, solid, yet lustrous life. It is amazing how much is done by nouns and verbs alone, and their vivid interplay within a lucid syntax sets going a continual dance: Pope's is a poetic universe alive with a myriad electronic solids. There is nothing academic, nothing static about it. If we say that his diction has 'lustre', we mean by this that it has life, like the sheen of life on a human body. And indeed, his employment of a style deriving from a rich assortment of well-chosen, well-handled and well-valued *words*, which themselves by association and heritage somehow do alone, as separate units or wholes, what is elsewhere done by metaphor, is exactly one with Pope's major statement on life; his concentration not on vast and settled, or unsettled, schemes of religion or philosophy, but rather on a world of separate, individual, free and autonomous, persons, as integral units within whom the universal purpose—for *that* is never forgotten—must be played out; and who, in their turn, are playing out their little destiny in face of a universal purpose.

But that more universal reality is not to be reached by leaping for it; it must be done through society and the nation. Pope was pre-eminently a patriot. He was associated with Bolingbroke and others who claimed the title of 'patriot', including that group of ardent young men who gathered together at Stowe under Lord Cobham, and were known as 'Cobham's cubs'.[1] Pope cannot be given a political label; and he was a poet not of war, but of peace; and yet he can be in general associated with that peculiar amalgam of aristocratic patriotism and liberal fervour which we find later in Earl

---

[1] See *Chatham: his Early Life and Connections*, Lord Rosebery (1910); also my account in *The Dynasty of Stowe* (1944), IV, 51–2; VI, 91; IX, 134–5.

Temple, Cobham's successor at Stowe, and in Pitt; men who willed imperial expansion, even at the cost of war, as a means to all the various arts and blessings of peace, envisaging a world close-linked by trade and freedom in a grand community preserving the heroic traditions, with peace still as a ruling concept, however strenuously to be bought.[1] Now, although Pope steered clear, except in his *Homer*, of warlike themes, his contribution as a, or rather *the*, poet of peace can only be properly assessed by realizing that peace was for him also a truly strenuous matter, demanding psychic integration and civic virtue. He is pre-eminently the poet of what Milton once, in his *Second Defence of the People of England*, called 'the campaign of peace'.[2] In this period our parliamentary system was first properly in action, and the liberties of the subject assured; and, though Pope outdistanced the best actuality of his day, as indeed a poet should, he was firmly rooted in its soil; he was not speaking to, or from, a void.

We have a graduation, as it were, from one concrete and living whole to the next; from words, concrete or abstract, nouns or verbs, to 'personification'; from 'personification' as a literary figure to dramatic entities such as the sylphs and gnomes of *The Rape of the Lock*; from these to a gallery of actual personalities, and thence to society and the nation; and finally, with no hiatus left unhealed, to the greater whole, with all its angelic and seraphic hierarchies, of the *Essay on Man*; where nevertheless the heart of its metaphysic is to be sought within the creative workshop of human personality.

Pope's diction is thus one with his general teaching; you might almost say that the teaching flowers from the diction, for his language grows plainer as his message becomes clearer. Both assert pre-eminently what might be called the *civic* virtues, his thought deriving from the city-states of those ancients whom he and Swift so deeply honoured: we have a sense of duty, honour, patriotism, just ambition, fame, nobility, and so on. Though these are interwoven with other, and more Christian, intuitions, they nevertheless take precedence over all individualistic aspirations. For Pope you

---

[1] As in Addison's *Royal Exchange*. See also *The Dynasty of Stowe* (1944), VII, 100–2; and *Hiroshima* (1946), II, iii, 'A New Whitehall'; and pp. 21, 23–4 below. Many of the issues involved have been discussed in Bonamy Dobrée's Warton Lecture, *The Theme of Patriotism in the Poetry of the Early Eighteenth Century* (1949); and in *The Broken Cistern* (1954).

[2] Discussed in *Chariot of Wrath* (1942), IV, 189.

feel that the highest virtue begins, like charity, at home. He is always, at the admittedly severe cost of sprinkling his page with a host of ephemeral names, calling his contemporaries back from the vast and varied speculations of the preceding century to their context as members of Augustan England, to the 'here' and 'now'. And yet that 'here' and 'now' is positively a-tingle with romantic excitement, ethical fervour, and cosmic meaning. In Pope religion and society, God and politics, spirit and body, converge. His world is compact, but burning; within its present humanity lies its eternal catholicism.

II

THE VITAL FLAME:

An Interpretative Study

II. THE VITAL FLAME[1]

I

Pope's *Pastorals* [2] (published 1709) are strikingly assured, and *Windsor Forest* (completed 1713) is a poem of first importance. Deep submission to nature is felt expanding into communal and national prophecy. The forest is a universal symbol:

> Not Chaos-like together crush'd and bruis'd,
> But, as the world, harmoniously confus'd:
> Where order in variety we see,
> And where, though all things differ, all agree.
>
> (13)

Those four lines, balancing man and nature with feeling for an enclosing and permeating whole, are the key to Pope's work.

Descriptive phrases are often somewhat general:

> Bear me, O bear me to sequester'd scenes,
> The bow'ry mazes, and surrounding greens . . .
>
> (261)

Instead of the chiselled image of Milton we have a queer refusal of visual outline, 'bow'ry mazes' being only superficially Miltonic. A quality rather than an object or set of objects is transmitted. Nor is the result necessarily vague:

> There, interspers'd in lawns and op'ning glades,
> Thin trees arise that shun each other's shades.
>
> (21)

General nouns balance a vivid feeling for natural life. Notice that

[1] First published in *The Burning Oracle*, 1939.
[2] The *Pastorals* are handled below, pp. 165-7.

the personification of the trees is not a weak artifice: rather their felt stillness, their living identities, are realized. Personification in Pope is never driven to any rigid extremes. When corn is seen 'in waving prospect' (39) we have movement and a whole, steady scene, together with an abstract [1] noun: and all, movement, wholeness, and the abstract well used in service to a physical impact, are characteristic. Notice that one word describes the object, one the unifying mind of the spectator: this union is often at the back of Pope's method, as in 'quivering shade' (135), where 'shade' touches human affections. There is precision without a materialized limitation. Even when Liberty leads 'the golden years' (92), though the phrase be ornate, the expressed quality is fairly exact. In Pope any humanizing of nature is really a partnership with nature: the condensation of feeling into a choice diction that already has classic impact assists, but the feeling is always there.

Moreover, phrases do not assert themselves in isolation; a 'predominating passion' renders every image soft, one inward life warming each unit of any single description. A vital context is ready for any striking impression, as in the generally admired lines on fishes:

> Our plenteous streams a various race supply,
> The bright-ey'd perch with fins of Tyrian dye,
> The silver eel, in shining volumes roll'd,
> The yellow carp, in scales bedropp'd with gold,
> Swift trouts, diversified with crimson stains,
> And pikes, the tyrants of the wat'ry plains.

> (141)

Here 'bright-ey'd' grades into 'silver' and 'shining', and sets a context for 'yellow', 'bedropp'd with gold', and 'crimson'.[2] There is nothing sudden or rigid; the whole movement being so organic, no complicated efforts at realization are needed; simple nouns and well-selected adjectives drop into place, and all, without strain, goes smoothly. The poet is well above his work, or rather, well inside it, or both. A lovely passage on reflections in water (212–18) pictures the miracle

---

[1] Geoffrey Tillotson has already drawn attention to Pope's use of abstract nouns in such phrases ('Language', 74).

[2] Pope's poetic use of *colour* has been excellently discussed by Norman Ault in *New Light on Pope* (1949). 'It would seem' he writes (v, 87), 'that Pope's conscious references to colour in *Windsor Forest* are carried to a pitch never before attained by any poet.'

of 'headlong mountains' and 'downward skies', trees that are 'absent', and 'floating forests' that 'paint the waves with green', while the water rolls 'slow' through the 'fair scene' which it holds. The description becomes a symbol of that repose mysteriously one with a vital yet undisturbing movement that characterizes Pope's major art-forms and tiniest phrases alike. The delineations, being inward, penetrate to the dynamic centres of life, and give, without effort, pictorial quality and action, as in the well-known:

> *See! from the brake the whirring pheasant springs,*
> *And mounts exulting on triumphant wings:*
> *Short is his joy; he feels the fiery wound,*
> *Flutters in blood, and panting beats the ground.*
> *Ah! what avail his glossy, varying dyes,*
> *His purple crest, and scarlet-circled eyes,*
> *The vivid green his shining plumes unfold,*
> *His painted wings, and breast that flames with gold?*
>
> (111)

Rich as is the description, the phrases work in obedience to a whole drawn directly from the energies of nature. Each image is apt, but none superlative. There is a reserve of power and a poetic humility, power being felt in the conception, not just in the expression. The regularity of couplet-rhyme helps in checking all separate excellences, levelling and subduing them, with a corresponding release to the central experience, while poignant action informs a poetic tranquillity; as in our former phrase 'waving prospect', where the still and vast abstract conception checks the more lively movement which is somehow then enclosed in stillness. This is Keats' 'might half-slumbering on its own right arm'.

Pope's animal apprehension is one with animal sympathy. The destruction of bird-life is again vigorously imagined when a fowler is described roving with 'slaughterous gun' in winter:

> *He lifts the tube, and levels with his eye:*
> *Straight a short thunder breaks the frozen sky:*
> *Oft, as in airy rings they skim the heath,*
> *The clam'rous lapwings feel the leaden death:*
> *Oft, as the mounting larks their notes prepare,*
> *They fall, and leave their little lives in air.*
>
> (129)

You could complain of 'tube', though the word may also mark an isolated visual exactitude. Pope is no specialist at mechanical imagery, and avoids it consistently. But the first couplet so precisely integrates action with atmosphere, the metallic suddenness of sound across the wintry landscape, that you almost smell powder in the keen air: a whole experience is given, an authentic instant of actual existence, a piece of a living universe. The realization is stark, sudden, and unerring; as, too, in the phrase 'leaden death'. 'Clam'rous' and 'mounting' are careful epithets, and 'little' denotes the sympathy implicit throughout, with a clever silhouetting of life's mystery in the thought of its loss, the birds as tiny flamelets puffed out in song. Animals are inwardly felt, as in the 'ready spaniel' shown 'panting with hope' (99–100) or the 'impatient courser'—'courser' because he is felt as kinetic—seen as excited in 'every vein', pawing the ground and tingling for 'the distant plain' (151). The animal's power and swiftness are admirably caught in 'earth rolls back beneath the flying steed' (158), the phrase aiming to net the paradoxical quality of speed. Animals are usually created in their vital and peculiar movement from an inward sympathy comparable with Shakespeare's, and continuous with the apprehension of dynamic quality, as well as shape and colour, in nature generally. The stallion and hare of *Venus and Adonis* are both recalled by *Windsor Forest*:

> *To plains with well-breath'd beagles we repair,*
> *And trace the mazes of the circling hare:*
> *(Beasts, urg'd by us, their fellow beasts pursue,*
> *And learn of men each other to undo).*

(121)

The animal's characterizing behaviour is noticed and exactly, though unobtrusively, recorded.

Such recognition will naturally widen beyond nature and animal life to a vivid feeling for human vitality in action, such as we find in Pan's pursuit of Lodona (171–218). A tense realization of movement and fear is projected through numerous precisions involving bird-comparisons, the sound of steps, Pan's shadow lengthened by the sun, the feeling of his very breath: it is vivid without being visual, an inward experience expressing itself freely and variously; and it should help us to understanding of Shakespeare's own similar mastery. The little drama leads up to Lodona's transmutation to a rivulet and this exquisite couplet:

The silver stream her virgin coldness keeps,
For ever murmurs and for ever weeps.

(205)

The real stream is in every accent. That process of nature-feeling which created the Greek myths, and which Keats understood so well in his own fluid personifications, enjoys an equal perfection here. The fusion of the human and the natural is not ever, in itself, a weakness; rather it is the farthest aim of all nature-mysticism, and, indeed, implicit in Wordsworth's own message.

The poem expands further, Windsor Forest becoming a national symbol, one with 'Britannia's goddess', Liberty (91). Oaks are 'future navies' (222), with no straining of association. An Elizabethan royalism is recaptured, Windsor boasting in Queen Anne 'as bright a Goddess and as chaste a Queen' as Diana in 'old Arcadia'; at once protectress of the 'sylvan scene', 'earth's fair light', and 'empress of the main' (159–64). So the courtier ranks above the poet, whose 'chymic art', reading magic lore from nature and history and associated with god-like excursions beyond earth and mortality, is a brilliantly characterized second (235–56). The Thames recalls past nobilities, river-feelings forming organically among the paradisal, yet contemporary, impressions. Again, as in the days of Elizabeth, 'discord' has been quelled, only this time by 'great Anna' (327); while the 'sacred' blessings of a peaceful reign are expected, the building of 'temples' replacing civil war and bloodshed (355–78). England is finally seen as supreme arbiter and 'great oracle' of the world (382). All evils are to be stilled on that day when

Unbounded Thames shall flow for all mankind.

(398)

The vision expands the Shakespearian prophecy in *Henry VIII*. Pope expects his country to oppose 'slavery' (408). He proclaims the end of conquest (408) and ambition (416), with the advent of universal peace.

The sense received of an organic continuity from nature, through animal-life, to human civilization, is most important. It is not a logical sequence; my quotations are drawn from various parts of what may well seem an untidy poem. The form is inherently, not studiously, organic. The generalizing tendency never loses contact with perceptual impressions. Feeling rather burrows into the underlying essence, catches the spirit and atmosphere, enjoys possession

21

with freedom, and so moves on to the universal. The process is Shakespearian, and the final inclusion a natural result of any contact with an inner vitality. *Windsor Forest* is felt as a teeming world: there are no limits to its boundaries. We are pointed on, through thoughts of imperial expansion as creatively interlocking one's own country with a great human whole, to the 'naked youths' (405) of America; and though the positive trust in a mercantile peace, to be grouped with Addison's *Royal Exchange* and poetically forecast by the glamour of Shakespeare's merchants, is, with much else in *Windsor Forest*, superficially reversed in Pope's later writings, the essential statement of the poem is never repudiated. Evils are keenly remembered: the forest's past as a setting for savagery and oppression (43–92) is set beside its present placidity and expected future. Such Shakespearian inclusiveness, covering a number of geographical references, points towards the *Essay on Man*. Pope's life-work is rooted in *Windsor Forest*. It holds the germ of all the rest, the satires too. The ultimate significance which Milton, starting with a religious poem, searched for in the organ music of his own mind, is here again sought in natural affinities. Nature and man are again in partnership: and this recaptured harmony is reflected with an assured poetic ease into the rose-chain and bowery prison of the couplet.

II

Shakespeare gives us drama and Milton epic, and Pope builds from both in *The Rape of the Lock* (1712–14). The poem has Lyly's feeling for the delightfully evanescent, the poignant attractiveness of a brilliant society.[1] Yet Lyly offered no strong action, and against this subtlest of poetic problems Pope very early pits his genius, preserving the essence of heroic poetry on condition of a semi-humorous treatment. Attempts to idealize the crown in Dryden's *Absalom and Achitophel* are weak, and in *Windsor Forest* the national fervour barely, if at all, carries off the more royalistic idealism. But, by full acceptance of a changed mental horizon, we may regain an integrity comparable with Shakespeare's:

> *Here thou, great Anna! whom three realms obey,*
> *Dost sometimes counsel take—and sometimes tea.*
>
> (III, 7)

[1] See my article on Lyly's plays in *The Review of English Studies*, April, 1939.

The compliment is made possible and even powerful by the joke. And by just such humour Pope integrates his whole poem into the heroic and religious traditions, religious tonings taking their place beside those royalistic and heroic, under similar semi-humorous conditions. The poem is not iconoclastic, but holds a warm humanism as surely as the somewhat similar *Love's Labour's Lost*. It is written not from a scorn but from a love. The whole is a flirtation with the sublime.

By seeing Belinda's toilet preparations as a ritual the poet channels reverend associations that build his scene and its action into both a more convincing and a more memorable impressionistic whole than would otherwise be possible. Nor is this merely a technical fancy, since the religion of post-Renaissance literature is, fundamentally, an Eros cult. So, in blending religious tonings with feminine vanity, Pope makes a synthesis of the Christianity-Eros conflict on a comparatively superficial, but delightfully human, plane, the rich humour being both the measure of a relation and the resolving of a conflict. Here it is:

> And now, unveil'd, the Toilet stands display'd,
> Each silver Vase in mystic order laid.
> First, rob'd in white, the Nymph intent adores,
> With head uncover'd, the Cosmetic pow'rs.
> A heav'nly image in the glass appears,
> To that she bends, to that her eyes she rears;
> Th' inferior Priestess, at her altar's side,
> Trembling begins the sacred rites of Pride.
> Unnumber'd treasures ope at once, and here
> The various off'rings of the world appear;
> From each she nicely culls with curious toil,
> And decks the Goddess with the glitt'ring spoil.
> This casket India's glowing gems unlocks,
> And all Arabia breathes from yonder box.
> The Tortoise here and Elephant unite,
> Transform'd to combs, the speckled, and the white.
> Here files of pins extend their shining rows . . .
>
> (I, 121)

He goes on to imagine a 'purer blush' suffusing her face, and 'keener lightnings' starting from her eyes. The delicate fun is obvious, but certain other significances may too easily be neglected. There is the same sense of wealth which we found in *Windsor Forest*: the poet feels his own corner of life interlocking with a vast whole of human co-operation. The use of perfumes is noteworthy: Pope consistently relies on them to establish his impressions. The whole passage is, to use the fine term applied by A. C. Bradley to the poetry of Keats, 'dense'. There is nothing visually flat. Pope is not a pre-eminently visual poet; rather he tells facts, names concrete objects, attaches needed epithets. But his reserve attains great richness, and his epithets modify with precision and force, as in the adjective 'mystic', both helping the main analogy and underlining the maid's professional care to serve a realistic purpose. The sacramental associations concretize, and give depth to, the whole business: objects are made alive, till they breathe out significant energy. Pope twice elsewhere in the poem uses such ritualistic colourings. There is the altar made of four French romances, and its offerings of love, in a passage to be quoted later, and here is a pretty description of coffee-making:

> *On shining Altars of Japan they raise*
> *The silver lamp; the fiery spirits blaze:*
> *From silver spouts the grateful liquors glide,*
> *While China's earth receives the smoking tide.*
>
> (III, 107)

This is symbolism in a very valuable sense of the word: dynamic associations are used to realize, seriously or humorously, some whole event or scene, objects and atmosphere, facts and implications, together. Here the ordinary and trivial spring to sudden life, a hidden magic released.

Warfare, so continual in heroic, and, given a more psychological significance, in dramatic, poetry, is likewise used, twice, the one instance forming a neat forecast of the other. First, there is the card-game. The emotionally heroic treatment of it is not illogical. Games are civilized substitutes for physical rivalry, and the kings and queens in chess or cards symbolize existent meanings, an age of settled culture, as Castiglione knew, needing an outlet for its warrior instincts. So phrases such as 'now move to war her sable Matadores' (III, 47) and 'th' imperial consort of the crown of Spades' (III, 68) reflect a truth. People *do* take their games seriously; they *have* been known to lose their tempers at bridge. Remembering this, ask whether the following lines overload their context, and if the rich humour is not dependent, as finest humour should be, on the holding up of a mirror to nature:

> And now (as oft in some distemper'd State)
> On one nice Trick depends the gen'ral fate.
> An Ace of Hearts steps forth: the King unseen
> Lurk'd in her hand, and mourn'd his captive Queen:
> He springs to Vengeance with an eager pace,
> And falls like thunder on the prostrate Ace.
> The nymph exulting fills with shouts the sky;
> The wells, the woods, and long canals reply.

(III, 93)

The ordinary word 'thunder', without any attempt at original phrase-coining, starts from its context with crashing impact; next, the movement curves over to the quiet end of a completed whole, the usual Shakespearian technique in the organizing of speech, scene, or play. The rich humour is proportional to our recognition not of a distortion but of a truth, depending, indeed, on a central, Shakespearian, humility before the simple and the vast in human instincts. It is a quality which tends to elude the puritanical consciousness.

Our other war-incident is the general mêlée in Canto V. Though feminine dignity may be for a while lost as 'whalebones crack' (v. 40), it is often cleverly preserved in delightfully mock-heroic terms, as when Thalestris 'scatters death around from both her eyes' (v. 58), or Belinda scores a victory with a charge of snuff thrown at the Baron till 'the high dome re-echoes to his nose' (v. 86). There is, too, the Shakespearian realization of personal dignity where you least expect it, in the brainless aristocrat Sir Plume, with 'earnest eyes and round unthinking face', who has nevertheless also the mystery of his own precise individuality, and therefore his own causes of pride:

> Sir Plume of amber snuff-box justly vain,
> And the nice conduct of a clouded cane.

(IV, 123)

The persons, it is true, are not strongly individualized except for this exquisite vignette of Sir Plume and his cleverly characterized words, but the presentation of people in general has a warmth, conviction, and sympathy that might well, at another time, have created drama on a wider scale. The fun is not derisive but cathartic.

L.P.—C

Pope's use of his supernatural 'machinery' is clever. These 'light Militia of the lower sky' (I, 42; observe the skilful 'i'-sounds) increase dramatic suspense, and therefore story-depth, since they foreknow and warn of the central disaster; help to universalize semi-humorously the whole action, forming, indeed, the binding symbolism of the little drama; are related to certain paradisal and, in Umbriel's journey, hellish colourings touching Dante, Shakespeare, and Milton; and finally reflect the implied belief of poetic art-forms in general that humanity and its sensible world do not exhaust the total of a comprehensive statement. They are of a race that lives in the pure upper light, that guides 'orbs' in heaven, like the child-spirit in Shelley's *Prometheus Unbound*, and follows shooting stars by moonlight. They are variously associated with rainbow, mists, tempests, earth, and the guardianship of the British throne (II, 77–90). They are explicitly related to traditional beliefs, both trivial and profound:

> *Fairest of mortals, thou distinguish'd care*
> *Of thousand bright Inhabitants of Air!*
> *If e'er one vision touch'd thy infant thought,*
> *Of all the Nurse and all the Priest have taught;*
> *Of airy elves by moonlight shadows seen,*
> *The silver token, and the circled green,*
> *Or virgins visited by Angel-pow'rs,*
> *With golden crowns and wreaths of heav'nly flow'rs . . .*
>
> (I, 27)

They are also spirits of the dead, now acting as guardian angels to the living (I, 47–66). They are in part quite seriously imagined, and exquisitely realized, with names delicately composed to suit their peculiar charges; Zephyretta, Brillante, Momentilla, Crispissa corresponding to fan, drops, watch, and lock. Nowhere is Pope's artistry in vowel-colour more evident than in the description of Belinda's setting out on the Thames by sunlight with sylphs invisibly attending. The passage is introduced by three lines of light 'i'-sounds, followed by weightier though soft vowellings to match the expansive peace:

> *But now secure the painted vessel glides,*
> *The sun-beams trembling on the floating tides:*
> *While melting music steals upon the sky,*

And soften'd sounds along the waters die;
Smooth flow the waves, the Zephyrs gently play,
Belinda smiled, and all the world was gay.

(II, 47)

Soon after, the Sylphs' introduction is accompanied by a growing accumulation of 'i' vowels, steadily increasing in clustered force for eight lines, before giving place to heavier sounds:

Some to the sun their insect-wings unfold,
Waft on the breeze, or sink in clouds of gold;
Transparent forms, too fine for mortal sight,
Their fluid bodies half dissolv'd in light,
Loose to the wind their airy garments flew,
Thin glitt'ring textures of the filmy dew,
Dipt in the richest tincture of the skies,
Where light disports in ever-mingling dyes,
While ev'ry beam new transient colours flings,
Colours that change whene'er they wave their wings.
Amid the circle, on the gilded mast,
Superior by the head, was Ariel plac'd;
His purple pinions op'ning to the sun,
He rais'd his azure wand, and thus begun . . .

(II, 59)

In the couplet starting 'While every . . .' heavy and light sounds interpenetrate to match the formation of deep colours from out aerial brilliance.[1] Continual change and movement is cleverly expressed in a various dance of evanescent impressions very different from Milton's more static, or at the best solemn, appeals. The final lines grow thicker with vowel-weight to establish a mock-heroic grandeur and cause the little speaker to swell out in close-up significance. So delicately rich and substantial an impressionism cannot be exhausted by categories of social satire: you could seriously compare this river-and-lady sun-piece with Shakespeare's Cleopatra on Cydnus. The description, as 'insect-wings' implies, depends on a close observation of nature. Pope's sympathy with small life-forms is

[1] In her 'Notes on Pope's Poetry', Edith Sitwell has commented on the 'texture' of this passage. She regards lines 59–68 as a crystallization of the poem's unique quality (*Alexander Pope*, 1930; XVIII, 272–3).

continual, and leads here to an exquisite apprehension of a sylph's (or fly's) punishment:

> *Gums and pomatums shall his flight restrain,*
> *While clogg'd he beats his silken wings in vain.*

(II, 129)

Heavy vowels oppose light ones. Later (II, 135) there is the horror and rounded sounds of 'fumes of burning Chocolate'. Triumphant Umbriel—another exquisite name—is shown mischievously clapping his wings 'on a sconce's height' during the mêlée (V, 54), and the sombre effects of his descent to Hell, with comic description of the objects there, are done with a glorious sense of the trivial sublimated to heroic stature. The dark and light tonings throughout expand far beyond 'mockery'; rather the humour is the condition of poetic achievement.

The poem has imaginative solidity, which is not the same as the imagining of solids in separation, presenting perceptual density and a close-packed unity. I have noticed the perceptual quality of Belinda's toilet, but, whatever is handled, the Lock itself, the guarded petticoat, Sir Plume's 'amber snuff-box' and 'clouded cane', bodkins, sconces, coffee-pots, all are rounded and convincing, and cohere together in their particular world. There is a heavy stress on bright substances, which are here peculiarly fitting. Silver is a persistent impression: 'The press'd watch return'd a silver sound' (I, 18), a 'silver token' (I, 32), 'each silver vase' (I, 122), the 'silver Thames' (II, iv), the petticoat's 'silver bound' (II, 121), the 'silver lamp' and 'silver spouts' of coffee-pots (III, 108–9). There is gold too: angels with 'golden crowns' (I, 34), 'golden scales' (V, 71), 'liquid gold' (IV, 45) in the Cave of Spleen, 'clouds of gold' (II, 60). It may take the form of gilt: 'gilded chariots' (I, 55), the 'gilded mast' (II, 69), the French romances 'neatly gilt' (II, 38). But these rich solids—there are jewels too—blend naturally into the silvery glinting wings of sylphs in sunlight, the recurrent 'i'-sounds, the 'lightning' of Belinda's sparkling eyes (I, 144), the glitter of poetic wit. Belinda dreams of 'a youth more glitt'ring than a birth-night beau' (I, 23), her jewellery is a 'glitt'ring spoil' (I, 132), the scissors to cut the lock a 'glitt'ring forfex' (III, 147). Over all is raised the Lock, itself finally carried with a 'radiant trail' of light (V, 128) to 'bespangle' the heavens. These impressions are gained almost entirely by naming appropriate objects; there is no over-plastering of descriptive imagery; nor is the aggregate result itself metallic, but rather warm with human contact, the prevailing impression being one of softness. Moreover, that most poignant method of bodying out the subtly atmospheric into poetic solidity, the use of smell, assists in 'Arabia' breathing from a box (I, 134), the 'imprison'd essences' (II, 94), and the 'fragrant steams' (III, 134) of coffee. A profoundly sensuous nature is creating.

Though the humour is never bitterly satiric, Pope does sometimes appear as an amused grown-up writing of children; but then each of us is a grown-up, and the rest all children, where romantic emotions are concerned. So we get a delicate treatment of girls' amours with suggestion that the Gnomes

> Teach Infant-cheeks a bidden blush to know,
> And little hearts to flutter at a Beau.

(I, 89)

A strangely purified sexuality is attained by this blend of child-innocence and desire, as in Byron's *Don Juan*. There is, as it were, a love for the object's very littleness, recalling the larks of *Windsor Forest* and the creation of the Sylphs themselves. The Sylphs protect young ladies from unchastity, by keeping their attention on the move:

> When Florio speaks what virgin could withstand,
> If gentle Damon did not squeeze her hand?
> With varying vanities, from ev'ry part,
> They shift the moving Toyshop of their heart.

(I, 97)

Though lightly, a deep enough human truth is hinted. The gentle mockery may be yet deeper, as in

> What guards the purity of melting Maids,
> In courtly balls, and midnight masquerades,
> Safe from the treach'rous friend, the daring spark,
> The glance by day, the whisper in the dark,
> When kind occasion prompts their warm desires,
> When music softens, and when dancing fires?

(I, 71)

It is the Sylphs who mysteriously save them, functioning as does the Attendant Spirit of *Comus*, and corresponding to what psychologists, who may not believe in such spirits, call 'inhibitions'. Notice especially the warm, sensuous creation here, the exquisite subtlety of verbal tone, consonants and vowels variously inter-shading.

In this last passage we may observe the central pauses in lines 2, 3, 4 and 6, and their comparative absence in lines 1 and 5. Such significant interplay is constant throughout Pope and should be carefully watched and followed in reading. Often contrasts are neatly balanced within one line. Here is another good example, where the antithesis of lines 1 and 2 with no internal pauses speeds up to internal antithesis in 3 and 4, gathers into the tripartite formation of line 5, and ends with a falling, run-on, pauseless unit in line 6:

> *Whether the nymph shall break Diana's law,*
> *Or some frail China jar receive a flaw;*
> *Or stain her honour, / or her new brocade;*
> *Forget her pray'rs, / or miss a masquerade;*
> *Or lose her heart, / or necklace, / at a ball;*
> *Or whether Heav'n has doom'd that Shock must fall.*

(II, 105)

The contrasts of the important and the trivial are vitally organic, one at least definitely balancing flirtation and religion, playing on the usual conflict. The use of caesura is interesting: often you have in reading to change your vocal colour, and even pace, in mid-line. Here pauses hold up the speed for couplet after couplet, with a final swift release, and run-on. You find something similar in Virgil, and my understanding has been assisted by my brother's study of Virgilian verse-groups,[1] from which I take the term 'release'. Other variations are employed. You can discover them by reading aloud, often altering the pace and vocal colour in mid-line, with close attention to the stops, commas especially, which are carefully placed. Striking subtleties will reveal themselves. You must, however, never ignore the couplet basis and its rhymes, since only in close reference to these do the variations hold their value.

The love-feeling, the erotic warmth, is at once soft and burning, while the poetic medium attains a perfect poise of relaxation and control. Indeed, the society Pope writes of is felt as eminently desirable. We may be amused at the Baron who builds an altar to love of 'twelve vast French romances nearly gilt' and lays on it

> *. . . three garters, half a pair of gloves;*
> *And all the trophies of his former loves.*

(II, 39)

[1] *Accentual Symmetry in Virgil* by W. F. Jackson Knight (1939).

Yet when Belinda's toilet is seen as a 'holy ritual' and her lock called 'sacred', it is not all comedy. She presides over the poem, with an especially spirited attraction:

> Her lively looks a sprightly mind disclose,
> Quick as her eyes, and as unfix'd as those:
> Favours to none, to all she smiles extends;
> Oft she rejects, but never once offends.

(II, 9)

Such is the vital centre of Pope's inspiration: Shakespeare's Rosalind might be so described, or Portia; they, too, are felt as all but divine, without losing humanity. Pope writes from a half-feminine gentleness, and can create sunshine feminine vitality from loving admiration. His light, humorous touch continually blends, as Milton, except once in Eden, cannot or must not, romantic and religious emotions; and so, in terms precisely suited to this glittering world, he sets on his heroine's 'white breast' a 'sparkling cross' (II, 7).

The manipulation of the action as a whole is dramatic rather than epic; and here, if we remember the comparative failure of long narrative in *The Faery Queen* and *Paradise Lost*, we may consider Pope's judgement sound. The excitement may be of a sort often found in epic, as at the vividly presented climax:

> Swift to the Lock a thousand Sprites repair,
> A thousand wings, by turns, blow back the hair;
> And thrice they twitch'd the diamond in her ear;
> Thrice she look'd back, and thrice the foe drew near . . .

(III, 135)

But this rises from a dramatically conceived whole, with Shakespearian forewarnings and fears. After the central event, the held-up suspense finds violent release in discordant passions and Umbriel's visit to the Cave of Spleen, as though a glittering outside had been shattered to disclose gloom; but there is a return to sympathy, dignity, and an almost tragic pathos. The poem is close knit, with a dominating central climax and a curve over, more like a Shakespearian play than any epic, and it concludes on a note of quiet power.

A deeper note is struck towards the end. Clarissa urges that women should be gentle, not angry, else 'why Angels call'd and Angel-like adored?' (V, 12). The thought recalls similar speeches at the

31

conclusions of *The Taming of the Shrew* and *Love's Labour's Lost*, where ill moods and superficial glitter are respectively reminded of the tragic undertones of human existence. She continues:

> *Oh! if to dance all night, and dress all day,*
> *Charm'd the small-pox, or chas'd old age away . . .*
>
> (v, 19)

—then, she says, gaiety alone might be our guiding star:

> *But since, alas! frail beauty must decay,*
> *Curl'd or uncurl'd, since Locks will turn to grey . . .*
>
> (v, 25)

Read the last line slowly, dwelling on the vowels and wistfully stressing 'will'. Pope's profound treatment of superficiality is to be rigidly distinguished from the more facile, and more usual, brilliance of a superficial treatment of human profundities. No poem ever had a more exquisitely sensitive introduction than that addressed to Miss Arabella Fermor, nor any ended with so sure and sweet a pathos that, in placing the heroine's beauty in a context of ultimate defeat, some-how crowns it with an immortal lustre. The poet imagines the Lock lifted as a starry constellation, which is also the constellation of his poem, glittering through the centuries:

> *Not all the tresses that fair head can boast,*
> *Shall draw such envy as the Lock you lost.*
> *For, after all the murders of your eye,*
> *When, after millions slain, yourself shall die:*
> *When those fair suns shall set, as set they must,*
> *And all those tresses shall be laid in dust,*
> *The Lock the Muse shall consecrate to fame,*
> *And 'midst the stars inscribe Belinda's name.*
>
> (v, 143)

'Consecrate': notice again the sacred and ritualistic colouring. Read-ing, let the commas hold up the movement with positionally varied pauses, changing your vocal colour deeply for 'as set they must', till in line 6 there is a quick release; then let the last couplet go with stately, measured emphasis. Again, notice the verbal statement and the concrete nouns. Though there is deepest sympathy, emotion never overspills the control; you read from a height, with sense of a unit completed at each instant, though each couplet is also organic to the paragraph whole. His 'holistic' instinct is, indeed, at the back of Pope's allegiance to the couplet.

A synthesis of the sexual and the religious is organic to the humour of *The Rape of the Lock*. The depths lightly tinted there are more richly blended in *Eloisa to Abelard* (1717), where the same balance assumes a poignant emotional and tragic force. This is certainly Pope's greatest human poem, and probably the greatest short love poem in our language. Pope's early development is peculiarly Elizabethan: from the idyllic nature of the *Pastorals* to the blend of rustic idealism and national vigour in *Windsor Forest*, through the scintillating and courtly, yet never superficially 'witty', *Rape of the Lock*, itself, like Shakespeare's comedies, showing deep tragic relations; and so on to the tragic music of *Eloisa to Abelard*.

Religion is early impregnated with sombre tonings:

> *In these deep solitudes and awful cells,*
> *Where heav'nly-pensive contemplation dwells,*
> *And ever-musing melancholy reigns;*
> *What means this tumult in a Vestal's veins?*
>
> (1)

Its sanctity is imbued with a Websterian grimness and pallor:

> *Relentless walls! whose darksome round contains*
> *Repentant sighs, and voluntary pains:*
> *Ye rugged rocks! which holy knees have worn;*
> *Ye grots and caverns shagg'd with horrid thorn!*
> *Shrines! where their vigils pale-eye'd virgins keep,*
> *And pitying saints, whose statues learn to weep . . .*
>
> (17)

Remorseless repetition and craggy consonants first toll the eternal sameness, rising to the thin tortured vowels of the last line but one. The nunnery is an old Websterian building, almost, you feel, a ruin, like Byron's Norman Abbey, whose 'moss-grown domes' and 'awful arches' (142–3) make of noon an eternal night, and whose 'dim windows', reversing the Miltonic pleasure, shed a grave-like calm (144). Watch now for the darkly rich vowel-colourings and held-up movement of this speech of death:

> *But o'er the twilight groves, / and dusky caves,*
> *Long-sounding aisles, / and intermingled graves,*

Black Melancholy sits, / and round her throws
A death-like silence, / and a dead repose:
Her gloomy presence / saddens all the scene,
Shades every flow'r, / and darkens ev'ry green,
Deepens the murmur / of the falling floods,
And breathes a browner horror on the woods.

(163)

My reading is as I have marked. The five strong internal pauses occur naturally where our text uses commas: the use is precise. Other internal pauses are slighter, and the last line shows a release, the assonance and close epithetical union of 'browner' and 'horror' forcing, I think, the run-on. Pope's full-throated mastery of vowel-colour is rich as Keats' when he needs it. Both favour a subtle interplay of light and shade, often a dark richness atmospherically suggesting woodland depths, with the same sacramental vowellings of emotions grave yet lovely. Both project the numinous and atmospheric through heavy sensuous perception, as many trees making one woodland company. Milton's exquisite, and, indeed, often Keatsian, solids are rarely so subdued, though his work was, no doubt, a most generous assistance to Pope. See again this labouring movement:

When round some mould'ring tow'r pale ivy creeps,
And low-brow'd rocks hang nodding o'er the deeps.

(243)

Nature is here part of a mood, one with an emotion. The created whole has a mysterious life Milton's grouped individual excellences do not normally attain, Pope's nature-paragraphs cohering to build a living, semi-human presence. Here a deathly stillness is required, but he was equally at home with the vital movement and sun-sparkling gaiety of *The Rape of the Lock*.

From this world of Websterian ruin and forbidding death Eloisa asserts poignantly her own, natural, desire:

Tho' cold like you, unmov'd and silent grown,
I have not yet forgot myself to stone.
All is not Heav'n's while Abelard has part,
Still rebel nature holds out half my heart.

(23)

The use of ruins, statues, and here 'stone' to build a specifically religious eternity in contrast with love exactly resembles Byron's in *Don Juan*. Eloisa accuses religion of killing those 'best of passions', love and fame, the erotic and power instincts, ideals of emotion and action. Married love she is proud of having refused, despising any such compact: 'Curse on all laws but those which love has made.' Honour and respect are nothing in comparison with so jealous a god. If the other God offered her Himself and the whole Creation, she would 'scorn 'em all'; would rather be a 'mistress' to the man she loves than a Caesar's empress (73–90). She aspires to absolute unmoral freedom in love's bondage. Yet this sin-tormented desire is close to Dante's, and indeed Milton's, Paradise:

> Oh! happy state! when souls each other draw,
> When love is liberty, and nature law.

(91)

But neither Dante nor Milton would dare a dramatic sympathy to Eloisa's over-leaping of moral canons in order to get there; and yet this imaginative willingness is precisely the condition of Pope's advance to the poetic stature of *Antony and Cleopatra* and *Don Juan*; a symptom, we can call it, of his clear, objective, ordering of emotions. Milton's ethical sense in *Comus* attempts a premature and disrupting resolution where Pope allows full speech to the opposing principles. When Eloisa, nearing the 'dread altars', made her final vows, her eyes were fixed, not on the Cross, but on Abelard (115–16). He is, to her, Christ. Sin or god, he remains 'delicious poison' (122), an 'unholy joy' (224). Her reason is shown as unable to fight her whole life, of which it is itself a part, a thought pointing on to the more explicit psychology of the *Essay on Man*. Desire she may conquer by day, but in sleep, when 'nature' is 'free'—and what power lies in this easy expression of a simple yet terrifying thought —it rises newly strong and unconquerable; for then 'all my loose soul unbounded springs to thee' (225–8). There is here more of a Byronic sin-sense in the protagonist than in *Antony and Cleopatra*: 'glowing guilt' itself 'exalts the keen delight' (230). But there is no imaginative confusion, however complex the issues, nor any pronouncing of judgement. It is interesting to find so Shakespearian an artist clarifying objectively the experience of sin *increasing* delight on so high a plane, since this it is which so troubles Spenser and Milton, and which Shakespeare leaves almost untouched, except

35

perhaps in Angelo, or the imaginative texture, as distinct from the persons, of *Antony and Cleopatra*; though, to be sure, Eloisa's 'delicious poison' was first spoken by Cleopatra of Antony. In her dream every 'source of love' is alive, she sees Abelard vividly present: 'I hear thee, see thee, gaze o'er all thy charms' (232–3); only to wake, phantom-deceived.

But from this burning conflict serene poetry may build in piling couplets a massed movement crowning human instinct with accomplished and inevitable victory:

> *I waste the Matin lamp in sighs for thee,*
> *Thy image steals between my God and me,*
> *Thy voice I seem in ev'ry hymn to hear,*
> *With ev'ry bead I drop too soft a tear.*
> *When from the censer clouds of fragrance roll,*
> *And swelling organs lift the rising soul,*
> *One thought of thee puts all the pomp to flight,*
> *Priests, tapers, temples, swim before my sight:*
> *In seas of flame my plunging soul is drown'd,*
> *While Altars blaze, and Angels tremble round.*

(267)

Never is Pope happier than when writing in terms of ritual. Here read the first four lines quietly, but let sound a heavier note thereafter. Notice the reliance on smell in the 'fragrance' of incense, and how the organ grandeur and the weighty nouns of sacred reference find each their place but no more, showing an effortless control of the magnificent comparable with Milton's, though less assertive than his, since no grandest part stifles, even for an instant, the breathing life of the whole unit. All dissolves into that whole, Abelard and Eloisa too, into a burning yet concrete whole, a human blaze that is its own flame-tipped altar, till angels themselves tremble at the might of a human sanctity. The solidity and crystallization of indefinable experience is maintained till the last; indeed, then most of all, with a rounded, effortless perfection, mastering and liberating the whole statement. This is an embodiment of Keats' counsel to surprise 'by a fine excess', though one, paradoxically, subdued to the whole movement always, as Keats, too, surely intended; his 'might half-slumbering on its own right arm', his rise and sunset fall of image.[1] Pope, as surely as any English writer, in his best work in

[1] To Taylor, 27 Feb., 1818; *Sleep and Poetry*, 237.

this kind, loads 'every rift with ore'.[1] You need to weigh every word in turn: how easy it is, for example, to miss here the terrific force in the admirably placed word 'plunging'.

Abelard is thus, to Eloisa, all but the divine, his voice heard in the hymn, his presence obscuring, replacing, God's, so that the opposition almost becomes a synthesis. Elsewhere, starting from the divine, we are made to imagine a blessed sanctity enclosing all human richness. Here it is, the other, and yet not dissimilar, synthesis, starting not from 'nature' but from 'grace', to use the terms of Pope's preliminary note. Eloisa describes the saintly life:

> *Desires compos'd, affections ever ev'n;*
> *Tears that delight, and sighs that waft to heav'n.*
> *Grace shines around her with serenest beams,*
> *And whisp'ring Angels prompt her golden dreams.*
> *For her th' unfading rose of Eden blooms,*
> *And wings of Seraphs shed divine perfumes,*
> *For her the Spouse prepares the bridal ring,*
> *For her white virgins Hymenaeals sing,*
> *To sounds of heavenly harps she dies away,*
> *And melts in visions of eternal day.*

(213)

'Melts': the warm sensuousness which we noted in *The Rape of the Lock*—'melting maids' and 'midnight masquerades'—here impregnates the divine with marriage-symbolism. Remember the earlier, erotic, phrase 'when music softens' (p. 29): here is the heavenly softness, 'wafts' at the start, 'melts' at the close, and, between, 'whisp'ring', 'rose', 'Hymenaeals', with numerous 'f's and 'v's. Again, observe the 'perfumes'. The lines are best given a slight midway pause until a delicate run-on for the last. Pope's angels, seraphs, altars, incense, all are vital beyond those of other English poets. They are sensuously felt, but the softness never becomes a total relaxation: the poetry controls its own sensuous abandon, at every instant objectifies and projects the dissolving subjectivity, crystallizing a melting emotion into verbal weight.

Pope is Dantesque, yet perhaps more human, to us, than Dante. There is no rigid line of demarcation to be drawn between his seraphs and delightful sylphs: his mind is all of a piece, his poetic world, nor only in this period, a single whole.

[1] Keats to Shelley, August, 1820.

37

About to surrender to this dream of the divine, Eloisa again rebels, crying, in the manner of Drayton's sonnet, even while 'dawning grace' is 'opening' on her soul:

> Come, if thou dar'st, all charming as thou art!
> Oppose thyself to heav'n; dispute my heart . . .
>
> (281)

'Penitence and prayers' are 'fruitless'. Therefore

> Snatch me, just mounting, from the blest abode;
> Assist the fiends and tear me from my God!
>
> (287)

I do not think another example in English of this recurring conflict strikes so shivering a climax. Notice the hampering pauses, aiding the sense, and how that last line of unsurpassed, perhaps unequalled, force is done almost entirely by plain concrete nouns and active verbs.

The general effect is one of sharp, agonizing conflict tragically resolved; though it is a conflict aspiring to a blend, as we have seen, since nature touches, or rather overwhelms, grace at one point, and grace absorbs nature at another. We who read feel a resolution Eloisa cannot be supposed to know. A vast nature broods over the whole: the dark eternity was from the start imagined largely in natural terms, and the conflict is unobtrusively related to tempests, seas, and winds. There is also a kindlier nature-imagery, of pines, wandering streams, and lakes that 'quiver' in the breeze (155-60); and a calm sea (253). The poem's end is calm. Abelard from the start is 'mixed' in Eloisa's mind with the image of God (12); he seemed 'angelic', as some 'emanation from th' all-beauteous Mind' (61-2), but she loves him as a 'man', not an 'angel', envying no 'joys of saints', nor any heaven in exchange for love (70-2). There is one resolution only wherein the divine hymenaeals will be one with the human: death, where frailties fall away, and it will be no longer sin to 'mix' with Abelard (176). A voice speaks to her, as she rests 'on some tomb, a neighbour of the dead' (304), and one who had suffered likewise calls her to peace. Is that peace a living heaven or an everlasting night? We are told:

> . . . All is calm in this eternal sleep;
> Here grief forgets to groan, and love to weep.
>
> (313)

And yet she who speaks is a living, 'sainted', maid. Anyway, in death God absolves all 'frailties'. So now Eloisa would die, with Abelard, in 'sacred vestments' and with 'hallow'd taper', presenting the Cross to her eyes, to symbolize the transition from lover to Christ (325–7). At this last moment, when tragic serenity holds all in a final union, comes that last withering bitterness, which is yet no bitterness but another blessedness, a paradox revolving on the very axis of death's mystery. Eloisa is dead. Let Abelard come:

> Ah then, thy once-lov'd Eloisa see!
> It will be then no crime to gaze on me.
>
> (329)

And yet, again, death 'all eloquent' proves 'what dust we dote on when 'tis man we love' (336). Death's very negation is a voice, a statement.

Heavenly love resembles Abelard's (342). Abelard, Christ, Death, each is all at the last, confusedly, mystically. But the whole poem is its own only answer. Our earlier passage of love's victorious powers must be felt as complementary to the Dantesque paradise, and both related to the conclusion. The unity within and controlling the conflict is remarkable, the very agony creating resolution before our eyes, nature and grace being felt as one at the sharpest moment of dispute. The more forceful the emotion, the more serene the poet's mastery. Certain couplet paragraphs attain to intense and well-varied dramatic expression, with a natural, almost Shakespearian, coherence and rhythmic subtlety;[1] others, as we have seen, build separate excellences of sensuous warmth. The poem is strangely serene. Its emotional structures form and dissolve, it lives with a softly beating movement, glowing and fading, like the pulsing of a star.

III

Superficial differences should not prevent our recognizing the Shakespearian affinities of Pope's first period in subject, emotional sympathy, and general control. His verse technique itself derives ultimately, it would seem, from Iago's speech to Desdemona after

---

[1] Our relegation of Pope's poetry to silent study has done it a grave injustice. Given an adequate vocal projection, with full attention to modulation of vowel colour and variation in pace and pause, *Eloisa to Abelard* will be found as powerful a dramatic monologue as any in our literature.

their landing at Cyprus, variations of a similar sort being woven across a similar regularity of couplet and caesura.[1] Therefore his two more philosophical poems, his *Essay on Criticism* and *Essay on Man*, can be supposed to reflect not only his own views on literature and life, but some part also of Shakespeare's; there is, probably, no nearer analogy. Although the two poems were written at different periods, the first when Pope was only twenty, they develop a single, coherent, argument. Pope resembles Shakespeare and Milton in his straight-line development, his axes of reference being the same from first to last. These concern (i) nature, and (ii) a sense of the whole; together with a heavy stress on pride as the main hindrance to creative understanding. I offer next, with apologies for what I none the less feel to be necessary and unavoidable, brief abstracts of the two poems.

The *Essay on Criticism* (1711) is strikingly relevant today, though it is, unfortunately, only too easy to let Pope's trenchant exposition pass over the surface of one's understanding. The argument is often challenging, and many of his points, if offered now, might incur the charge of an excessive romanticism.

The critical intelligence is severely handled. Let those censure, we are told, who can write themselves; 'false learning' has damaged good sense; much poor criticism derives from inferiority and jealousy. Pope's centre of operation is an implanted faith in 'unerring nature': that is, creative life. This is the 'source', 'end', and 'test' of all art. Nature always 'works without show and without pomp presides', which is true enough of Pope's work, but less so of Milton's; it informs the whole organism as 'soul' a living 'body'; 'unseen', it yet imparts vitality to all else. But instinctive power is not by itself enough. 'Wit' (i.e. native ability) needs the control of judgement, and the two should work in harmony: "Tis more to guide than spur the muses' steed.' Nevertheless, nature remains primary and is only restrained, as Shakespeare's Polixenes also tells us, by laws of her own making, critical precepts coming, not from man's reason, but from Heaven: that is, nature in its widest sense (68–99). Too often critics, being creative failures themselves, seize on rules easy to understand,

---

[1] This has been remarked by Geoffrey Tillotson, and by someone else earlier, though who it was I cannot recall. I am not, of course, denying the vast difference between Pope and Shakespeare in terms of period and taste, and for a valuable side-light on this difference would point to John Butt's *Pope's Taste in Shakespeare* (1936).

pronounce judgement on their betters, and 'write dull receits how poems should be made'. If you should respect Homer, that is merely because Homer—we today might add Shakespeare—introduces you direct to nature. But no 'rules' are absolute; there is a 'grace beyond the reach of art' and any licence that works is itself a 'rule'. Rules are aids to expression, not limitations of it, and the end, not the means, is important (105–180).

Pride blurs understanding and leads to folly, but, pride once banished, 'truth breaks upon us with resistless day' (201–12). That is, many universal truths which cannot be positively demonstrated are self-evident once certain rigid mental hindrances related to intellectual pride are removed. Truth is in this way almost a moral quality. The thought relates to the New Testament and Pope's own *Essay on Man* very closely. Much faulty criticism, we may suggest, is due to the critic's not being able to conceive that a writer has touched an apprehension beyond his own, and a consequent unconscious abstracting of what he himself can most easily receive, the usual stressing of Perdita to the neglect of the Hermione-resurrection in *The Winter's Tale* being a modern instance. Which leads us to Pope's next point.

The art-form must be understood in the spirit of its composition and seen, or felt, as a *whole*. If it is vitalized by 'nature' and warmed by feeling, 'slight faults' are irrelevant. Cold correctness is not art. Parts, as parts, do not count in themselves, any more than a 'lip' or an 'eye' can make human beauty. Therefore no single element should obtrude overmuch. But critics, too often themselves 'fond of some subservient art' (e.g.—as we may suggest—history, theology, economics, biography, stage-technique, psychology, or indeed literary criticism—or interpretation—itself), some private interest of their own, 'still make the Whole depend upon a Part' (233–66). This continual doctrine of the whole is, of course, complementary to Pope's emphasis on a central life-force, 'nature', with derogatory remarks concerning the 'false learning' (19–27) of critics: since, as Pope observes, it is the unifying life that makes any whole organic. As a corollary, it follows that excessive ornament and verbosity are bad, departing from nature, that is, from sincerity: we may remember Pope's own instinctive reliance on nouns and verbs. Too much concentration on 'language' is bad; originality is as dangerous a temptation as copying; avoid 'laboured nothings' (289–336).

Critics who think only of surface smoothness and metrical delight miss many more important substances:

> *In the bright Muse though thousand charms conspire,*
> *Her voice is all these tuneful fools admire.*

(339)

Notice the word 'thousand'. That is, they miss the statement of the whole comprised, we may add, of sense-suggestion, subtle associations, ideas and symbols of all sorts, and much else; so dissolving it away into metrical and verbal technique, as people go to church for the music rather than the doctrine and substance. Literary cliques, we are told, are a danger, since 'wit' (i.e. poetic talent) becomes the supposed possession of a few with the rest damned. Do not ask whether a work be new or old: ask only if it be true. Critics who judge an author according to his personal importance rather than his works are a 'servile herd'. The vulgar err by imitation, the learned by a forced, inorganic, originality; rather than follow the crowd they 'purposely go wrong' (394–429). Praise is of little value that waits till others approve (474–5). A critic should preserve humanity and good sense: if all 'seems infected', the disease may be not in the object, but in the critic's own eye (558–9). Right criticism is as much a matter of moral fibre as of learning, and true counsel is not effective unless offered with tact (560–77). Pope's emphasis is everywhere *vital*. Every point scores, though I doubt if the last caution is sufficiently observed in such lines as:

> *The bookful blockhead, ignorantly read,*
> *With loads of learned lumber in his head . . .*

(612)

In Horace cool judgement was one with poetic inspiration, whereas today, says Pope, the reverse holds: critics judge violently, but write weakly.

The contemporary challenge to us is obvious. A creative intelligence opposes the academic and formalized mind. It is the old unfortunate opposition of the New Testament and it seems impossible to advance, though some good might come of attending to Pope's own clarifying of the issue in terms of two specific concepts: (i) nature, or vital power, and (ii) the whole. These may be considered respectively centre and circumference of Pope's universe. It is clear why 'the last and greatest Art' is the 'Art to blot',[1] since concern for the whole organism must sometimes involve the removal of some cancerous growth, itself aspiring to an independent, and therefore hostile, organic life of its own; like Milton's Satan, though we can be heartily glad of the fault. 'Nature' and 'judgement', power and control, instinct and art, may be unified under the holistic concept, since control of any part is constituent to the organic quality of a whole existing, as an organism, through the infusing power of its own central, and instinctive, life. Control acts in service to nature, not to dominate it, as Pope clearly asserts, and his own paragraph-units illustrate the maxim.

The *Essay on Man* (1733–4) is a precise development of the same doctrine on a wider front. It is not only a poetic philosophy, but the universal philosophy, not so much of poets as of poetry; and is, exactly, the philosophy implied by Shakespeare's work. Epistle II starts with a reaction from Milton ('presume not God to scan'), the more clear from the earlier claim (I, 16) to 'vindicate' instead of 'justify' His ways.[2] Pope still stresses the whole, nature, and the opacities of pride.

In the first Epistle our attention is drawn early to the vast cosmic whole, a 'mighty maze, but not without a plan', recalling *Windsor Forest*. To criticize it from the limitations of human reason is absurd:

> He, who thro' vast immensity can pierce,
> See worlds on worlds compose one universe,
> Observe how system into system runs,
> What other planets circle other suns,
> What vary'd Being peoples ev'ry star,
> May tell why Heav'n has made us as we are.
> But of this frame the bearings, and the ties,
> The strong connexions, nice dependencies,
> Gradations just, has thy pervading soul
> Look'd thro'? or can a part contain the whole?

(I, 23)

With what imperturbable and untroubled ease, comparable to that of Shakespeare's 'cloud-capp'd towers', the couplets roll out their

---

[1] *Horace, Ep.* II, i, 281.
[2] See Warburton's note to I, 16.

mighty images. So the poet asks why man complains. Weak though he be, why expect to be strong? Just as the lamb is ignorant of human purpose, so is man of the divine. The lamb 'licks the hand just rais'd to shed his blood', a merciful Providence blinding it: Pope's sympathy with small animals is again noteworthy. But, small or large, it is the same to God, whom we are shown in a great passage intent on His purposes, seeing 'with equal eye' either 'a hero perish or a sparrow fall', atoms or whole systems destroyed, 'and now a bubble burst and now a world' (1, 35–90). The smooth and controlled statement here lifts the mind to that final serenity conditioning tragic art. Death will answer questions. Meanwhile a life-force beats in us with resurgent hope, and to that we must trust (1, 95). Pope's vitalistic philosophy is at once vast and simple, working from the patent fact that the race does not commit suicide. It aims at interpreting life itself.

As before, the hindrance to cosmic receptivity is 'reasoning pride', pride working through reason. Thus order is disturbed: 'Rejudge his justice, be the God of God.' Man would invert the universal laws. In pride he assumes the world was created for him alone, that nature's riches are all for him. Yes, but what of nature's cruelty? Of earthquakes and tempests? Are not these natural as a spring morning? If so, why should not human evil, that of a Borgia or a Catiline, form needed part of the one great design? Notice (i) the reference of human evil to earthquakes and tempests, as in the Shakespearian symbolism; and (ii) the preliminary forgiveness of all evil which we may suppose to be at the back of Shakespeare's work. Sound reason, says Pope, must 'submit'; and indeed Jesus' doctrine of God's non-human justice was very similar. To Pope, conflicts are necessary. The great 'all' is based on elemental strife, and 'passions' are the *élan vital* of existence: the Shakespearian analogy is again obvious, passionate conflict being the very hub and axle of Shakespearian drama. All this, whatever, if any, its limitations, is a philosophy integral to tragic art. Moreover, though these disquietudes occur, the 'general order' in nature and man, the stability of the whole, is not in danger, as in *Richard II, Julius Caesar, Hamlet, Macbeth*, where order is felt as ultimately and inevitably undisturbed (1, 113–72).

The nice balance of human and animal faculties is analysed. Do we envy the fly's 'microscopic eye'? Given a more delicate sense-perception, who knows but that we might 'die of a rose in aromatic pain'? Were our hearing keener, tuned to a different wave-length, we might be stunned by the thunders of the cosmic music. Each life-form has its gifts, the lynx its sight, the hound his keen scent (I, 193–214). Great nature beats in the poetry, its vast and tiny miracles inspiring equal awe:

> *The spider's touch, how exquisitely fine!*
> *Feels at each thread, and lives along the line.*
>
> (I, 217)

Man's sense-perception and thought are subtly balanced with thin division. In this vast mystery of air, ocean, earth, all alive and pregnant with creative energies—'all matter quick and bursting into birth'—this *living* universe, where life is graded step by step upward, magnificently ordered into an 'amazing whole', where one disruption might upset all, why should man complain? Pope senses those same creative forces that so tingle in Goethe's *Faust*, however they be levelled under his own smoother harmonies. Would you have angels and suns, he asks, reorganized for your needs? That were at once madness, pride and impiety. It is as though the 'foot' or 'hand' should rebel against the head; the thought is continually of nature and organic life (I, 233–60). The 'great creating nature' of *The Winter's Tale* is Pope's explicit theme.

Pope attacks man's self-confident *reason*. It was, earlier, his violent aversion:

> *In Pride, in reas'ning Pride, our error lies;*
> *All quit their sphere, and rush into the skies.*
> *Pride still is aiming at the blest abodes,*
> *Men would be Angels, Angels would be Gods.*
>
> (I, 123)

Which may be read as an unintended criticism of Milton, whose nature is so continually humanized, eternalized, and in whom human impulse is all but petrified through a too tyrannic 'reason'.[1] The truer wisdom is piety towards God, or Nature. For

> *All are but parts of one stupendous whole,*
> *Whose body Nature is and God the soul.*
>
> (I, 267)

---

[1] For Milton's own *use* of the concept, see my note on p. 174 below.

An inexhaustible and magical life-force 'operates' ubiquitous and eternally 'unspent':

> *As full, as perfect, in a hair as heart:*
> *As full, as perfect, in vile Man that mourns,*
> *As the rapt Seraph that adores and burns.*

(I, 276)

The natural and the divine are not in conflict; there is a graded ascent, but no opposition. Therefore:

> *Submit—In this, or any other sphere,*
> *Secure to be as blest as thou canst bear:*
> *Safe in the hand of one disposing Pow'r,*
> *Or in the natal, or the mortal hour.*
> *All Nature is but Art, unknown to thee;*
> *All Chance, Direction which thou can'st not see;*
> *All Discord, Harmony not understood;*
> *All partial Evil, universal Good:*
> *And, spite of Pride, in erring Reason's spite,*
> *One truth is clear, Whatever is, is right.*

(I, 285)

See how the thought moves in terms vast and unethical corresponding to the symbolisms rooted in Shakespearian drama. This trust, lucid and impregnable in its cosmic grip, is necessary alike to any poetic or religious conception of the whole. It may be related in particular to the New Testament, Shakespeare, and Shelley's *Defence of Poetry*.[1] Such pre-eminently positive and vitalistic works might today be grouped together to form the basis of a new classicism, at once naturalistic and religious: that is, a body of doctrine which can be accepted, normally, by every educated person. There are few safer guides to such a faith than Pope, since he is never submerged by his own ocean-roll of rhythm, as Milton, nor burned by his own fire, as Shelley. He offers what is perhaps the most valuable of all insights: a coherent romanticism. This is reached through (i) a sense of ever-springing life in nature, the continual miracle of existence, and (ii) a dominating sense of the cosmic whole. Each, of course,

---

[1] The comparison of Pope's lines and Shelley's *Defence of Poetry* has since been developed in *Christ and Nietzsche* (1948), I, 20; III, 104. For Shelley, see also V, 175, note; 179; 201–2.

involves the other. The doctrine is positive, not negative; interpretative, not critical; got by a humility washing the mind transparent to see what is before its eyes. It is the conditioning starting-point for all wisdom.

Why, then, does it fail to satisfy? Only because a static philosophy, as such, must; must, indeed contradict itself. If all is perfect, how complain of man's absurd pride? Why indeed write any poem at all, since all action implies dissatisfaction? Yet Jesus' philosophy of love fails before the Pharisees who raise his wrath: there is always a good and evil while man remains an active force. Universal acceptance will never lead to an ultimate placidity in, at all events, a western mind; and observe that the discrepancy involves the problem of *action*. And yet this very discrepancy points us back to a provisional solution, for the final test is not static either. We should not ask 'Is the world as I see it perfect?' but rather, 'Does the belief in a final harmony *in practice* lead me to action that proves, however illogically, creative?' The problem centres finally on this question of subjective experience, and it will be seen how Pope in his second Epistle takes more precisely into account the dynamic of the human mind or soul. That is not, however, his business here.

As a statement of a positive acceptance conditioning creative action, the *Essay on Man* and Jesus' central assurance God = Love remain impregnable, and likewise appear to condition any satisfactory creations of epic or dramatic force in poetry. But, again, it is one thing to know God's love when you read a ghastly news-story in the morning paper, and quite another to feel the same when such a shadow creeps near your own life: trust in the universal harmony, though it may readily be known, is rarely to be lived through to the end. The best philosophic poetry, even the creative psychology which we shall study in Pope's second Epistle, leaves a want: if it did not, there would be no need for the New Testament drama, as complementary to its doctrine, Shakespeare's plays, or *Eloisa to Abelard*. These hold an extra dimension of shared action and shared experience: we are made to feel, however weakly, the hero's agony, whilst at the same instant knowing, however confusedly, the more inclusive harmony. The sharing is now part of our acceptance; dramatic, not philosophic, with an emotional validity beyond static theory. Hence *Paradise Lost* must be considered a far greater work than Pope's *Essay*, since, even though Milton be wrong and Pope right on the most crucial of poetic issues, Milton's Satan remains of more worth than any philosophy.[1] This is, fundamentally, the cause of the disparity between Jesus' simple doctrine and the complexities of Christian ritual and dogma, and it perhaps follows that the Christian Church errs in opposing pantheism rather than working for an inclusive assertion. Pope's first Epistle remains, like Jesus' faith, as true as any such philosophic statement can be: though itself static, it takes fully into account the dynamic of life, stressing the upsurging forces of nature continually, and specifically including evils. As a static philosophy, it will never be superseded while the human race is here to philosophize; but such philosophy, as we know it, may, and indeed must, be complemented by a more dynamic, subjective thinking such as Pope moves to in his second Epistle; which will depend also on our understanding of the New Testament drama, religious ritual generally, and especially tragic literature. Milton flies, like a moth to a flame, and with something of the same noble and selfless perversity, into the very centre of this problem, always working from the disharmony between nature and God, and caught in the spidery web of the problems involved by human free will and action. He is in *Paradise Lost* too much involved in his own fiction; Pope in the *Essay on Man*, if only because it is an essay and not a drama, too little; blend the two and you get Shakespearian tragedy, Milton's own Satan, or *Eloisa to Abelard*.[2]

Pope, indeed, once finely approaches the mystery in his Essay:

> *So Man, who here seems principal alone,*
> *Perhaps acts second to some sphere unknown,*
> *Touches some wheel, or verges to some goal;*
> *'Tis but a part we see, and not a whole.*

(I, 57)

This darkly shadows a very great truth indeed, the exploration of which is the central purpose of all my interpretations, for this sense

---

[1] The thought here is intricate, but its validity has since been supported by Maynard Mack who follows my argument in using a similar contrast of Pope's statement with Milton's Satan in point of 'dramatic' depth, his word 'ceremonial' balancing my use of 'ritual' below (*Twickenham* edition, Int., lxxiii).

[2] The central problem discussed in this paragraph has since been neatly handled by R. J. Z. Werblowsky, in *Lucifer and Prometheus* (1952). He argues that the acceptance of evil must always be limited to the past, and that in any 'concrete situation' involving choice such an acceptance must, failing some 'radical psychological revision of the values of good and evil', remain inapplicable (VI, 100).

of some new dimension beyond direct knowledge exactly corresponds to the shared, lived, mystery of tragic ritual, whether religious
or artistic. See how a geometrical and mechanical symbol, so unusual
in Pope, assists for once this deliberate penetration. Such a penetration is often reflected in literature into some cogent, often supernatural, symbolism thrown up by the dramatic conflict, and yet also
the very heart of the work concerned: the voice of eternity in the
'sainted maid', together with earlier similar impressions, is such an
integrating and resolving symbol in *Eloisa to Abelard*. Throughout
the *Essay on Man* there is an explicit belief in extra dimensions of
existence beyond the sensible-human, of angelic hierarchies and purposes. They are, unlike Milton's divine beings, left undefined, and
this lack corresponds precisely to that sense of a great otherness so
often given negative definition by a work of tragic art. Indeed, all
art works as much through what it leaves unsaid as through what it
says, and hence the positive force so mysteriously inhering in the
baffling technique of reserve generally which Pope so finely masters.
Our four lines accordingly express the fundamental meaning of
tragic art: the revelation, through experience, of some purpose,
beyond the individual, fulfilled by suffering.

In Epistle II Pope concentrates on man. He attacks science, con-
trasting its supposed certitudes concerning the majestic and mysterious universe with man's hopeless ignorance of, and lack of
mastery over, himself. It then concentrates on the instinct of self-love
as the primary thrust of human nature. Reason, we are told, can
look ahead and guide, but is not the motor force. Pope sternly
reproves thinkers who regard instinct and reason as enemies: 'More
studious to divide than to unite', they are happiest when 'at war
about a name'; and we may say the same about certain critical concepts that have since helped to fog the naturalistic synthesis of Pope's
own *Essay*. So Pope's attack is levelled against reason *in isolation*,
when out of touch with the creative principle (II, 1–92). When he
rejects a virtuous stoicism 'fix'd as in a frost', we may be reminded
of Milton's motionless and resisting Lady in *Comus*, and Jesus in
Paradise Regained. In a passage closely following a speech of Nestor in
Troilus and Cressida we are shown the grandeur of 'exercise' under
spiritual 'tempest', when God himself 'mounts the storm, and walks
upon the wind'. All passions can be directed for good, they are
indeed the necessary gale to drive on the ship; various emotions may
be harmoniously blended; man cannot, we are told, destroy what he

is himself composed of. We are urged towards a light-and-shade harmony tuned, with reason's help, to natural and divine purpose.

There follows a piercing analysis of dangerous 'master passions', explaining how they draw to them all natural forces of the personality with deadly success, and how, mothered by 'nature' and nursed by 'habit', they grow stronger by the help of other faculties. Evil is here deliberately related to nature; but Pope's ordering and directing of the psychological drama are very different from Milton's. He repudiates mental for more vital categories: 'rules' are no help where 'arms' are needed; to 'mourn' is not to 'mend'; reason, (here = conscience) may be 'a sharp accuser but a helpless friend'. He suggests that such thinking may prove deceptive, and insidiously make matters worse, as indeed seems to happen with Milton and Marlowe, whose poetry is far more dangerously sensuous than Shakespeare's or Pope's, as though they are simultaneously condemning and enjoying (II, 101–60). Pope's way is eminently practical. Nature's road 'must ever be preferred'. Reason by itself is here not even a 'guide', of no *positive* help, but it may well be of negative use, and 'guard' against disaster:

> 'Tis hers to rectify, not overthrow,
> And treat this passion more as friend than foe.
>
> (II, 163)

We have a psychology of integration that fits Shakespearian tragedy, and the sense we receive that the energy there displayed, as Keats once said in another context, remains, in essence, fine. It also ranges itself with Pope's holistic arguments elsewhere. We begin to see how, through the medium of a personal psychology, Pope has gone far to blend a universal acceptance with moral categories. He does not repudiate his first Epistle, but shows how, even though 'nature' may originate evils, the trust in her harmony may remain *creatively true*; and he next outlines examples of dangerous passions proving creative if well used. A virtue rooted in instinct, almost, one might say, in vice, grows strong, body and mind acting as one whole, 'wild Nature's vigor working at the root', the fine naturalistic emphasis recalling certain of Jesus' parables. Lust, we are told, may become love, sloth turn into philosophical meditation, while thought of what vices lie at the root even of our virtues may serve as a salutary check to pride. As for any more immediate and practical distinctions of good from evil, that is left, as indeed it must be, to 'the God within the mind'; probably a more secure trust than modern scepticism would allow. It is admitted that vice, as vice, can be real and increase through habit, though it should, normally, be instinctively hated and therefore, we may suppose, transmuted, in so far as seen and understood; the implication being that virtue is fundamentally the more instinctive. Yet we are told to remember always that virtue and vice are both parts of the self, and each self part of a greater whole, with which Heaven is mainly concerned, using different personalities for different, subsidiary, purposes, and building from defects the glory of creation (II, 175–248). The thought reflects the Shakespearian integrity while helping to define the Miltonic indecision. In Epistle II *the good-and-evil antinomy is all but resolved through a dynamic psychology serving as a transition from total acceptance to ethical discrimination.*[1]

So the third Epistle widens again from the individual to society, itself part of a cosmic drama felt as *positive activity*, wherein atoms cohere, matter blends with matter, dying vegetation produces new life, and all perishing forms are aspects of one vast vitality like bubbles on water: 'by turns we catch the vital breath, and die'. All parts blend into a single whole, one 'soul' connecting and preserving all, nothing, and the rule is observed by Pope's own poetic phrases, existing for itself alone. Man must not centralize nature in himself, as Milton's imagery tends to do, the bird does not sing primarily for him, the horse enjoys the ride. However, man alone attains unselfishness and imaginative power: the jay cannot admire the 'insect's gilded wings'. Animals preserved for slaughter have a good time first and do not foresee the doom man ultimately shares with them; and, by a similar prevision of nature, death never *seems* near to man. Notice the illumination of a simple but vast human truth through a natural analogy (III, 1–78).

There is again an emphasis on the respect due to instinct. Reason —we should say 'intelligence'—is generally slow to serve, but 'honest Instinct comes a volunteer', and, moreover, invariably hits its mark: the contrast is that between intuitive genius and laboured skill in any activity whatsoever, in life, art, or play. Instinct is 'quick' and tireless, reason 'heavier', and soon weary. Instinct makes for action; reason

---

[1] This, the core of my interpretation, has been accepted, with acknowledgment, by Maynard Mack as the core of his own: 'One of the functions of this epistle is to effect a transition from a mood of theodicy ("submit") to a mood of ethics' (*Twickenham* edition, lxi).

is merely a 'comparing' power. The one is permanent and 'must go right', whereas the other is intermittent and 'may go wrong' (III, 79-96). So

> . . . *Reason raise o'er Instinct as you can,*
> *In this 'tis God directs, in that 'tis Man.*

(III, 97)

'This' means, of course, 'instinct' in Pope's latinized syntax. The argument is part of a general tradition, or development, from the New Testament to Blake and Nietzsche. Nor is it quite so mad as it sounds: Keats likewise urged the sanctity of the heart's instinct. Nature that made the 'spider' design his 'parallels' (III, 103) can look after men. Pope, unlike Shakespeare and Swift, seems to have a warm corner in his heart for spiders. In this, as in much else, he is with Byron.

God, in designing the great whole, plants various bounds to the nature of all beings, whose bliss depends on mutual help. Union is really an instinctive end, since one nature feeds the vital flame of all creation:

> *Whate'er of life all-quick'ning aether keeps,*
> *Or breathes thro' air, or shoots beneath the deeps,*
> *Or pours profuse on earth, one nature feeds*
> *The vital flame, and swells the genial seeds.*

(III, 115)

In the 'fierce embrace' of sexual love nature's essential harmony is realized. This expands to love of children and, with reason's help, farther. Men know 'habitual' as well as 'natural' love: that is, lasting and deep emotions. From these charity is born. This use of parental love as a transition from the sexual-erotic to what St. Paul called 'agapé' is most important, but the use of 'habitual' is also neat, since the deeper love may often develop through habit alone (III, 119-46).

Nature's absolute rule was God's rule, and at first all was peace. But, since then, man has fallen to blood-sacrifice, slaughtered beasts for food, and become an enemy to himself (III, 147-68).[1] Pope does not reconcile this directly with his former optimism and the many obvious cruelties within nature. Man's slaughter of animals has from

---

[1] In his valuable study *The Golden Feast* (1952), Mr. Roy Walker has collected a wealth of material from mythology and poetry supporting the vegetarian philosophy. Pope is writing in this tradition.

the start troubled him, and may seem to dislocate the precision of his *Essay* considered as a whole. But he has been steadily making a most difficult transition from general acceptance to moral distinctions. We have already suggested that no static conception can do this, and we must not contrast Epistle III with Epistle I without remembering Epistle II. Until the very complex implications of this process are fully grasped, the separate Epistles are perhaps best read as independent approaches to the mysteries of human life: the first philosophical, the second mainly psychological, the third ethical. 'Nature' is throughout a binding and fusing concept, and the whole poem may be, provisionally, allowed to enjoy an artistic rather than a purely logical coherence. Yet perhaps nowhere in literature can we so clearly see, by regarding the place of Epistle II in the sequence, how there is logic of the most subtle and profound sort within the *arrangement* of any true artistic whole. We are watching something very rare: a poetic genius of the first order deliberately setting himself in maturity to create a compact and coherent system from his own creative centre.

Pope next describes man's progress to civilization, how human art copies birds, ants, and bees, the close reference of human and natural communities reminding us of *Henry V*. Nature, with finer laws than man, knows 'anarchy without confusion', a phrase throwing back to *Windsor Forest*; and this cannot be improved on by reason, which only entangles 'justice' in 'law' (III, 169–98). So societies and kings come into being. At first the patriarch was 'king, priest, and parent' in one, and led to the worship of a single father-God. All was well before 'wit oblique' scattered the 'steady light'. Disasters follow: tyrants, conquests, superstitions, devils. Pride and force come into play; emotional directions go crooked, 'fear' makes 'devils', and 'weak hope' constitutes religious faith. The divine is now felt as 'partial, changeful, passionate, unjust', gods are made in the likeness of 'tyrants', 'pride' builds a heaven and 'spite' a hell. Some of this fits pre-Christian theologies, but if we remember Milton's excessive and barbaric royalisms, Pope may be felt closer to his own day whenever he refers to force, or when he sees 'zeal' rather than 'charity' at the helm of religion (III, 199–262). Now all naturalistic faith is quickly lost:

Then sacred seem'd th' ethereal Vault no more.

(III, 263)

Remember how the elements of nature are in *Paradise Regained* (II, 121–6) under demonic domination. Pope, like Milton, believes in a 'fall', but there is a vast difference. His centre of judgement is never the fallen consciousness, which cannot prescribe to man's sinful state any more than the blind can lead the blind. Rather he is to be ranged with Keats in his emphasis on a past naturalistic piety; with Byron in his horror of blood-sacrifice; and with Shelley in his hatred of theological tyrannies. Milton, of course, has similar 'romantic' directions, and probably later poets owe him more than they think, but his poetic faith is disrupted by the attempt to force together incompatible systems.

To continue. That self-love driving man to crime makes him also protect himself against it: 'all join to guard what each desires to gain'. The bad logic and suicidal quality of selfishness is, indeed, excellently shown. Any great 'follower of God', 'poet' or 'patriot', aims only to rekindle nature's ancient light, to restore mankind as a whole to its fundamental instinct, the doctrine of both Jesus and Shelley. All Pope's thought is based on such vast natural directions: so, though different forms of government and religion arise in turn, that man 'can't be wrong whose life is in the right'. Truth is felt as a vital direction, not a mental concept or any arrangement of concepts, and the resolution of the *Essay's* central paradox is again implicit. So charity, which involves action, is greater than faith or hope, being 'all mankind's concern', inevitably and instinctively, however little they know or like it. Man, 'like the vine', can only gain strength from an 'embrace', self-love and social love being, at the last, identical (III, 269–312). The argument has a beautiful simplicity and precision, and may be profitably related to-day to our economic and international problems. One passage (III, 289–302) on order recalls Ulysses' order-speech in *Troilus and Cressida*.

The *Essay's* four parts are alternately general and personal, and the last Epistle treats of happiness:

> *That something still which prompts th' eternal sigh,*
> *For which we bear to live, or dare to die,*
> *Which still so near us, yet beyond us lies . . .*
>
> (IV, 3)

The touch is wistful, humble, and deeply understanding. Pope brings a Shakespearian insight to this simple yet vast issue, on which the 'learned' are consistently 'blind', taking extreme positions, either trusting in 'everything' or utterly agnostic (IV, 19–26); nor should a proper sympathy with Pope's whole argument accuse his own *Essay* of the facile trust indicated, since it shirks no tragedies of mortal existence, nor any moral evils, but rather sees into and through them. Behind the isolated selfishness of robber, tyrant, hermit, or proclaimed hater of man, he sees a lurking love, a desire for admiration or friendship. One common longing is felt behind all humanity. Happiness is not a matter of material circumstance, which indeed tends to negate itself, since wealth of any sort leads to fear and lack of it may condition hope. But the final peace rests in simplicity and virtue: 'And Peace, oh Virtue! Peace is all thy own.' Virtue naturally meets man's approval (IV, 39–88). The statement bears to the acceptance of moral evil in the first Epistle precisely the somewhat obscure relation borne by Macbeth's, or Richard III's, necessary condemnation within the play to the equally important artistic delight the spectator derives from his crime, Pope's thinking all along running parallel to the issues raised by study of Shakespeare, or any great tragic artist. We are reminded that noble self-sacrifice proves rather a willing 'contempt of life' than the inefficiency of virtue (IV, 102). God is next cleared, not altogether satisfactorily, of responsibility for certain evils in terms of general law, in that He does not abrogate the law of gravitation to prevent a death, the thought again involving the concept of the whole (IV, 111–30). There follows an incisive argument on simple virtue's essential independence of outward suffering or rewards, giving instead 'the soul's calm sunshine, and the heart-felt joy' (IV, 168). It is acutely observed that fame is really a matter of one's own circle, since the rest does not touch you (IV, 239). A striking autobiographical paragraph asserts that superior gifts bring only trouble: 'All fear, none aid you, and few understand' (IV, 266). An expanded contrast of simple integrity with the shams of worldly place and power follows Wolsey's advice in *Henry VIII*, and points towards Pope's own doctrine in the *Satires* (IV, 269–326). The way to happiness is through identity with the vast chain of being and rising whole that is the *Essay's* main argument. Our very aspirations are evidence of something beyond, since nature does not implant meaningless faculties; as so often, the thought is flashingly new. We are last brought to a vision of widening circles of altruism and a reiteration of the claim implied in nearly every line of the poem to have held up 'Nature's light' instead of 'Wit's false mirror' (IV, 327–

372; 393). 'Wit' in Pope is variously used: here it means 'human reason', normally something like 'intellectual talent', sometimes even 'poetic genius'.[1] It is here felt as specifically academic, perhaps contemporary: Pope's thought is probably dwelling on writers of his own day.

Pope's mature theory on man and his universe relates exactly to his *Essay on Criticism*, his own poetic practice, and his satires: to his nature-feeling, sympathetic human warmth, and sense of the artistic whole. His *Essay* is far from easy, but much of its difficulty is removed once it can be felt as a dynamic rather than a purely static statement. He works to substitute vital directions and a living psychology for dead concepts, with a strong sense of the marsh-like insecurity of rigid terms, as in his suggestion that the ethical reason alone may surreptitiously pander to the very vice it condemns (II, 155–60); or when he considers arguments concerning the 'forms of government' mere folly whilst putting emphasis instead on the *way* those forms are administered (III, 303). He keeps his eye steadily on the final test of action, individual or communal. The cosmic trust throughout may be related both to Bacon's *Advancement of Learning* and to Shelley's *Defence of Poetry*, and clearly touches certain modern tendencies with which it has not been as yet associated; as, for example, the naturalism of Henri Bergson; the holism of Jan Smuts, whose remarkable book *Holism and Evolution* adds a valuable concept to our vocabulary; and the all but excessive vitalism of Lawrence's *Fantasia of the Unconscious*. This only those, to use Pope's phrase, 'more studious to divide than to unite' (p. 49), can fail to recognize. Such rigid divisions are, it would seem, rooted in an unconscious fear that wills the dispersal of positive forces in order to avoid their massed significance.[2]

IV

The Dunciad (1728; final version, 1743) stands apart from both the *Essay on Man* and the satiric epistles. In handling with a poetic sublimity those personalities of the book-world whom he most despises, the poet fuses extremes to give us a mock-heroic of the

---

[1] Pope's use of 'wit' has now been discussed by William Empson in *The Structure of Complex Words* (1952).

[2] Additional remarks on the *Essay on Man* are offered on pp. 169–82 below. For its relation to 'religion' as normally understood, see especially p. 178.

same genre as *The Rape of the Lock*, but with a diametrically opposite tone. It is Pope's attempt to fit his worst particular experiences into the harmonies of great art after the universal principle symbolized by Dante's final vision of the divine circle mysteriously fitted to and enclosing, though how the poet cannot say, the human form. The resolving medium is humour as rich in its way as that of *The Rape of the Lock*. The particular references, on understanding of which the humour must partly depend, are unfortunately somewhat tedious, though they give rise to some entertaining notes by the author. That the subject should be so personal may seem regrettable, but the peculiar nature of the poem may be supposed to define the conditions under which alone a work of narrative, and even more one of heroic, art was felt by the poet to be possible. As in Dante, the poet's own negative experiences force themselves shamelessly forward; but, while personal records are certainly involved, general experiences, and not persons, are really in question, though the poet himself cannot quite be expected to know this. Literature was at this period the medium through which an old culture was felt to be in transit to a new, and the nature of its contemporary practitioners was intuitively recognized as a matter of vital national, if not racial, concern. *The Dunciad* objectifies the genius of its age and is an artistic document of considerable importance.

The irritating preponderance of forgotten names is, as one of the notes all but suggests, itself part of the design, the persons seeming the more boring and therefore fatuous for our ignorance. The prevailing darkness of the poetic atmosphere is thereby increased, since you are forced to wade through a stifling, clinging, muddy, bog-like substance of intractable references. The poem has also actual bogs, mud, and even 'mud-nymphs' (II, 332). It is couched in Pope's more sensuous, rich-throated, slow manner, and loaded with naturalistic and biological reference. Pope's work never shows the Miltonic emphasis on the hard or metallic: 'brazen brightness' and 'polished hardness' are terms of exact critical opprobrium (I, 219-20), while his own impressions are naturalistic. The atmosphere is thick and heavy with fogs, clouds, 'rolling smoke' (I, 248), 'vapours blue' (III, 3), and, generally, palling darkness; a 'veil of fogs dilates' the awful face of the Goddess of Dulness (I, 262); people move in a 'black troop' (II, 360); the darkly-vowelled name 'Mundungus' (I, 234) sets the tone. Many small or supposedly dull-witted animals are used with the normal derogatory associations, as in the second book of *Gulliver's Travels*: such are donkeys, apes, puppies, owls, crabs, bugs, maggots. A strongly physical impact is usual, as in the exquisite

> *Round him much Embryo, much Abortion, lay,*
> *Much future Ode, and abdicated Play.*
>
> (I, 121)

The animals may, when more fully realized, both help the poem and yet show Pope's own natural sympathy, as in

> *So watchful Bruin forms, with plastic care,*
> *Each growing lump, and brings it to a Bear.*
>
> (I, 101)

Or in the picture of 'huge Lintot' running:

> *As when a dab-chick waddles through the copse*
> *On feet and wings, and flies, and wades, and hops.*
>
> (II, 63)

The cramming of jerky monosyllables into one line is a usual trick in Pope where absurdity is to be indicated, and the awkward motion implied may recall his own expressly athletic grace, sense of vital movement, and consummate ease: correspondingly he sees his opponents as dull, and heavy in motion. Mechanic imagery is a precise association for the dull and inorganic, and so bad poetry makes the muses 'scream like the winding of ten thousand jacks' (III, 160); dull, creaking, brains work strangely, like 'ponderous slugs' of lead (I, 182) pumped into motion by an air-gun, or clocks that go by the movement of a weight beneath (I, 183–4); the hero's head, guided by the Goddess, is as a bowl that goes 'obliquely waddling to the mark in view' (I, 172); Dulness 'lumbers' like a 'rolling stone' (III, 293–4). The joy lies in translating to clear physical terms the cumbersome inefficiencies of so abstract an art as literature: Pope makes the ordinary man realize how a bad artist appears to himself, and the humour is often richly satisfying. All movement is slow, as when old Dulness 'heaved the head' (I, 257); the world of *The Dunciad* is ludicrously harmonious and organic, being all stupid, dull, sleepy, with its sleepy 'poppy' (III, 317), 'sacred opium' (I, 288) and 'drunken vine' (I, 303). The Dunces start their ludicrous harmonies, like asses braying:

So swells each wind-pipe; Ass intones to Ass;
Harmonic twang! of leather, horn, and brass.

(II, 253)

Subtle nasality and inanimacy ('brass') are used by a poet of warm
natural affinities to convey his impression of a dead art. But the
impression may be more naturalistic, as when

Keen, hollow winds howl thro' the bleak recess

(I, 35)

to signify music caused by emptiness. The poetry relies throughout
on heavy sensuous appeal, as when, again, the authors drive their
audience to sleep:

Then mount the Clerks, and in one lazy tone
Thro' the long, heavy, painful page drawl on;
Soft creeping, words on words, the sense compose;
At ev'ry line they stretch, they yawn, they doze.

(II, 387)

Which we must read very, very slowly, giving the vowels and 'z'
sounds their full chance. *The Dunciad* is the condemnation, by as
vital a poet as any in our literature, of the insidiously academic
writer, the poet of outward form lacking spiritual energy, in short,
the charlatan; one who, because he is out of contact with the springs
of life, is necessarily dull.

Heroic action is strongly physical; indeed, you may feel, too much
so, when we come to Curll's misfortune in the race, his prayer to
Jove, and subsequent recovery of speed 'renew'd by ordure's sympathetic force' (II, 103), and his later engaging in competition with
'salient spout' (II, 162) for a well-known authoress 'with cow-like
udders and with ox-like eyes' (II, 164). The booksellers' competition
is not for the squeamish. Sensibilities may well be offended, even
when we rule out all consciousness of contemporary and personal
reference; and yet the references are often such as, being fictional
physical impressions of an inward reality, ought not to hurt more
than direct reference to the vice intended, which is normally both
dangerous and respectable. Pope gives full reasons in his notes, and
we must suppose him sincere. Where there is a true humour, the
physical images perform a cathartic purpose of the most general
kind. The mud-diving competition, with the exquisite 'mud-
nymphs', is surely most happily conceived to objectify the

muck-raking of slanderous authors, and attains a mock solemnity that is too deeply humorous to be finally cruel:

> When lo! a burst of thunder shook the flood;
> Slow rose a form, in majesty of Mud;
> Shaking the horrors of his sable brows,
> And each ferocious feature grim with ooze.
>
> (II, 325)

To be read with a reverential and measured sonority. The humour depends on a discrepancy between true dignity and Pope's long-standing *bête noire* of unjustifiable and ludicrous pride. It can scarcely have done these heavy gentlemen harm for once to see themselves sinking 'with all the might of gravitation blest' (II, 318). A fine Miltonic transposition shows us one of them waiting his turn at the dive:

> In naked majesty Oldmixon stands . . .
>
> (II, 283)

What soft cohesive grandeur in the stately utterance! The image remains a noble warning to the human race.

The epic's beginning sets the note of gravity and bathos in happy balance:

> The Mighty Mother, and her Son, who brings
> The Smithfield Muses to the ear of Kings,
> I sing.
>
> (I, 1)

Book II starts with a Miltonic parody. But the essence of grandeur is quite purely transmitted: it is real, though its application be mockery. Just as the Goddess' temple has its 'sacred Dome' (I, 265), so the poetry has its own sanctity and shadowed grace, often with a mighty voice softened to nature's splendours:

> . . . in yonder cloud behold,
> Whose sars'net skirts are edg'd with flamy gold,
> A matchless youth! his nod these worlds controls,
> Wings the red lightning, and the thunder rolls.
>
> (III, 253)

Which seems almost wasted in a passage which is, as a whole, a magnificent exposure of absurd stage elaborations that make 'a new world to Nature's laws unknown' (III, 241). As in *The Rape of the Lock*, ritualistic dignity is used, though with a greater satiric intention. So we watch our hero setting the flames to his sacrifice of unsuccessful plays:

> *And thrice he lifted high the Birth-day brand,*
> *And thrice he dropt it from his quiv'ring hand;*
> *Then lights the structure, with averted eyes:*
> *The rolling smoke involves the sacrifice.*
> *The op'ning clouds disclose each work by turns. . . .*

(I, 245)

The first two lines are a parody on epic narrative that may remind us that the satire is throughout two-edged: there is a criticism of vacuous sublimity as well as criticism of trivial substance. But we can also feel, in these—to borrow Keats' phrase—'huge cloudy symbols' of an absurd pomp, these domes, temples, and altars, or the 'rev'rend flamen' of II, 354, a rich, indeed Keatsian, apprehension of the sacred.[1]

The whole work has, to quote Flecker's *Hassan*, a 'monstrous beauty like the hindquarters of an elephant'.[2] It moves with a similar cumbersome ease. The imaginative consistency recalls Dante's *Inferno*, which it resembles far more closely than Milton's Hell. Like Dante's poem, it is, to quote this time from *The Testament of Beauty* (III, 244), cluttered with 'earthly tangle', though whether it lie equally near to the 'throne of God' will perhaps be questioned. It has at least one claim to lie nearer, since there is a strange and happy absence of the sadistic.[3] The comedy is not precisely cruel: the dunces are all happy, are not shown as realizing their absurdity, and are allowed to maintain a certain physical, though ludicrous, dignity. Pope respects the physical to this extent, whereas he is merciless

---

[1] I have emphasized the sensuous qualities in Pope's poetry. Both J. Middleton Murry, in his essay 'The Poetry of William Collins' (*Countries of the Mind*, First Series, 1931), and F. R. Leavis, in *Revaluation* (1936), have stressed a relationship to the Metaphysicals. See also Maynard Mack's contribution to *Pope and his Contemporaries*, ed. J. L. Clifford and L. A. Landa (Oxford, 1949). Dr. Leavis' argument has been opposed by F. W. Bateson in *English Poetry* (1950; XIV, 254).

[2] Edith Sitwell, probably the first to appreciate this quality, has observed 'a kind of smoky and appalling beauty' permeating the poem (XVIII, 276).

[3] A penetration of the sadistic element in Dante's *Inferno* is one of the many profound insights of John Cowper Powys' *The Pleasures of Literature* (London, 1938; New York, under the title *The Enjoyment of Literature*, 1938).

when explicitly referring to ethical or artistic faults; and so Cibber, Oldmixon, and even Curll, have, in a sense, their own personal rights, like Sir Plume (p. 25). Dante's whippings and bodies stuck upside-down are, of course, part of a deadly serious statement, but Pope's delicate emotional and sensuous touch, felt in the softness, the nature-tone, of the whole atmosphere, is witnessed by his avoidance of what in his poem of mainly humorous intention would have been dangerous indeed. His few but somewhat callous references to poverty may be regarded as part of the metaphoric scheme in that they help to underline a mental and spiritual poverty. Shakespearian phrases often ring similarly callous with less excuse, offending a certain delicacy which has now become natural, whereas in the social consciousness of the past vagabondage and villainy had been identified. *The Dunciad* is Pope's *Inferno*, his *Macbeth*. That it refuses any violent evil is characteristic, for he writes from a mental horizon where such depths are not of primary importance: he feels, to adapt a phrase from Lyly's *Campaspe* (I, i, 82), 'letters' taking the place of 'lances'; and that is why his accusation of 'dulness' goes deeper than you might think, implying, as it does, a lack of mental vitality, and therefore of all those cosmic contacts on which the *Essay on Man* insists. Moreover, the poet's most intense personal antagonisms are next lifted as a weighty mallet to drive in his more general challenge, the whole mass of his emotional abhorrence in Books I to III—and they are mainly emotional and impressionistic, with slight attempt at rational analysis—being propelled in the subsequently added Book IV (1742) to establish a more philosophical charge, levelled at a whole culture.

In Book III the duncial are warned 'not to scorn your God' (III, 224). Book IV at once introduces us to abstract terms: Science in chains, Logic 'gagged and bound', Rhetorick stripped and languishing, Morality strangled, 'Mathesis' alone given freedom for her madness, but the Muses in 'ten-fold bonds' (IV, 21–36). The charge later emphasizes all the usual complaints, flattery in a 'sacred gown' (IV, 97), and, 'last and worst', that hypocrisy of the Muse, 'wit' without 'soul' (IV, 99–100). School education has become a meaningless discipline:

> To ask, to guess, to know, as they commence,
> As Fancy opens the quick springs of Sense,
> We ply the Memory, we load the brain,

Bind rebel Wit, and double chain *on* chain;
Confine *the thought, to exercise the breath;*
And keep them in the pale of Words *till death.*

(IV, 155)

I romanize crucial concepts. Universities come off no better. They dole out 'fragments, not a meal' (IV, 230). The 'critic Eye' acts as a 'microscope of Wit', studying 'hairs and pores', while quite missing how 'parts relate to parts or they to the whole', blind to 'the body's harmony, the beaming soul' (IV, 233-6). Something of the sort, surely, has happened with the study of Pope's own work, weighting him with labels. His own emphasis is still on the organic, the vitalistic, and set dead against all rigidities that would '*petrify* a Genius to a Dunce' (IV, 264; italics mine); against the 'cement' that binds together and reduces all mentalities to 'one dead level' (IV, 267-8). The stony and infertile are images of evil. The poetry, as before, is scattered with animal references, though these scarcely always maintain the precise animal tonings of Books I–III: to the silkworm (IV, 253), the adder (IV, 373), the fox (IV, 351), the humming-bird (IV, 446), with a delightful couplet on bees (IV, 79-80). There are exquisite descriptions of an exotic flower and a butterfly, which a scientist is satirized for having killed (IV, 403-36). We must not let Pope's or Swift's seeming over-stress of scientific indictment blind us to the substantial truth of their charges, at least where the humanities are concerned:

> *'Tis true, on Words is still our whole debate,*
> *Disputes of* Me *or* Te, *of* aut *or* at,
> *To sound or sink in* cano, O *or* A,
> *Or give up Cicero to C or K.*

(IV, 219)

God is replaced by a mechanic causality, and concepts of 'matter' and 'space' (IV, 475-6), pride making man 'the final cause' of the universe (IV, 478). Scientists are ironically commanded to

> *See Nature in some partial narrow shape*
> *And let the Author of the Whole escape.*

(IV, 455)

The proper *Dunciad* atmosphere is, on the whole, maintained, but the verse gets more taut and swift, as in the *Imitations of Horace*, and the book's more philosophic statement neatly links it with the *Essay on Man*: 'Be proud, be selfish, and be dull' (IV, 582).

We end with a prophecy of utter chaos, the heavy abstractions falling like the vast folds of a curtain to blot out the shows of human civilization:

> *Thus at her felt approach, and secret might,*
> *Art after Art goes out, and all is Night.*
> *See skulking Truth to her old cavern fled,*
> *Mountains of Casuistry heap'd o'er her head!*
> *Philosophy, that lean'd on Heav'n before,*
> *Shrinks to her second cause, and is no more.*
>
> (IV, 639)

All knowledge, losing contact with its true centre, turns 'giddy', turns in on itself, as today we have seen it do so clearly:

> *See Mystery to Mathematics fly!*
> *In vain! they gaze, turn giddy, rave and die.*
>
> (IV, 647)

The exact penetration into the chaotic and undisciplined, because unrooted, thought of the next two hundred years is almost uncanny. And now, since without the inner pulse of vital experience all sanctities are nothing,

> Religion *blushing veils her sacred fires,*
> *And unawares* Morality *expires.*
>
> (IV, 649)

'Chaos', the great 'anarch', rules. It is only too easy to shirk this challenge to our whole culture; to deny its precise relation to the warnings of Bacon's *Advancement of Learning*; and to Shelley's *Defence of Poetry*; to forget that respect for secondary causes still lingers deep in the twentieth-century mind, and that Pope's message stands above us, and beyond us, today.

V

From *The Rape of the Lock* and *Eloisa to Abelard* Pope moves, through *The Dunciad*, to philosophy and satire. Of these, the one is merely the obverse of the other, they are complementary, the *Essay on Man* being timeless and universal, and the satires particular

and contemporary. This general move towards teaching, or prophecy, may be thought to register, in one sense, a fall, as Pope's
compact line half-acknowledges, saying how, leaving 'Fancy's maze',
he 'stoop'd to Truth and moraliz'd his song.'[1] But that is not the
whole story. We watch poetry discarding heroic themes and aiming
to achieve direct social impact; rather than describe actions, it
becomes itself active. The pen was rapidly becoming a force comparable with the sword, and more is involved than literary jealousies or
personal antagonisms. Besides, the nature of Pope's attack is of an
importance reaching far beyond his own age. The *Essay on Man*
presents a substantially new and vitalistic synthesis, which, though
in spirit deriving from the New Testament, was nevertheless
academically unorthodox and did not find another full poetic voice
for half a century; and which is, moreover, of a positive power to
meet with misunderstanding, resistance, and even hatred, in any age.
Only in terms of this visionary positive can the satires receive a
precise understanding.

Pope's negative position may be more closely defined, and is
therefore more valuable, than Swift's.[2] Images of disgust are rather
ethical than physical in their direction, resembling Shakespeare's,
and the attack is strictly limited. Full-blooded crimes we have already
seen equated with tempests and set among the harmonies of the
Essay. These, being easily recognized, are of comparatively slight
danger, and the attack concentrates on the more insidious and respectable vices, seen as some form of untruth to nature, loss of vital
centres, insincerity, dishonesty, or pride. The conception is never
rigid; we find rather an attempt at a very subtle, though often
virulent, diagnosis. Society is shown as intrinsically self-contradictory, and individuals as lacking any wholeness of personality, any
health.

We pass now to the *Moral Essays* (1731–5). In his *Epistle to Lord
Cobham*[3] Pope attacks those who concentrate on second causes, and
continues with a profound commentary on human nature. Personality, he says, cannot be reduced to reasoning and principles, any
more than the dissecting of an animal can isolate its life for analysis.
In personal relationships all is relevant to the observing subject, and

[1] *Epistle to Dr. Arbuthnot*, 341.
[2] See my essay 'Swift and the Symbolism of Irony', in *The Burning Oracle*
(1939).
[3] *Moral Essays*, I.

we are very far from attaining to clarity concerning even our own motives (23–50). Men change from hour to hour, according to their employment, the time of day, the company they mix with, and reasoning can never bring down the elusive essences of such 'flying game' (63–98). All who argue from data and facts with 'retrospective eye', attempting to find the cause from inspection of the thing, the 'motive' from the 'deed', are on insecure ground (99–102). A good action need not originate from true goodness, nor does wise reasoning prove wisdom (109–18). We are urged to discover, presumably through intuition, a man's 'ruling passion', the centre of energy, when all should fall into perspective: otherwise you mistake 'the scaffold for the pile' (174–227). We may suggest that the discovery of certain centres of energy in Shakespeare and Pope serves similarly to clear up many confusions on the plane of conscious intention.[1]

Pope's emphasis on vital direction rather than any moral absolute or set of absolutes determines his human analysis. He sees wealth, as in the amazingly compact narrative of Sir Balaam,[2] doing the devil's work. His sense of the concretely vital is used to expose the appalling dangers inherent in the ever more abstract tendencies of finance, a hundred oxen being ironically imagined as arriving at a statesman's levee from a foreign country,[3] and the essential intangibility of the most dangerous vices being shown to work in double harness with the growing intangibility of wealth. Pope's positive emphasis is simple and concrete:

POPE: *What Riches give us let us then enquire:*
     Meat, Fire, and Clothes.
BATHURST: *What more?*
POPE: *Meat, Clothes and Fire.*
                              (*Moral Essays*, III, 79)

In opposition, he paints the typical vulgarities of his age in *Moral Essays*, IV, with a description of a garden-design showing no 'art-ful wildness', each 'alley' symmetrically balanced by a 'brother', and 'trees cut to statues, statues thick as trees', the last image compressing his habitual aversion from the statuesque to any denial of organic life (IV, 113–20). We are taken to a library well stocked with unread books, a lavatory where 'gaping Tritons spew to wash your face',

[1] Pope's arguments here may be aligned with what I have called the 'spatial' approach to literature or biography; see *Lord Byron: Christian Virtues* (1952), I, 47.
[2] *Moral Essays*, III, 339–402.   [3] Ibid., III, 58.

and a dining-room of solemn grandeur more appropriate to a
'temple' or 'hecatomb' (IV, 133–56). It is all insincere and out of touch
with the real situation, a forced hospitality:

> In plenty starving, tantaliz'd in state,
> And complaisantly help'd to all I hate.
>
> (IV, 163)

Against this we have a characteristic longing for golden corn again
to 'embrown the slope', and wave above the forgotten ruins of a
fallacious gaudiness (IV, 173–6).

The conception is Shakespearian: in *Timon of Athens* wealth and
entertainment depend on living sincerities and, those gone, the palace
crumbles; just as Enobarbus' allegiance to Antony's fortunes is conditioned by Cleopatra's faith. Pope's close kinship to Shakespeare
is felt again in his *Epistle to a Lady*.[1] The feminine temperament is
vividly and variously characterized: Atossa is an amazing study of
dangerous vitality; Chloe is drawn from a violent reaction to the
non-vital, recalling the Messenger's description of Octavia in *Antony
and Cleopatra*; and a sympathetic treatment (269–80) of feminine
complexity fits Cleopatra neatly. Pope senses a vital positive, and
his view of women does not take the Miltonic turn, though he can
be severe, as Byron seldom is. All Pope's most violently satirized
people, even Chloe, are very much alive, though the most vivid are
perhaps scarcely credible. Dryden in *Absalom and Achitophel* perhaps
gains as a dramatist what he loses as a satirist, his Achitophel and
Zimri being too well rounded, too composed, for the intended condemnation, at least for the kind of condemnation Pope brings to the
creation of Sporus, his satiric portrait of Lord Hervey, in the *Epistle
to Dr. Arbuthnot* (1735).

But Sporus is no mere personification of a thesis, nor even a type.
He could not properly be fitted with a Jonsonian label:

POPE: *Let* Sporus *tremble—*
ARBUTHNOT: *What, that thing of silk,*
           Sporus, that mere white curd of Ass's milk?
           Satire or sense, alas! can Sporus *feel?*
           Who breaks a butterfly upon a wheel?
POPE: *Yet let me flap this bug with gilded wings,*
           This painted child of dirt, that stinks and stings;

[1] Ibid., II.

Whose buzz the witty and the fair annoys,
Yet wit ne'er tastes, and beauty ne'er enjoys. . . .

(305)

That he should be shown as not enjoying any full-blooded pleasures is necessary. Smiles show his emptiness 'as shallow streams run dimpling all the way'. He is created largely from vivid impressions of disgust, and is a 'toad half-froth, half-venom', who 'spits' himself abroad

In puns, or politics, or tales, or lies,
Or spite, or smut, or rhymes, or blasphemies.
His wit all see-saw, between that and this,
Now high, now low, now master up, now miss,
And he himself one vile Antithesis.

(321)

He is utterly insincere, a 'cherub' face disguising a serpent nature. The study has a striking and unforgettable vitality drawn from the poet's intense loathing, expressed first in jets of venom, then speeding into accumulations that whirl giddily, inducing sickness at an ever-lasting self-contradictory Nothingness. An utter lack of self-realization, of psychic wholeness, is indicated, together with a failure to fuse the masculine and feminine elements ('master' and 'miss' and, later, 'head' and 'heart') in the personality. 'Antithesis' sums the indictment, its strong force yet weak vowels reflecting a psychic discrepancy which has not attained the status of conflict: the subject is *content*, yet every instant offends against and denies Pope's philosophy of integration in the *Essay on Man*.[1] The use of monosyllabic jerks both makes for a puppet-like movement, though Sporus is more than a puppet, and acts as a fusillade of scorn; and what vitriol charges the exactly placed 'blasphemies'! Whatever or whoever the human prototype, or prototypes, this is scarcely a rounded study, but neither is there any single *idea* behind its creation, as there is, for example, behind Sir Epicure Mammon; rather is it caught straight from contact with those human personalities stated by Pope himself to be irreducible to concepts or principles of reason. It holds a more intense poetic energy, a greater compression of passion, than does Dryden's Zimri: that glows, this is white-hot. Dryden draws a real man, but Pope distills, compresses, and ejects through one per-

[1] For a closer discussion of Sporus as a dissociated personality, see *Christ and Nietzsche*, IV, 125.

son, the living essence of a whole poisoned society. Sporus, set between Shakespeare's Lucio and Byron's Steno, is a poetic archetype.

The creation is paradoxical, since its very intensity is set to constitute a condemnation of not-being: Sporus is vigorously inactive
and powerfully a nothing. The lively essences are, of course, Pope's,
and these are strongly emotional. Had the condemnation depended
on pure reasoning rather than on an analytic impressionism it would
have cut across the poet's own human understanding as expressed in
his *Epistle to Lord Cobham*.[1] The emotional and sensory nature, the
personal and relative quality, of the portraiture, indeed save it from
certain charges, since there is no claim to a dispassionate consideration. The feeling is directed against a person, or society, not being
properly itself, and the more cool, less sensory, yet equally un-
reasoned, scalpel, incisiveness of the Atticus analysis earlier, being a
study of insincerity, lukewarmness, and petty pride, is at root a
similar indictment. Both, being creations drawn from real persons,
are, as such, scarcely charitable, and we may find it difficult to isolate
a purely receptive and imaginative understanding. Yet we can never
exactly know the provocation, and any final judgement on the
original situation must, it seems, include information of a subtle sort
quite impossible to obtain. All fiction has its germ in personal experience, and Lord Hervey may well have provided merely a release-
moment to a piled-up disgust of society as a whole, like the bursting
of a dam. The compressed venom resembles that of Shakespeare's
final period, and substantially the same experience is being transmitted. Conditions now force, or at least allow, a shameless, to us
it seems a libellous, directness of reference: the context is different,
but Pope is perhaps no more to be blamed than Shakespeare. For all
we know there may have been living originals of Osric and Oswald
—or Caliban!

The *Epistle to Dr. Arbuthnot* itself gives us Pope's most comprehensive defence:

> *Curst be the verse, how well soe'er it flow,*
> *That tends to make one worthy man my foe.*

(283)

Here and elsewhere he is quite certain of his rectitude. This epistle
shows a blend of violence and gentleness, varying between attack
and pathos, social criticism and autobiography, swelling and subsiding

---

[1] *Moral Essays*, I.

69

with an undulatory movement, whose balance repays attention. His chief boasts, of looking after his mother to the last and cherishing a deep friendship, are not those of a misanthrope: he is never submerged by his own satire, but well above it. He may have been mistaken in actual judgements—how can any man be certain of another's worthiness or knavery?—but his personal reactions are being used as the explosive force behind a satire which becomes elsewhere a quite general indictment. I believe a final understanding will acquit him of unnecessary cruelty, though it might have to be couched in intellectual terms which his more intuitive sense of his own righteousness need not have taken into account. Anyway, his persons are today as fictional as Iago and Cloten, and the writing indisputatably holds the kind of integrity needed for great poetry. I ask that we bring such a view to a short inspection of Pope's *Imitations of Horace* (1733–8). Such a view is at least fictionally forced, since these epistles, like that to Arbuthnot, sometimes dramatize the poet himself, showing him in a favourable light.

They enjoy a strange agility and happy freedom, together with a strangely non-sensuous appeal and a vivid use of abstract nouns; a continual, if reserved, nature-reference helping to preserve the usual Shakespearian kinship. They are often dramatic with a dialogue structure showing Pope's discussion with some friend on his own position as satirist. Dissatisfaction with his calling alternates with sublimation of it, the central stimulus being at once a general irritation and a happy sense of power. Though he knows himself part of the process he deplores, the loss of contact, the flinging apart of ideals and actions, literature and life; though he is forced back continually on discussion of great writers or himself instead of other heroisms; yet now his ethical mission grows clearer and his verse becomes more sinewy, purposive and fast. As dynamic ideals are pitted against a putrefying society, so the language, like that of Shakespeare's later style, is continually at work to transmute living essence into a compact yet lightning phraseology, as in the pith and pregnancy and mastery of the abstract and universal in 'puff'd prosperity',[1] or

> *Oh Impudence of wealth! with all thy store*
> *How dar'st thou let one worthy man be poor?*
> (*Horace, Sat.* II, ii, 117)

[1] *Horace, Sat.* II, ii, 126.

These vast yet feather-light abstractions flash like a club: 'prosperity', 'impudence'; or again, 'violence', 'antipathy' (as on p. 76 below). Pope fights material inertia with a spiritual energy, aiming to inject poetic vitality into the communal mind without any reliance on fiction.

These self-dramatizing epistles are as little negative as *Timon of Athens*, a play which covers Pope's major attacks. There the positive, the purposeful direction, is in the hero; here in Pope himself. He becomes his own protagonist, and separate satiric thrusts are subsidiary to discussion of their own nature and necessity. Having followed his own teaching in Epistle II of the *Essay on Man* by trusting those ruling and envenomed passions that can simultaneously create a Sporus, he also rises beyond them, mounts on his own emotions, brings his whole self to the launching of a less personal, yet even more virulent, attack. The sublimated emotion, though continuous with the other, is qualitatively different, the expression less sensuous and the emotion impersonal:

> *Farewell then Verse, and Love, and ev'ry Toy,*
> *The Rhymes and Rattles of the Man or Boy;*
> *What right, what true, what fit we justly call,*
> *Let this be all my care—for this is All.*
>
> (Horace, *Ep.* I, i, 17)

He feels newly grown up, and his poetry takes on a Pauline fervour, the new inclusiveness making his earlier work seem to him, though not necessarily to us, comparatively weak. There is a delighted excitement, with a corresponding lessening of personal hostility, his interlocutor sometimes interrupting to create a subtle humour. The impersonality is one with the drama. He is now more interested in himself as satirist than in any satire, but only because he is presenting himself as a dramatized universal, as the voice of a communal vitality divorced from the community. This, the objective viewing of his own vital direction, is the true gist of the little dramas. They are therefore in essence positive and impersonal.

The explicit attacks continue as before against luxury and corruption, with usual reminders of temperance and simplicity. Commercial enterprise has become a mad race for wealth at whatever physical risks,[1] flattery has undermined Church teaching [2] and

---

[1] *Horace, Ep.* I, i, 67-72.
[2] Ibid., II, ii, 218-25.

letters.[1] Crown and politics are alike corrupt.[2] The old aristocracy has fallen before a new order of 'booby' lords.[3] So

> In Soldier, Churchman, Patriot, Man in Pow'r,
> 'Tis Av'rice all, Ambition is no more!
>
> (Epilogue I, 161)

The throne itself is vigorously attacked, especially in the Epistle to Augustus, where the old thought of England as a dominating and central influence recurs with ironic intention.[4] The swing-over from Elizabethan royalism to the piercing revolutionary visions of the early nineteenth century pivots on Pope's work. He writes of war like Byron:

> . . . let Jove encrust
> Swords, pikes and guns, with everlasting rust!
> Peace is my dear delight. . . .
>
> (Horace, Sat. II, i, 73)

His 'Yes, the last Pen for Freedom let me draw' [5] suggests that pen to be rather the first of a new, than the last of an old, order.

Since the main complaints date back at least to the New Testament, though as far from satisfaction now as then, they are not in themselves so important as is their vigour of transmission. Besides, the aim is towards an emotional redirection more fundamental than any specific teaching. Certainly what Pope regards as ugly, stupid, evil, or what not is, to any right-thinking person, ugly, stupid, and evil. There is no indecision: ethical fervour and imaginative virility are co-active in as sure and indissoluble a partnership as you will find anywhere. But the vigour is the teaching. That is why personal disgusts must still be allowed reference, and Pope refuses to limit himself to attack on abstract sins,[6] since that lets slip the very dynamic he would exploit. The concentration on such is itself a danger: the 'fear' of desiring advancement as bad as the desire, since each equally argue an admiration;[7] and this is not to be cured by any thinking, by any static doctrine. No attack is levelled against obvious crime. The dispute seems to involve an essence at once more than mental and less than instinctive: 'a fool quite angry' is 'quite

[1] Horace, Sat. II, i, 21–2.
[2] Epilogue, I, 105–10.
[3] Horace, Sat. II, ii, 175–6.
[4] Horace, Ep. II, i, 394–419.
[5] Epilogue, II, 248.
[6] Ibid., II, 13.
[7] Horace, Ep. I, vi, 18–21.

innocent' in the *Epistle to Dr. Arbuthnot* (107). Purposive vitality gets respect: it is the test of highest poetry.[1] After all, Pope had praised Sir John Blunt in a difficult passage [2] for rationalizing a 'ruling passion' into a mad scheme, with sharp condemnation of purposelessness, even though purpose be taken to 'extremes'. This comes during a discussion of the motives and rationalizations of avarice,[3] where the subtleties involved force a treatment in personal and narrative terms. Pope's ultimate gospel is not reducible to a static logic, and must be referred to the dynamic psychology in Epistle II of the *Essay on Man*. In both this and his doctrine of the universal balance and 'power',[4] he draws close to the teaching of Nietzsche.[5]

The poetry, though tense with passion, is always superbly at ease. There is a white purity as well as a white fury. It is, indeed, itself happy, with a gay variation, showing often a delightful friendship in the manner of address, with diction chatty, forceful, amiable, and resonant, by turns. Separate lines exert a stripped athletic grace, as in the clean action of, 'The devil is in you if you cannot dine',[6] or 'The worst of madmen is a saint run mad'.[7] There is a Shakespearian control of vast concepts, as in this reminiscence of *Troilus and Cressida* followed by one of Pope's new running lucidities:

> This subtle Thief of life, this paltry Time,
> What will it leave me if it snatch my rhyme?
>
> (*Horace, Ep.* II, ii, 76)

A darker, though no less brave, cosmic apprehension than that of the *Essay on Man* draws him now closer to *King Lear*:

> This Vault of Air, this congregated Ball,
> Self-center'd Sun, and Stars that rise and fall,
> There are, my Friend! whose philosophic eyes
> Look thro', and trust the Ruler with his skies,
> To him commit the hour, the day, the year,
> And view this dreadful All without a fear.
>
> (*Horace, Ep.* I, vi, 5)

[1] Ibid., II, i, 338–47.
[2] *Moral Essays*, III, 151–62.
[3] Attacked at *Horace, Ep.* I, i, 65–84.
[4] *Moral Essays*, III, 159–68.
[5] The complexities of Pope's ethical thinking forecast Nietzsche's, and for a further elucidation I must point to my analysis of *Thus Spake Zarathustra* in *Christ and Nietzsche* (v).
[6] *Horace, Sat.* II, ii, 148.
[7] *Horace, Ep.* I, vi, 27.

See the careless handling, the reckless poetic out-tossing, of immensities together with the new intensity shadowed of a *Macbeth* fear, as again in the solemn meditations of his epistle to Colonel Cotterell:

> *Does neither Rage inflame, nor Fear appal?*
> *Not the black fear of death, that saddens all?*
> *With terrors round, can Reason hold her throne,*
> *Despise the known, nor tremble at th' unknown?*
> *Survey both worlds, intrepid and entire,*
> *In spite of witches, devils, dreams and fire?*
> *Pleas'd to look forward, pleas'd to look behind,*
> *And count each birth-day with a grateful mind?*
>
> (*Horace, Ep.* II, ii, 308)

We may leap the centuries to find a quatrain of Byronic detonation:

> *Say, does thy blood rebel, thy bosom move*
> *With wretched Av'rice, or as wretched Love?*
> *Know, there are Words, and Spells, which can control*
> *Between the Fits this Fever of the soul.*
>
> (*Horace, Ep.* I, i, 55)

The word music is precisely one with meaning: it is rather a vibrancy than a music. There are swinging blows and hammering repetitions. The couplets break free of old constraints, they ripple, ring, dance, volley, joke, and reverberate, using a whole armoury of technical resource; scatter a hail of monosyllables, tilt with alliteration. Scorn of militaristic heroisms rolls out in the heavy ironic assonance of

> *Rend with tremendous sound your ears asunder,*
> *With Gun, Drum, Trumpet, Blunderbuss, and Thunder . . .*
>
> (*Horace, Sat.* II, i, 25)

Or equal scorn is meted to Miltonic excellences of

> *Gold, Silver, Iv'ry, Vases sculptur'd high,*
> *Paint, Marble, Gems, and robes of Persian dye . . .*
>
> (*Horace, Ep.* II, ii, 264)

Pope's own mind runs rather to nature and man than to inventions, crafts, and arts. But a different appreciation, together with hint of an earlier style, murmurs in the delicate fervency of 'Then Marble, softened into life, grew warm'.[1]

---

[1] *Horace, Ep.* II, i, 147.

The best strength does not show itself in short quotation, but rather in paragraphs, where couplet-modulation is malleable as in any Shakespearian sequence, a muscular cohesion rippling vertically down the page. Such evolve organically, couplet answers couplet, as in the run-on movements of the conclusion to the epistle to Bolingbroke.[1] The dialogue form may assist delightful humour as at the conclusion to the epistle to Mr. Fortescue,[2] or the split line-units and tennis-ball toss and return within and across the couplet in the second *Epilogue*, 10–27. Pope's humour is never unhealthy, never itself cruel, though on occasion he himself is: nor is it ever far off.

There is no bitterness, since at every instance there is creative direction, but neither is there any weakening of scorn. He would 'cure the arrant'st Puppy of his Pride',[3] and plant a scorching, branding impress:

> *Yes, while I live, no rich or noble knave*
> *Shall walk the World, in credit, to his grave.*
>
> (*Horace, Sat.* II, i, 119)

Yet all must be felt as flotsam on the torrent of the one forthright passion. He answers objections from an impregnable ethic: if a distasteful image turns your stomach, so, he replies, 'does Flattery mine'[4]. His calling is one of national importance, 'useful to the state' as any soldier's,[5] provided that it does not sink to praise of some 'monster of a king', or turn virtue or religion to sport.[6] In straight-line development from *Windsor Forest*, Pope's patriotism is no whit abated, though now his 'country's ruin' makes him 'grave'.[7] Friends recognize and acknowledge his integrity;[8] they are dramatized as warning him against the dangers that must certainly have been risked,[9] but he insists on driving his attacks far beyond personal animosities against people in high position against whom he has, as an individual, no possible complaint,[10] following only 'Virtue' and her friends,[11] indebted, 'thanks to Homer', to 'no Prince or Peer alive'.[12] Enjoying a brave independence won by his pen, he feels that pen as a pistol,[13] or a sword,[14] and satire a 'sacred weapon'.[15] Grouping St. Paul with Aristippus, he acknowledges no final intellectual

---

[1] Ibid., I, i, 161–88. [2] *Horace, Sat.* II, i, 143–56. [3] *Horace, Ep.* I, i, 60.
[4] *Epilogue*, II, 182. [5] *Horace, Ep.* II, i, 204. [6] Ibid., i, 210–11.
[7] *Epilogue*, II, 207. [8] *Horace, Sat.* II, i, 138. [9] Ibid., i, 101–4.
[10] *Epilogue*, II, 157–67. [11] *Horace, Sat.* II, i, 121. [12] *Horace, Ep.* II, ii, 69.
[13] *Horace, Sat.* II, i, 105. [14] *Epilogue*, II, 248. [15] Ibid., 212.

authorities except 'righteousness',[1] and that 'priestless Muse' which preserves good men with fire caught from her 'shrine', and opens the 'Temple of Eternity'.[2]

So a happy valiancy, a buoyancy and triumphing certitude, ring from a confidence resting on 'the strong Antipathy of Good to Bad'.[3] Though he is surely too bold, trusts too uncompromisingly in a human intuition, and thus himself incurs the charge of pride, he makes of his answer at once a final defence and a further thrust:

> Yes, I am proud; I must be proud to see
> Men not afraid of God, afraid of me.
>
> (Epilogue, II, 208)

He is proud, as St. Paul is proud, with a righteous, because now wholly impersonal, intolerance. The lines speak with a vigour and transparency of syntax deriving from the simplicity and force of the indictment. The teaching is never static, since that is the way to a thousand self-deceptions, mistaking the 'reverse of wrong for right'.[4] The burning sincerity of a more dynamic gospel is implicit throughout these epistles and shines in their very militancy. His aim is single: to set 'the Passions on the side of Truth',[5] and take Heaven by 'Violence of Song'.[6]

The keen religious fervency that projects itself into such phrases as 'virtue', 'Heaven', 'priestless Muse', 'Temple of Eternity', these last coming, as a climax, in the second Epilogue (234–5), may recall Pope's own early Dying Christian to his Soul (1712), his Messiah (1712), and The Temple of Fame (1711–1715), a poem deserving close attention for its vital and spiritualized use of the architectural. These poems stand slightly apart from Pope's naturalistic development. But in the Messiah the divine is itself a super-sun: there was never a final antagonism. In Milton a great force turns inwards, becomes rigid; in Pope an original gentleness widens to an overpowering prophetic challenge. His life-work shows a steady expanding, a flowering, of natural impulse into the ethical fervour of the Horatian epistles. Nor must we forget his Universal Prayer (1738), which states the centre and circumference of his doctrine.

[1] Horace, Ep. I, i, 23–34.   [2] Epilogue, II, 232–5.   [3] Ibid., II, 198.
[4] Moral Essays, III, 198.   [5] Horace, Ep. II, i, 218.   [6] Ibid., i, 240.

III

SYMBOLIC ETERNITIES:

An Introduction to 'The Temple of Fame'

III. SYMBOLIC ETERNITIES

I

AT the conclusion to our last essay we referred to *The Temple of Fame* with its 'vital and spiritualized use of the architectural'. This is Pope's only poem to concentrate at length on works of spatial artistry, and a separate treatment of it is needed.

This is not his normal *genre*. He was interested in the laws of architecture,[1] but as a poet he generally preserves a direct and unmediated approach to the human problem, whether in fiction, psychological diagnosis or satire, eschewing all facile symbols of transcendence and leaving the harmonizing and eternalizing to diction and couplet. His instinctive interests are nature and man; he has none of the previous century's delight in gadgets and artefacts. Too exact a formality in gardens or house-design repelled him, and he had little mercy on a nobleman's grounds full of 'trees cut to statues' and 'statues thick as trees'[2]; and he could write of metallic arts with scorn.[3] His poetry is not, any more than Shakespeare's or Byron's, dominated by other arts. And yet their *vitalities* fascinated him. In *Windsor Forest* he could endue 'a new Whitehall' with visionary meaning, and see 'temples' rising as 'the beauteous works of Peace' (378–80); he could compose the exquisite line, 'Then marble, soften'd into life, grew warm'[4]; and see the 'priestless Muse' opening the 'Temple of Eternity'.[5] He was interested in the new landscape gardening, columns, terraces and all, provided that it was a true collaboration of art and nature, as at Stowe.[6] He was himself a practitioner and innovator, making his own grounds at Twickenham a model, and devoting himself for many years to the artistry

---

[1] Tillotson, quoting Spence, 'Design', 95.
[2] *Moral Essays*, IV: see p. 66.
[3] *Horace, Ep.* II, ii, 264; see p. 74 above.
[4] *Horace, Ep.* II, i, 147.
[5] *Sat., Epilogue*, II, 235.
[6] *Moral Essays*, I, 47–70.

of his Grotto. He painted, too. Of his youthful experience as a painter and his passionate concern, both in poetry and in painting, for colour, Norman Ault has recently given us a valuable account, quoting his lines (1714-17) to Charles Jervas, his art-master:

> Smit with the love of Sister-Arts we came,
> And met congenial, mingling flame with flame;
> Like friendly colours found them both unite,
> And each from each contract new strength and light.

Thus smitten, they will tread together 'th' Eternal Alpine Snow', Pope's image for man's furthest endeavour, as in the *Essay on Criticism*.[1] So their track is pursued 'from art to art'.[2] Like Blake and Rossetti, Pope served both arts, glimpsing a wondrous possibility in their union; and in his address to Addison (1715-21) called for a revival of sculpture, honoured equally with poetry (51-8). The lines to Jervas have already been referred by Professor Tillotson to *The Temple of Fame*, in the *Twickenham* edition (1940; 231). But this artistic marriage raises so many fascinating questions that we must preface our discussion of the longer poem by a review of such symbolic fusions in the work of other poets. Without such a preparation, the peculiar importance of Pope's contribution cannot be assessed.

II

All art may be defined as the attempt to fuse 'space' with 'time'. Music and literature exist primarily in time, as sequences; sculpture, painting, and architecture, in space. But this is not the whole story. Each aims to transcend its limitations in space-time. Thus the temporal arts attain 'form' or 'structure', and are rich with all those meanings which I have regularly defined as 'spatial', while the spatial arts tend to suggest narrative, or at least to hold some vital significance that trembles on the brink of motion[3]; or again, even when this is least obvious, as in architecture, it is clear that they need time, as Byron observes when writing of St. Peter's in *Childe Harold* (IV, 153-9), for their mental reception.

[1] *Essay on Criticism*, 232; and compare the 'eternal snows' of *The Temple of Fame*, 57.

[2] *New Light on Pope* (1949); v, 72-3. These last phrases are quoted from an early, and in parts, it seems, superior, draft of the poem.

[3] For a modern analysis of the process, see Sir Herbert Read's *The Meaning of Art* (1931, Pelican edn. 1949); paras. 22, 26a.

Music speaks to the ear and painting to the eye; but single senses give us glimpses only, and the reality may be supposed to correspond rather to whatever might be reported by all the senses, if such could be, working in artistic unison. Nor have we any reason to suppose that it would be exhausted by that. It is best to admit frankly that all art is necessarily inadequate, since the super-sensuous reality cannot be captured and held by our minds; but it remains a valid approximation. The greater reality is not, however, to be supposed as in opposition to sense experience, but rather as some richer dimension of that experience: it exists in the eternal dimension, which contains, and surpasses, time, but it is not to be thought of as static: it exists in space-time. Space-time is eternity, and art an approximation to its expression.

The 'interpretation' of art must therefore be called more than ancillary; it is rather, as has always been recognized in practice, however often denied in theory, a needed auxiliary. It will, moreover, be clear that such interpretations inevitably tend to concentrate on the spatial properties of a temporal art and the temporal properties, as in Lessing's and Ruskin's interest in the moving qualities of painting, of a spatial art. Interpretation assists the art under discussion to say more clearly what it is aiming to say, but cannot quite say, though it does suggest, by reason of its own peculiar limitation.[1]

There have been, of course, attempts in every age to harmonize various arts into some greater and more inclusive art: such is the attempt of opera, of ballet, the music dramas of Wagner, and certain interesting modern advances by the cinema. But, though the blend of music, poetry, and ritual dance appears to have attained a high measure of success in the drama of the ancients, our modern attempts generally leave something to be desired, since we find either that one art tends to dominate at the expense, and sometimes to the serious indignity, of the rest; or that, even when all are working together, the mind cannot assimilate more than is contained in artistic experiences of a simpler kind. This is, however, no reason for giving up the attempt, and we may expect future developments of greater achievement.

Poetry, with its extension in Shakespearian drama, has perhaps come as near as may be, for us today, to a wholly satisfying inclusion. All writing, as Joseph Conrad tells us in his preface to *The Nigger*

[1] For my own methods, see *Essays in Criticism*, Oct., 1953 and April, 1954; also, on *The Scholar Gipsy*, *R.E.S.*, probably Oct., 1954.

of the Narcissus, 'must strenuously aspire to the plasticity of sculpture, to the colour of painting, and to the magic suggestiveness of music'. Poetry in particular offers an experience which is mysteriously both sound and colour, time and space: music, imagery, and meaning are often inextricably entwined, indeed identical, and in it we have the heart of our mystery. Sometimes, as pre-eminently in a great speech of Shelley's *Prometheus Unbound*,[1] it deliberately plays on a confusion of sense-impressions (e.g., in Shelley, 'the music of the living grass and air', IV, iv, 257) to crash the barrier shutting man's sense-locked consciousness from what lies beyond. Nevertheless poetry is, in hard fact, a temporal art, composed of sequences in logic and narrative, its spatial qualities being only spatial by metaphor; they are, to use a paradox, inwardly and spiritually spatial. It is therefore the especial business of interpretation to wrest the deeper meanings from its various patterns in rhyme and stanza, its colourings, its half-visualized scenes, its massing of associations, its structure. We have already seen (p. 53) how Pope's *Essay on Man* exists less as a logical proposition, or set of logically cohering propositions, than through a juxtaposition of contradictory philosophies to make a greater, beyond-philosophy, statement: it is the work of a man with the mind-structure of a poet using philosophic sequences for his purpose. There is here a vital distinction, which applies also to poetic inter-pretation, since interpretation does not reduce poetry to philosophy, but rather uses philosophic thinking to assist our responses to a com-prehension that philosophic thought alone could never attain, and might even have to repudiate; the comprehension, that is, of what the work of poetry is striving, and no art can do more, to realize. It gives the poetry spatial projection, puts it, inwardly, on the stage of our imaginations, *produces* it for us. We all know how a work in dramatic form may reveal unsuspected riches under visual and spatial projection: interpretation merely extends the process to poetry in general.

It is often observed that the importance of a work of art lies not in what it says, but in what it *is*. But poetry clearly says something too; and since a work of art is an organic whole, what it says must be related very closely to what it is. That Shelley should choose to write of the skylark and Keats of the nightingale had something to do with the bright-ethereal and dark-woodland qualities of their re-spective manners. We could, indeed, define poetry as 'an arrange-

[1] IV, iv, 236-69; *The Starlit Dome* (1941), III, 219-23.

ment of words which is what it says'; or, put the other way, 'which is always saying the reality which it is'. Therefore, since, as we have seen, poetry is a space-time reality, we shall not be surprised to find it offering, with what might be called a kind of introspective self-consciousness, a number of precise symbolisms of the space-time dimension which it exists to embody. These symbols I have already, in various works, discussed in detail, but a short retrospective re-grouping and commentary will prove a helpful preliminary to our study of *The Temple of Fame*.

The Christian Trinity itself might, in its fusion of unity with diversity, its dramatic formation, be called an archetype of all such symbolisms. It is as a living and ceaselessly interacting, yet ever-still, complexity in self-union, and in Dante's *Divina Commedia* the central mysteries of the faith are presented in similarly paradoxical terms involving fusions of action with harmony, duality with unity, and so on; as in descriptions of the Gryphon, of Beatrice, in the circular schemes used throughout, and in the final vision of the human form set within the divine 'circling'.[1]

Renaissance poetry is often found to speak through a number of related symbolisms in attempt to blend the arts of space and time within some highly charged unit. These we may for simplicity group under two main headings, human and transcendental—the word perhaps says too much, but there is none better—as: (i) the action-pose, and (ii) musical buildings.

Shakespeare has comparatively little to offer in description of the visual arts, though the Sonnets use the eternal connotations of monu-mental architecture to point a negative; both *The Merchant of Venice* (III, ii, 114–18) and *Timon of Athens* (I, i, 31–9) offer descriptions of motion within painting; and significant sculptural miniatures occur in the Final Plays, as with Marina called 'a palace for the crown'd Truth to dwell in' and compared with 'Patience gazing on kings' graves' to outface 'extremity'.[2] Shakespeare's main symbols, corresponding roughly to our two divisions, human and transcen-dental, are: (i) the King, or the Crown, and (ii) Tempests and Music. For the rest, I would point here to two peculiarly relevant occasions. The first is Hamlet's address to the Players,[3] on the knife-edge balance of power with control, of action with grace, to attain

[1] *The Christian Renaissance* (1933), VII, 146–53; XII, 319–23.
[2] *Pericles*, V, i, 123, 140: and see *The Winter's Tale*, V, ii, 107; *Cymbeline*, II, iv, 72–85, 89; *The Crown of Life* (1947), II, 64–5; III, 118; IV, 174–6. [3] *Hamlet*, III, ii.

artistic poise; a passage which must be understood in direct relation to the play's central problem.[1] The second is the coming to life of Hermione's statue in *The Winter's Tale*, with all its sharp underlining in the dialogue of the space-time paradoxes being enacted, to make what might be called an extreme development of the 'action-pose'.

Statues are always likely to assume importance in humanistic poetry. Byron has some valuable statue-descriptions in *Childe Harold* (IV, 49–53; 160–3), the *Venus*, the *Laocoon*, and the *Apollo*, seeing the sculptor's art as an incarnation of the divine, and noticing in one of them its moment of action ('the shaft hath just been shot'); a yet finer tribute to the 'divine' import of the 'poesy' within the 'kindled' brow of sculpture occurs in *The Prophecy of Dante* (IV); and he has left us some interesting prose comments on the art.[2] The symbolic heart of *Marino Faliero* is an equestrian statue (III, i). The use of plastic suggestion to print eternal significances on his human delineation becomes emphatic in Byron's latest work. There are examples in *Sardanapalus*, and in *Don Juan* they abound. The poem's delicate feeling is concerned throughout with 'the precious porcelain of human clay' (IV, 11), surely never more exquisitely realized in poetry than in the lines:

> *A pure, transparent, pale, yet radiant face,*
> *Like to a lighted alabaster vase.*

> (VIII, 96)

Juan and Haidée are imaged as a statue group (II, 194); Aurora is spiritualized by descriptions on the brink of sculpture and specifically related to the eternal (XV, 43–7; 58); the ghostly paintings of Norman Abbey are alive with poignant meanings (XVI, 19); and at the poem's climax, through a fine stroke of metaphysical humour, we discover that the mysterious figure thought to be a ghost, and at one point sculpturally conceived, is a warmly living, and amorous, duchess (XVI, 120–3). Throughout *Don Juan*, as was shown at length in *The Burning Oracle*, the clustering sculptural impressions serve to impart some feeling of eternal essences, or significances, within the poem's keenly visualized descriptions.

The other great Romantics, though in their main emphases less humanistic, were nevertheless sensitive to the eternal, space-time,

---

[1] '*Hamlet* Reconsidered', *The Wheel of Fire*, 1949 edn.
[2] The Bowles Controversy, LJ, V, 547–51, 557. For the Bowles Controversy, see pp. 113, 137 below.

properties of the action-pose. Wordsworth's description of Newton's statue with its prism and silent face, as

> *The marble index of a mind for ever*
> *Voyaging through strange seas of Thought, alone*
>
> (*The Prelude*, III, 62)

is unforgettable. Andreas, the blazing centre of Coleridge's *Zapolya*, is described in statued action:

> *So looks the statue, in our hall, o' the god,*
> *The shaft just flown that killed the serpent.*
>
> (I, i, 258)

The god is Apollo: Coleridge may have been thinking of the same statue, the Apollo Belvedere, as was Byron. Shelley's transcendental intuitions in *Prometheus Unbound* find expression through a remarkable description of chariot-figures whose very speed appears, under poetic pressure, to freeze them in a living stillness; and there are descriptions of wondrous palaces richly engraved with 'Praxitelean shapes' and 'Phidian forms'.[1] Keats' poetry works continually through what I have called 'tip-toe' effects, little pictures of poised motion, his *Ode on a Grecian Urn*, with its action snapshots of passionate humanity for ever fixed within a rondure equating beauty with truth to make a neat miniature of Dante's final vision, offering the most obvious example of a general tendency.[2]

In Browning's *The Statue and the Bust* we have a satiric opposition of statue-forms against the dynamic of human existence, though *Pippa Passes* shows a fine insight into the vitalities of sculpture. Opposite views of painting are presented in *Andrea del Sarto* and *Fra Lippo Lippi*, and *all* the arts work together in *Cleon*, in direct relation to life, death, and immortality. The statue-piece of the Resurrection central to Ibsen's last work *When We Dead Awaken* recalls *The Winter's Tale*, and the dialogue at key moments plays on and into the most subtle and secret balances of art and life.[3] Living statuary is an important element in the semi-transcendental humanism of Shaw's *Back to Methuselah*; and the 'phantom' of Yeats' *Resurrection* is similarly conceived. A modern poem of first importance, Francis Berry's *The Iron Christ*, specifically defines the attainment of a harmony beyond war in terms of a giant effigy of Christ

[1] *Prometheus Unbound*, II, iv, 129–40; III, iii, 161–6; III, iv, 108–21; *The Starlit Dome*, III, 205, 214–15.

[2] *The Starlit Dome*, IV, 294–6.   [3] *Christ and Nietzsche*, V, 179, 182.

hauled with great labour up the Andes, and gradually, precariously, hoisted and tilted into position to reach a balanced and lasting poise upon the heights.[1] Poise and peace are inter-affective and inter-illuminating concepts.

So much for our 'action-pose'. Next, we have our 'musical buildings'. In *The Burning Oracle* I discussed Milton's poetry in terms of his passion for artefacts and music in *disjunction*, his solids being static and cold in proportion as his music is overpowering. But there is a noble union within the cathedral description of *Il Penseroso*, and *Paradise Lost* shows at least three notable successes. One is the massing of Satan's hosts into a solid array which next moves lightly to flute music, the power of this particular description helping us to understand the universal meaning of pageantry and processions; the next is the building of a great structure by organ-music, the music being conceived as the building power; and the third, the creation of the world to the accompaniment of song and music.[2]

Such symbolisms are developed by the Romantics, whose insight delights to express itself, as Shakespeare's does not, in the vertical dimension. So we have our mountains, domes and temples. Our most compact unit is Coleridge's *Kubla Khan* with its mystic and marvellous dome once glimpsed and now only to be built with the aid of the Abyssinian girl's music in 'air', or poetry. It is a musical, poetic, transcendental dome, contrasted with the river of life and nature generally; the solid and stable with the fluid. Wordsworth's life-work shows a gradual shift from nature-poetry to works describing the arts of design, and edifices in especial; and in his preface to *The Excursion* he described his life-work as a cathedral, with ante-chapels. His most striking symbolic successes in this *genre* are probably the 'imperial palace' of his *Immortality Ode* and the fine comparison of dawn on the clouds and mountains to a number of palatial fabrics all 'molten together', in *The Excursion* (II, 831–60). Shelley's poetry is full of domes, of which 'life' as a 'dome' refracting 'eternity' in *Adonais* is the best known; and he has temples too, to which his paradoxical rivers flow *up*; and there is his marvellous passage already mentioned (p. 82) in which a confusion of impressions intermingles nature with orbs, spheres, and even axles to 'drown the sense'.[3] Such mechanisms help us to understand the peculiar nature of

[1] Francis Berry's collected poems, *The Galloping Centaur*, Methuen, 1952.
[2] *Paradise Lost*, I, 531–71; I, 705–17; VII, 252–60, 557–640.
[3] *Prometheus Unbound*, IV, iv, 236–61.

Keats' poetic magic flowering from a moment-by-moment fusion of the opposites in play. His buildings, interiors (as in *The Eve of St. Agnes*), urns (in the odes *On Indolence* and *On a Grecian Urn*) are warm with human vitalities, and his trees sculptural; nature, man, and art are intrinsicate and each at every instant endowed with the properties of the others. We have a fine example of a magical building flowering into creation, with a 'haunting music' as sole supporter of its 'faery roof', in *Lamia* (II, 119–41). Wordsworth is eminently a poet of *sound* and wrote an ode 'On the *Power* of Sound'. The symbolisms of these four poets are discussed throughout *The Starlit Dome*.

Byron takes a similar course in his own different manner. In aesthetic theory he supports the rights of architecture as against nature,[1] and uses architectural metaphors as when he compares Pope's work to a Greek temple, to establish his poetic and political judgements (see pp. 148, 150 below). He was fascinated by the definition of architecture as 'frozen music', and anxious to discover its origin.[2] In *Childe Harold* (IV, 156) he extends himself in description of St. Peter's in Rome, 'all musical in its immensities'; his handling of Venetian architecture in *Marino Faliero* (III, i; IV, i) is dramatically and atmospherically important; and so is his wonderful realization of Norman Abbey, on whose ruins the winds harp an 'unearthly' and mysterious music beneath the moon recalling Butler's *Erewhon*, in *Don Juan* (XIII, 55–74).

The meaning of our many 'musical buildings' is most clearly set down in Browning's *Abt Vogler*, where the experience of the eternal dimension reached by and through the musician's art is exactly, and in detail, described as a throwing up of a palatial structure; and in *An Epistle of Karshish* this dimension becomes a 'vast distracting orb' around time's 'meagre thread'.

Old legends tell of cities built by music,[3] the thought being recaptured by Tennyson's *Tithonus*:

> . . . *that strange song I heard Apollo sing*
> *When Ilion, like a mist, rose into towers.*

---

[1] The Bowles Controversy, LJ, 546–8, 552. See pp. 138–9, below.

[2] Journal, 17 Nov., 1813; LJ, II, 326.

[3] Compare my remarks on the magical properties of music in *The Shakespearian Tempest*, VI. We must remember always that music, like thunder, is a Shakespearian power, and accompanies the resurrections in *Pericles* and *The Winter's Tale*. Note, too, the title of Wordsworth's Ode above.

You get it again in O'Shaughnessy's 'We are the music makers', wherein 'great cities' are said to be builded by poetry:

> *We, in the ages lying*
> *In the buried past of the earth,*
> *Built Nineveh with our sighing,*
> *And Babel itself in our mirth . . .*

Yeats' man-transcending 'starlit' or 'moonlit' dome in *Byzantium*, which may suggest the dome of the heavens as well as a building, for all human domes imitate the sky, is associated with the music, if such we can call it, of the 'great cathedral gong'. As a climax to our story we have Francis Berry's *Fall of a Tower*, throughout constructed round an exact use of these symbols, its theme reaching fulfilment in the building of a Temple blending Sun-worship with Christianity to the music of violins and flutes:

> *A spiral-fluted Temple with a Dome*
> *Of patterned glass to take the varying shine*
> *Between the green far hills and crystal seas.*

This particular example of our recurring symbol is remarkable for its easy compacting of a number of meanings, natural, human and divine.

Architecture, springing from king and ancestor worship and the will to establish for them cenotaphs and memorials, asserts the vertical against the horizontal, flowers into the eternal meanings of temple and cathedral, and finally embeds itself in poetic symbolism. Shakespeare's use of monuments in the Sonnets and 'king's graves' in *Pericles* (v, i, 140) provides a good commentary on the process.

Metaphysical poetry shows a dearth of such major symbols, since its concern with the eternal dimension is conceptually explicit. It uses whatever minor conceits or images come to mind, and counters its transcendental themes with colloquial rhythms and vocabulary, so reversing the usual process whereby a poet eternalizes a realistic theme with pattern, music, and symbol.

Though metaphysical in sympathy, Eliot's work is also rich in the romantic tradition. Thinking of our two divisions, human and transcendental, I would select: (i) *La Figlia che Piange*, as good an example as we shall find of Eliot's skilful use of feather-light balances in image and thought, here serving a sculptural centre of momentary poise to mark a choice and divergence of the ways; and (ii) the *Four*

Quartets, so rich in meditation on different varieties of time and that which is beyond time, and in the balanced identities of motion and stillness, of action and inaction (*Burnt Norton, The Dry Salvages*), to create a vital eternity; also expressed by the thought of words reaching the 'silence' through their patterned form or music (*Burnt Norton*), and of music itself heard so deeply 'that it is not heard at all' (*The Day Salvages*); by various symbols of dance (*Burnt Norton, Little Gidding*), and by the Chinese vase moving 'perpetually' in its own 'stillness' (*Burnt Norton*). Eliot and Francis Berry stand as our two finest modern exponents of the symbols we are discussing.

Our brief account may be summed up by a couple of prose quotations from my own *Atlantic Crossing*. Here is the first:

'And in wider issues too, you must, in order to be true to the surface of life, work from some universal centre: not a static centre, but a centre which is itself movement. A rhythmic centre, or heart. You must find the centre not of a static pattern alone, but of the unfurling movement of patterns; not the outward brilliance, but the inward core of music, the ship's throbbing engines, the blood-infusing and colour-shooting heart. You must aim to know the patterned growing and musical petal-design, the pulsating solidity, of the flower-building you would create.'

(VII, 214)

And here is the other:

'But it is a moving, developing pattern, its colours fed from inward wells of passionate significance like dark blood sent blushing to the face from the heart's deep music. The rich colours seen by the mystic impel him to action. Our cosmic scheme must never remain static. It is not only a design, but a drama too, the quintessence of whose imagery is verbal music. The only purely unspatial and temporal art, that of music, must be added to, or rather inwoven with, our scheme of elements, not only in the sense of an immediate harmony and ever-springing dawn, but in wider rhythms of day and night, life and death, and the sun-cycle of the seasons, till, as fine architecture to the inward eye, the universe of earth, fire, air and water is felt thrusting itself up, second by second, hour by hour, aeon by aeon, which is its rhythmic nature and eternity quality, its music. For the space-time dimension is eternity, which is why it curves over, a sweeping rainbow arc. There is thus no final antagonism between philosophies of space and time, which are twin approaches to a more richly dimensional whole.'

(VII, 215)

These pieces, published in 1936, describe, far better than I could say it today, the *alpha* and *omega* of my own writings, and what they claim to reveal. At the heart of my other original work, *The Dynasty of Stowe* (VI), part of the mansion's North Front is imagined as dissolving to reveal the living persons of its past owners, and the personification of Stowe, again flowering from the structure, proceeds to speak its oracles in such paradoxes as we have been discussing.

But though such symbols are centres of considerable importance, they cease to be so the moment we forget their circles. Valuable though it may be to describe, or create, such revealing paradoxes, it is still finer to work up, as Shakespeare and Byron work up, the action-pose of a human drama into the musical building of some expanded artistic form. Ivory towers, as Tennyson wrote his *Palace of Art*, itself rich with these symbolic properties, to demonstrate, are a second-best, and may be a danger. They symbolize man's relation to eternity; but they do no more; they do not fuse his most pressing concerns, as does drama, with the eternal dimension.

Before approaching Pope's poem, I would call attention to three theorists of importance in our present context. One is, naturally, Lessing, whose *Laocoön* is the classic document on the interdependence and inter-relationship of the arts of space and time, and of the ways in which they can, or cannot, encroach on one another. Two scenes from Elizabethan drama make interesting dramatic footnotes, or forecastings, of Lessing's book. One is that remarkable dialogue between Hieronimo and the Painter occurring in the anonymous additions to *The Spanish Tragedy* (III, xiia); the other, the dialogue between Poet and Painter in *Timon of Athens* (I, i). Though they do not develop Lessing's thesis, these scenes serve to throw up, in sharp dramatic terms, the nature of his problem.

The next is Nietzsche's *The Birth of Tragedy*. Nietzsche sees drama, and indeed life in general, as composed of two powers, or principles. The first is the 'Dionysian': the dark origins of creation, numinous and mystic, energic, even violent, orgiastic, unmoral, of sound rather than sight, of 'the unconscious', as we should say. The other is the 'Apollonian': the created ideal, the vision in and beyond creation; conscious, intellectual, of daylight. The one is dynamic, the other, in comparison, static; the typifying art of the one is *music*, of the other *sculpture*. Though here Nietzsche is at pains to emphasize the importance of the Dionysian, his aim is the fusion of the two; and in his other great imaginative work, *Thus Spake Zarathustra*, he celebrates and defines the fusion in terms, recalling Pope's *Essay on Man*, of human psychology; in terms, we might say, of the human workshop.[1]

Our third theorist, unfortunately little known though a thinker of great importance, is the French aesthetic and dramatic theorist of the last century, François Delsarte, whose three basic principles were drawn from the study of ancient statuary. They are (i) opposition, (ii) sequence, and (iii) poise. 'Opposition' in statuary is normally apparent in a certain sympathy existing between the head and lower limbs, and countered by a torso tending differently. 'Sequence', being temporal, can in statuary, as opposed to dramatic art, be only suggested. In 'poise' these two principles are blended; and somehow this blend gives us a breath of eternal life.[2]

III

Such is our introduction to Pope's *Temple of Fame* (1711–1715). We shall proceed to show, though his favourite field is the far harder one of strict human delineation, yet that he has, in his one attempt at such symbolic writing, shown himself a master of it.

Pope's poetry, irrespective of its subject, holds just such a 'poise' as Delsarte has defined. In terms of the Delsartian trinity we can, indeed, draw a useful contrast between the poetic styles of Milton and Pope. To use his own words from the preface to *Paradise Lost*, Milton's *forte* lies in 'the sense variously drawn out from one line to another'; it is, as my essay 'The Frozen Labyrinth' in *The Burning Oracle* argued, essentially narrative and winding, even music in *L'Allegro* being defined as a 'winding bout of linked sweetness long drawn out'. 'Sequence' clearly tends to dominate. But since literature is already and inevitably a temporal art, this is dangerous; and the danger is countered by weight of diction, solidification of image, and various other means, as it were, of weighting down, clogging, the forward progress; of putting on the brake. The result is control

---

[1] *Christ and Nietzsche*, v.
[2] I hope to discuss Delsarte, who himself published nothing, later. My present section condenses a typescript entitled *Space, Time and Poise in English Poetry*.

rather than balance. In Pope, however, we have a very clear sense of opposition and balance, as with the two halves of his regularly divided line-units and of the rhymed couplet itself. Each, line and couplet, is, in itself, a balanced unit. His verse paragraphs are also units, succeeding each other, as, pre-eminently, in *Eloisa to Abelard*, in alternate, balanced, pieces, like a graceful walk. Writing of Pope's use of variation, George Sherburn tells us that 'eighteenth-century art depended not on long crescendoes leading to orgiastic climaxes, but on balance and alternation of tone'.[1] In a temporal art sequence is anyway assured, and Pope shows no lack of smooth continuity. As a result, we have poise or grace, rather than control; and this is what we mean, or should mean, whenever we think or talk of peace. Writing of the happier, non-satiric, types of eighteenth-century poetry, Sherburn relates the moment of poetic release to a 'consciousness of being perfectly poised in life, perfectly at peace in its green pastures'.[2]

Pope's world shows a harmony as assured as, though less geometrical than, Dante's. His poetic philosophy rests on two basic principles as centre and circumference: (i) the secret impulses of nature within man, and (ii) the cosmic whole. Man is the centre, as in Dante's final vision. But Pope is far more humanist, Greek, Renaissance, in emphasis. Man is allowed greater status as a dynamic unit. How is Pope to be placed in our present context?

We need not, I think, be surprised to find that, in the one poem in which he so engages himself throughout, published at the height of his interest in painting, he should have left us a handling and grouping of symbolisms surpassed by none of the various treatments which we have passed in review. *The Temple of Fame* compactly includes all the effects in question, neatly grouped, inter-related with each other, given exact place in a rational and time-honoured scheme, and finally pointed to ethic: that is, they are valued. I am not arguing that Pope's peculiar excellence in this province proves him an abler poet than those who have achieved less in it. But I do assert that *The Temple of Fame* serves to compact and crown our present study.

Here are some preliminary points. *The Temple of Fame* contains some of our very finest realizations of the action-prose, together

---

[1] *Selections from Alexander Pope*, New York (1929); Int., xxxiii.
[2] *Selections*, xxxvi. F. R. Leavis in *Revaluation* (1936) at one point uses the word 'poise' to characterize Pope's artistry.

with perhaps our finest example of a living architecture. The Greek and Medieval may be supposed as to this extent balanced. Though the architecture is rather classic than Gothic, the Gothic is included; and, indeed, the whole design, though humanist in content, is medieval in conception, and directly derived from Chaucer's *Hous of Fame*, to which, however, its main excellences owe nothing. But it is romantic too: we have not only a sacred structure, but a structure placed on the summit of a mountain; and though in this Pope is following a medieval tradition, for you find the same in Chaucer and the throne of Fortune in *Timon of Athens* (I, i, 65), Pope's mountain is very much more exciting in the romantic manner. So much for the major substances. In detail, *The Temple of Fame* avoids all the limitations and weaknesses, intentional or unintentional, that are liable to attend such impressions. Though many of the Miltonic elements are included, there is no trace of stiffness in use of artefacts, gems, or bejewelled mounts; nor any undertone of decadence, laziness or premature solutions, as, variously, in the intentional impressions of artificiality to which C. S. Lewis has drawn our attention [1] in Spenser's 'Bower of Bliss', or those of Tennyson's *Palace of Art*, Browning's *The Statue and the Bust*, or Yeats' *Sailing to Byzantium*; nor any of that unintended facility in use of the dome or other architectures which might be a charge levelled at the Romantics in general. Our symbols are as highly charged as those in *Kubla Khan*, Keats' *Grecian Urn*, or *Abt Vogler*. The exploitation of sounds, both dulcet and jarring, challenges comparison with Milton and Wordsworth (e.g. in his ode *On the Power of Sound*). Human energies are included at every instant and the major statement as deeply relevant to world affairs as that of *The Iron Christ*. There is a sense of the transcendent as surely as at the conclusion to *The Winter's Tale*, in Byron's statue poetry, and *Abt Vogler*. But it is not exactly mystical, nor metaphysical; the abstruse metaphysics of Donne and Eliot are avoided, though much of their basic thought subsumed. There is throughout a stern realism. Though presented in full power and authority, the symbols are deliberately valued. The Goddess of Fame is exactly what the title implies; no more, and no less. 'Fame' is a great concept, piercing the eternal dimension; but the Goddess remains enigmatic, sometimes, it is true, felt as the personification of divine justice, but sometimes shown as irresponsible.

There is, however, no uncertainty in the moral. Our symbolisms

[1] *The Allegory of Love*, VII, 324-9.

are related to ethic, to virtue; but not to any static or theoretic
virtue; the great strivings of man's past are given concrete and
individual embodiment and finally judged, if not by the Goddess,
by the poet. The conclusion witnesses a selfless humility. The poem's
manner itself possesses the reserve Lessing noted as a characteristic of
ancient sculpture, not only in descriptions of the action-pose, but in
its own technique, its every moment of poetic poise. Spatial and
temporal conceptions and substances intermix, as in Keats, only with
a far greater relevance to human actuality, without becoming fluid,
or ceasing to be themselves. There is a supervening harmony, as in
Dante, but with all human energies and rights preserved. The whole
is lucid, coherent and objective. A child could understand it.

We next offer a brief commentary. The poet, vaguely located
'betwixt earth, seas and skies', surveys 'the whole creation' in
panorama:

> In air self-balanc'd hung the globe below,
> Where mountains rise and circling oceans flow;
> Here naked rocks, and empty wastes were seen,
> There tow'ry cities, and the forests green:
> Here sailing ships delight the wand'ring eyes:
> There trees, and intermingled temples rise.

(13)

He is startled by a strange sound, like 'broken thunders' or the
murmuring of ocean—the sounds throughout are important—and
suddenly sees a 'glorious pile' piercing the clouds:

> High on a rock of Ice the structure lay,
> Steep its ascent, and slipp'ry was the way;
> The wond'rous rock like Parian marble shone,
> And seem'd, to distant sight, of solid stone.

(27)

On it he could see names inscribed; most were obliterated by time,
and some appeared only to dissolve. Some were worn or melted by
storm or sun, these corresponding precisely to the twin dangers of
hostility and excessive adulation, but others survive despite all trials:

> Yet part no injuries of heav'n could feel,
> Like crystal faithful to the graving steel:
> The rock's high summit, in the temple's shade,
> Nor heat could melt, nor beating storm invade.

Their names inscrib'd unnumber'd ages past
From time's first birth, with time itself shall last;
These ever new, nor subject to decays,
Spread, and grow brighter with the length of days.

(45)

It is a spiritual mount, resembling in its impressions of ice certain favourite poetic intuitions of Coleridge, especially his 'sunny pleasure-dome with caves of ice' in *Kubla Khan*:

So Zembla's rocks (the beauteous work of frost)
Rise white in air, and glitter o'er the coast;
Pale suns, unfelt, at distance roll away,
And on th' impassive ice the lightnings play;
Eternal snows the growing mass supply,
Till the bright mountains prop th' incumbent sky:
As Atlas fix'd, each hoary pile appears,
The gather'd winter of a thousand years.

(53)

The word 'eternal' is important, and it recurs. On this white mountain-rock stands the Temple of Fame, 'stupendous', 'not rear'd by mortal hands' (62), and surpassing the finest creations of Babylon, Greece, or Rome.

The 'dome', a word which sometimes means no more than house (Latin, *domus*), is square, with four 'faces', each different, and with four brazen gates (65-7). The Western front is of Greek architecture:

Westward, a sumptuous frontispiece appear'd,
On Doric pillars of white marble rear'd,
Crown'd with an architrave of antique mold,
And sculpture rising on the roughen'd gold.

(75)

Our dominant visual impressions throughout are of white and gold, signifying a rich spirituality, or purity. On this front are sculptured mythical heroes: Theseus, Perseus, Hercules. The sculpturings, with a subtle enjoyment of artistic mingling, or interplay, show music functioning as a creative force, as trees 'start from their roots' to Orpheus' art and Amphion's 'creating lyre' is seen making Thebes to rise (79-88). The impressions are of vivid, immediate, up-springing vitality. It is all happening while we watch, with a kinship to that

peculiar immediacy that so characterizes Goethe's poetry. Here is
Thebes, flowering to, and from, music:

> *There might you see the length'ning spires ascend,*
> *The domes swell up, the wid'ning arches bend,*
> *The growing tow'rs, like exhalations rise,*
> *And the huge columns heave into the skies.*

(89)

A lovely description recalling our other buildings to music, in
Milton, Coleridge, Browning, Keats, and O'Shaughnessy. The *still
sculpture* itself catches the *action* of *architecture* springing from *music*,
and all this is reported in *poetry*: we could scarcely have a more
complex, and yet so lucid, compacting of our various themes.

The Eastern front is more gorgeous, 'flaming' with diamonds and
'barbaric gold', like certain spectacular pieces of *Paradise Lost* (III,
505–8; V, 753–63). On it we have Ninus the Assyrian, Cyrus of
Persia, the 'royal Magi' in 'long robes', while, with a finely characterizing action, 'Grave Zoroaster waves the circling wand' (93–8).
There are Chaldeans in white, and Brahmans in their forests, adepts
at magic, at raising the dead, men who

> *Made visionary fabrics round them rise,*
> *And airy spectres skim before their eyes.*

(103)

But, with a reminder typical of Pope's approach, we are told that
Confucius stands apart, 'superior and alone', being rated above the
rest in view of his more 'useful science' of ethical teaching (107–8).
The Southern front, which is Egyptian, shows priests in gilded
niches, learned in geometry and astronomy. Here is a good
miniature:

> *High on his car Sesostris struck my view,*
> *Whom scepter'd slaves in golden harness drew:*
> *His hands a bow and pointed javelin hold;*
> *His giant limbs are arm'd in scales of gold.*

(113)

Every time you feel the action of the people depicted, without forgetting that it *is* depicted. The poetry gets the essence of each action-
pose, as such.

On the North, there is Gothic art 'o'erwrought with ornaments of barb'rous pride' (120). We have Zamolxis, student of immortality, with 'erected eyes' (123), and Odin shown falling into one of his 'trances' (124): every detail is alive and active, yet never is the picture forgotten. There are 'Runic characters' (122), grim Scythians on iron blood-smeared columns, Druids and Bards, and many more of what Pope, with his hatred of militarism, calls 'doubtful fame' (129). The wall is interesting:

> The wall in lustre and effect like Glass,
> Which o'er each object casting various dyes,
> Enlarges some, and others multiplies:
> Nor void of emblem was the mystic wall,
> For thus romantic Fame increases all.
>
> (132)

The wall is 'mystic'; its supernatural powers are not doubted, and yet Fame is called 'romantic', because it sometimes romanticizes. Notice how subtly our sense-impressions and various solids are impregnated with exact meaning.

The living structure—it functions as a live thing—opens to reveal its interior:

> The Temple shakes, the sounding gates unfold,
> Wide vaults appear, and roofs of fretted gold:
> Rais'd on a thousand pillars, wreath'd around
> With laurel-foliage, and with eagles crown'd:
> Of bright transparent beryl were the walls,
> The friezes gold, and gold the capitals:
> As heav'n with stars, the roof with jewels glows,
> And ever-living lamps depend in rows.
>
> (137)

The roof is a sort of heaven, and the lamps 'ever-living'. Inside, we find sculptures of 'sage Historians in white garments' who have conquered time:

> Grav'd o'er their seats the form of Time was found,
> His scythe revers'd, and both his pinions bound.
>
> (147)

We have Alexander throned, with feet on subject sceptres and tiaras; and Caesar, master of the world and himself, 'unmoved' and 'superior' (157). But most important, we are told, the strong ethical

97

emphasis persisting, are the more selfless heroes, Epaminondas, Timoleon, Scipio, and Aurelius of 'unbounded virtue'. The valuation is at once heroic and Christian, with particular honour to 'those of less noisy, and less guilty Fame' who silently serve virtue; and so we pass to 'the godlike Socrates', Phocion, Agis, Cato and Brutus (159–77).

We have next some beautiful studies of great writers, placed on pillars arranged in a *circle* round the Temple's centre, nearest, as Pope's note tells us, to the throne of Fame. 'Mighty Homer' is set high on a throne of 'eternal Adamant' (183), solidity being exactly used to signify spiritual with lasting fame. Our impressions are here to be peculiarly rich, with a fine sense, not merely of action, but of inward, spiritualized, qualities pictorially and dramatically expressed, as in the second line of an earlier couplet of remarkable power:

> *Heroes in animated marble frown,*
> *And Legislators seem to think in stone.*

> (73)

So now, of Homer:

> *Father of verse! in holy fillets drest,*
> *His silver beard wav'd gently o'er his breast.*

> (184)

True, Homer is not so deeply spiritualized as some others, since his work is mainly on the more simple, heroic, level: so, 'Tho' blind, a boldness in his looks appears' (186). As a great poet, he is venerable, but his themes are violent:

> *The wars of Troy were round the Pillar seen:*
> *Here fierce Tydides wounds the Cyprian Queen;*
> *Here Hector glorious from Patroclus' fall,*
> *Here dragg'd in triumph round the Trojan wall,*
> *Motion and life did ev'ry part inspire,*
> *Bold was the work, and prov'd the master's fire.*

> (188)

'Motion and life': the lines apply both to the Homeric poetry and to its visual presentation. The actions are left rather vague since Pope remains distrustful of militaristic emotions. He wants the art without any close-up of its subject. When we come to Virgil we find less disparity between art's serenity and warlike action—Pope is, one feels, troubled by this paradox—and we are aware of a new depth, a dignity different in kind, directly related to the poet's artistry. He is found in a shrine 'of purest gold' showing exquisite finish, 'with patient touches of unweary'd art':

> The Mantuan there in sober triumph sate,
> Compos'd his posture, and his look sedate;
> On Homer still he fix'd a rev'rend eye,
> Great without pride, in modest majesty.
> In living sculpture on the sides were spread
> The Latian Wars, and haughty Turnus dead . . .
>
> (200)

Again, the brutality of war is slurred. As for the 'living sculpture', that is our reiterated emphasis, rising to a climax in the succeeding lines, wherein Pindar is felt with an extraordinarily interesting distinction from the other figures exactly relevant to Nietzsche's thesis in *The Birth of Tragedy*, as *melting into his own music*:

> Four swans sustain a car of silver bright,
> With heads advanc'd, and pinions stretch'd for flight:
> Here, like some furious prophet, Pindar rode,
> And seem'd to labour with th' inspiring God.
> Across the harp a careless hand he flings,
> And boldly sinks into the sounding strings.
> The figur'd games of Greece the column grace,
> Neptune and Jove survey the rapid race.
> The youths hang o'er their chariots as they run;
> The fiery steeds seem starting from the stone;
> The champions in distorted postures threat;
> And all appear'd irregularly great.
>
> (210)

This passage is of considerable importance. Nietzsche distinguishes the dithyramb and lyric, and to this *genre* Pindar's poetry pre-eminently belongs, from epic, in that the lyrist is identified with the music, is one with the Dionysian 'I am', whereas the epic poet composes more externally, is more objective.[1] Now this identification with the music is also the theme of Browning's *Abt Vogler*, where the artist both creates and *is* the music, for a while; it is also what Eliot means by 'music heard so deeply that it is not heard at all' and 'you are the music while the music lasts'.[2] Pindar, the prototype of such

[1] *The Birth of Tragedy*, v, vi.   [2] *The Dry Salvages*, v.

art, is, with exact import, shown accordingly as melting into his music; letting, with a grand abandon, the music speak through him, as subject. His theme is, like Homer's, physical action, but there is a difference. Athletics replace war, and a strong representation is the more readily allowed. We may think that Lessing's principle, drawn from his study of the *Laocoön* group and other ancient works, on the importance of avoiding the moment of physical violence, is here ignored. But observe that all Pope's other miniatures show a fine reserve; the power of Pindar exists in his careless, yet bold, *relaxation*. Violence is, however, in place for his 'champions', since neither the actual bloodshed of war nor the spiritual connotations of art are involved. The very violence ('distorted') suggests a deliberated and controlled presentation to give a sculptural equivalent to the subject: it is the business of such contestants, as it is not the business of a Laocoön, to look like that. Such are the exactitudes characterizing Pope's impressions.

With Aristotle, the philosopher, there are naturally no such complexities:

> *Here in a shrine that cast a dazzling light,*
> *Sate fix'd in thought the mighty Stagirite;*
> *His sacred head a radiant Zodiac crown'd,*
> *And various Animals his sides surround;*
> *His piercing eyes, erect, appear to view*
> *Superior worlds, and look all Nature through.*
>
> (232)

And we have a beautiful example of the pure, suggestive, action-pose, in description of Cicero:

> *Gath'ring his flowing robe, he seem'd to stand*
> *In act to speak, and graceful stretch'd his hand.*
>
> (240)

A positive treasure-store of noble sculptures exists in this richly compacted poem.

These plastic yet ever-living figures are being used for a transcendent purpose as surely as the statue of Hermione in Shakespeare, or the snapshot actions on Keats' Grecian urn; they serve to realize an intuition of eternal validity in the great persons concerned. The Temple is itself a spiritual temple, a kind of temple of eternity, to be equated with other such throughout poetic symbolism, though never was there a finer presentation. The descriptions are loaded with impressions of gold and rich gems set against the prevailing whiteness, and the architectures are felt as living. The main fabrics resemble those of the magicians who, as we have seen, 'made visionary fabrics round them rise' (103); and when we hear that 'six pompous columns o'er the rest aspire' (179), the purposeful, living impact of 'aspire' is organic. The specifically architectural descriptions culminate in a circular, or spherical, impressionism, rising to a noble climax:

> These massy columns in a circle rise,
> O'er which a pompous dome invades the skies:
> Scarce to the top I stretch'd my aching sight,
> So large it spread, and swell'd to such a height.
> Full in the midst proud Fame's imperial seat,
> With jewels blaz'd, magnificently great;
> The vivid em'ralds there revive the eye,
> The flaming rubies shew their sanguine dye,
> Bright azure rays from lively sapphyrs stream,
> And lucid amber casts a golden gleam.
> With various-colour'd light the pavement shone,
> And all on fire appear'd the glowing throne;
> The dome's high arch reflects the mingled blaze,
> And forms a rainbow of alternate rays.
> When on the Goddess first I cast my sight,
> Scarce seem'd her stature of a cubit's height;
> But swell'd to larger size, the more I gaz'd,
> Till to the roof her tow'ring front she rais'd.
> With her, the Temple ev'ry moment grew,
> And ampler Vista's open'd to my view:
> Upward the columns shoot, the roofs ascend,
> And arches widen, and long aisles extend.
> Such was her form as ancient bards have told,
> Wings raise her arms, and wings her feet infold;
> A thousand busy tongues the Goddess bears,
> And thousand open eyes, and thousand list'ning ears.
> Beneath, in order rang'd, the tuneful Nine
> (Her virgin handmaids) still attend the shrine:
> With eyes on Fame for ever fix'd, they sing;
> For Fame they raise the voice, and tune the string;

With time's first birth began the heav'nly lays,
And last, eternal, thro' the length of days.

(244)

As in Byron's description of St. Peter's, the building's size is conditioned by the onlooker's gathering assimilation. It is not merely an object, but an experience, and the experience involves effort as the 'aching sight' pierces upward. The temple is more mystical, more symbolical, than Byron's St. Peter's, and it is vividly alive. We must not for one instant forget that this is the Temple of Fame, and that she is *exactly what her name implies.* So the gems and colours are all 'lively' and shown in ceaseless interplay, as though the richly accumulated values of the human tradition across the centuries were always both borrowing from and lending each other new splendours of meaning. It is, you see, the creative process and eternal purpose behind these rich and inter-active accomplishments of great men that the poet's artistry expresses. That is why the Temple grows moment by moment larger as subsequent insight gradually, as, for example, with the reputation of a Shakespeare, clarifies, and significance matures. Its expansion is both vertical and horizontal ('Upward . . . extend'), both eternity and time being under survey. The Goddess herself is visualized in phrases reminiscent of Biblical prophecy. She is mistress of a multitude of human tongues, eyes, ears; all the creative activity and sense-impressions of mankind are her implements; almost she is That for which man's consciousness exists. In especial, the arts, or Muses, serve her in interpreting, ratifying, and perpetuating, indeed all but creating, the values in question. Such 'Fame' may be called a supreme value for which other lesser values exist; it was born at time's origin, but its life is 'eternal'. See how our living and mainly spherical architecture generates itself while we watch—it is all dramatic, in the ever-present 'now' of dramatic art —and how the whole is crowned by song and music; while the concluding impact of the word 'eternal' supervenes on, or rather flowers from, a ceaseless activity, rather like the vivid interplay of swirling, dance-like action and supervening harmony throughout Dante's *Paradiso.*

Such is the wealth of meaning smoothly housed in Pope's most elaborate use of this symbolism. We have here a good example of what Byron meant by calling Pope's a 'poetry without fault' (p. 130 below).

Here the poem could have ended, and some of us might wish that it had. But this is not Pope's way: for one thing, he does not base his art on the climax, his favourite technique being undulatory; [1] for another, he is not quite content with his goddess, great though she be. Even though she be all but equated with eternity, it is only his own intuition of the eternal. Besides, can we trust in anything called Fame as wholly reliable? And if we could, would this be enough? Are there not other, more purely ethical, compulsions to be watched? Is this goddess *moral*?

She is enigmatic. 'All the nations' come at the sound of her doom-like 'trumpet' (277–8), 'millions' of suppliants attending of every conceivable variety:

> Their pleas were diff'rent, their request the same:
> For good and bad alike are fond of Fame.
>
> (292)

We find her disgracing some and honouring others: 'unlike successes equal merits found' (295). The line is ambiguous: has she, or has she not, her own good reasons for her decisions? There is a certain doubt.

> Thus her blind sister, fickle Fortune, reigns,
> And, undiscerning, scatters crowns and chains.
>
> (296)

That seems clear enough, but it is not the whole truth.

After all, she has so far been shown as an able goddess, with our historic figures well ordered and grouped. Moreover, she is next shown ratifying the finest values. When the learned come pale with study to ask her reward, her reception is described in a noble passage introduced, again, by the authoritative word 'eternal', and rich with circular impressions and a subtle use of sound and smell:

> The Goddess heard, and bade the Muses raise
> The golden Trumpet of eternal Praise:
> From pole to pole the winds diffuse the sound,
> That fills the circuit of the world around;
> Not all at once, as thunder breaks the cloud;
> The notes at first were rather sweet than loud . . .
>
> (306)

[1] See p. 92 above: and also Geoffrey Tillotson's section, 'Design'.

103

Though at first the choice few alone recognize the merit in question, the power grows, the notes get stronger:

> *By just degrees they ev'ry moment rise,*
> *Fill the wide earth, and gain upon the skies.*
> *At ev'ry breath were balmy odours shed,*
> *Which still grew sweeter as they wider spread;*
> *Less fragrant scents th' unfolding rose exhales,*
> *Or spices breathing in Arabian gales.*
>
> (312)

The truly virtuous are likewise honoured:

> *Next these the good and just, an awful train,*
> *Thus on their knees address the sacred fane.*
> *'Since living virtue is with envy curs'd,*
> *And the best men are treated like the worst,*
> *Do thou, just Goddess, call our merits forth,*
> *And give each deed th' exact intrinsic worth.'*
>
> (318)

That is exactly how we want her, as Goddess of true Fame, or valuation, to function. But she does not always do so. Another virtuous band appears, only to have their claims ruined by slander:

> *But straight the direful Trump of Slander sounds;*
> *Thro' the big dome the doubling thunder bounds;*
> *Loud as the burst of cannon rends the skies,*
> *The dire report thro' ev'ry region flies,*
> *In ev'ry ear incessant rumours rung,*
> *And gath'ring scandals grew on ev'ry tongue.*
> *From the black trumpet's rusty concave broke*
> *Sulphureous flames, and clouds of rolling smoke:*
> *The pois'nous vapour blots the purple skies,*
> *And withers all before it as it flies.*
>
> (332)

Again, a fine exploitation of sound. But we may, indeed, wonder why the Goddess allows such slanders to obscure true merit, since she functions normally as a just arbiter, never more so than when she disappoints the expectations of great conquerors, crowned and armed, proud and defiant, men who for fame 'swam to empire thro' the purple flood' (347), and expect renown:

'Ambitious fools!' (the Queen reply'd, and frown'd)
'Be all your acts in dark oblivion drown'd;
There sleep forgot, with mighty tyrants gone,
Your statues moulder'd, and your names unknown!'
A sudden cloud straight snatch'd them from my sight,
And each majestic phantom sunk in night.

(350)

What they did *seemed* to be virtue (349), and they *are* majestic (355). We watch Pope making an advance beyond the heroic tradition; while using its terms, he is redirecting it. Fact is falsified, since great conquerors *have* been remembered, but he is really out to define a result that should be, not only what is. His whole poem is, as it were, a search for just fame, for eternal virtue. Therefore those who were indifferent to fame and followed virtue for its own sake are greeted by a 'trembling music' that spreads 'triumphant',

> *So soft, tho' high, so loud, and yet so clear,*
> *Ev'n list'ning Angels lean'd from heav'n to hear.*

(374)

Here, again, the Goddess fulfils our expectations, functioning as an eternal rather than as a temporal arbitress.

But we are next again surprised to find her allowing the claims of certain fashionable young men, who, unsuccessful in love, yet wish to have the reputation of amorous conquest; and their claim is allowed, even at the expense of the ladies' honour (378–93). There appears to be some justice at work here, since another group, 'unlearn'd in arts to please' (396), is peremptorily dismissed. Traitors certainly get their deserts:

> *Last, those who boast of mighty mischiefs done,*
> *Enslave their country, or usurp a throne;*
> *Or who their glory's dire foundation lay'd*
> *On Sov'reigns ruin'd, or on friends betray'd;*
> *Calm, thinking villains, whom no faith could fix,*
> *Of crooked counsels and dark politics;*
> *Of these a gloomy tribe surround the throne,*
> *And beg to make th' immortal treasons known.*
> *The trumpet roars, long flaky flames expire*
> *With sparks, that seem'd to set the world on fire.*

At the dread sound, pale mortals stood aghast,
And startled nature trembled with the blast.

(406)

Again we are satisfied.

As though to attempt a clarification, our scene, following Chaucer (III, 822 ff.), shifts from the Temple of Fame to another temple, or centre, of Rumour. It is called

a structure fair
Its site uncertain, if in earth or air.

(420)

The 'mansion' whirls round 'with rapid motion' (422), and there is continual noise. This is a receptacle, a magnet, drawing all *sounds* whatsoever to itself from the earth:

Nor ever silence, rest, or peace is here.

(435)

The passage grows metaphysical, out of all proportion to the subject. Pope was apparently attracted by an earlier passage of Chaucer's poem (II, 257-314) on sound, and works it in here. Just as a stone dropped in water makes widening and ever-widening circles, so sound, we are told, impresses itself on air:

Thus ev'ry voice and sound, when first they break,
On neighb'ring air a soft impression make;
Another ambient circle then they move;
That, in its turn, impels the next above;
Thro' undulating air the sounds are sent,
And spread o'er all the fluid element.

(442)

The 'soft impression' suggests Rudolf Steiner's theory that sounds actually carve corresponding shapes, or figures, in the air. We are faced by an interesting attempt to feel sound spatially; it functions in circular, spatial, waves. The passage accordingly falls neatly into place for our general purpose.

As for Rumour, the thoughts are fairly obvious, and not unlike the Shakespearian exposition in the Induction of 2 *Henry IV*. A list of falsities is presented, with their snowball tendency to grow worse duly noted. False news flies fast, spreading like fire. Such lies reach the home of Rumour, who returns them to earth when perfected. And all this appears to be allowed, even controlled, by Fame:

> Fame sits aloft, and points them out their course,
> Their date determines, and prescribes their force.
>
> (483)

'Date' means their date of expiry. Some soon die. Others—Pope may be thinking of the reputation of poets—'wane and wax alternate like the moon' (486). Sometimes you see a lie and truth 'contending' for passage, both finally going forth 'inseparable' or 'for ever join'd' (494–5); an exquisite penetration of what does, in fact, often happen, especially with the reputations of men of genius.

Our conclusion is spoken in the poet's own person. He is warned that the favour of Fame is, after all, a vain quest:

> How vain that second life in others' breath.
>
> (505)

It can be a mad pursuit, attended by much disquiet, much hostility. The final passage makes a perfect statement:

> Nor Fame I slight, nor for her favours call;
> She comes unlook'd for, if she comes at all.
> But if the purchase costs so dear a price,
> As soothing Folly, or exalting Vice:
> Oh! if the Muse must flatter lawless sway,
> And follow still where fortune leads the way;
> Or if no basis bear my rising name,
> But the fall'n ruin of another's fame;
> Then teach me, heav'n! to scorn the guilty bays,
> Drive from my breast that wretched lust of praise,
> Unblemish'd let me live, or die unknown;
> Oh grant an honest fame, or grant me none!
>
> (513)

Our conclusions serves, if not to elucidate, certainly to crown, our earlier ambiguities.

The goddess Fame appears to fulfil incompatible functions. She is both (i) a goddess of eternal valuation ratifying the true and denouncing the false, and (ii) a personification of the random action of fame, or rumour, on earth.[1] Perhaps the two may be assimilated under the heading of 'realism', since, in actual experience, good name and lasting preservation is, on the whole, a resultant and an assessment of one's actions, though we are also aware of many injustices. We can say that Pope, working in a humanist tradition, and building on Chaucer, starts to write an allegorical poem on Fame; and in the process, not only does his symbolism outdistance Chaucer's, since the peculiar excellences which we have noticed, except for the passage on sound, are not in Chaucer, but even where he to some extent follows, as he does, the earlier master in delineation of the Goddess and her actions, his thinking adds a new intensity to the enigma which she presents as symbol simultaneously of divine authority and the perversities of fortune. The whole reflects Pope's own survey, from a personal view, and the conclusion tidies everything, with its assertion of righteousness and humility as the only certainty. If the Goddess is ambiguous, the moral of the poem is not.

The poem's first half, concluding with the great temple description, is concerned with what is known from the past, and it would seem that the Goddess is, so far, considered a divine dispenser of justice. Her actual accomplishments are before us: Homer and Aristotle are, in fact, remembered. But the poet may next be felt wondering if she is always just. Have other good and great men been either forgotten or slandered? You cannot be sure. He is, perhaps, thinking now of himself and of the present, or future, and in so thinking deliberately discusses the Goddess' apparent irresponsibility. There is always, in these matters, a vast difference between past records and present anxieties, as with the easy acceptance of destructive forces as part of God's scheme, provided it all be an old story, but the far harder matter of acceptance for ourselves, here and now. That is another way of looking at our problem.

There is yet a third, perhaps the most important of all. Even if Pope's Goddess is regarded as only in part reliable, that does not mean that his greater passages are less meaningful, nor any the less symbols of the eternal. The fame which interests Pope is poetic fame; the Temple's centre, with its poets and philosophers, makes that abundantly clear. Now poetry and philosophy are themselves techniques of traffic with the eternal, and any fame so won is necessarily a fame close to eternal status. We have, accordingly, a clustered

[1] Tillotson observes 'an incompletely stated connection between the two temples, that of Fame and that of Rumour', 'Design', 55.

association of poetry, fame and eternity. But, and even if this be an expansion of Pope's explicit meaning, it most certainly touches the *reasons* lying beneath his surface, Pope may, without any slighting of its importance, yet be felt as unwilling to give this 'cluster' unqualified homage. Why? Because eternal insight is not enough. *Kubla Khan* had that, and so has Keats' *Grecian Urn*; but do either make any contact with morality? Confucius' teaching was considered as more important than miracle and magic (107). Life to Pope, as to Byron, takes precedence over art, even though that very precedence becomes again art's subject. 'Eternity' may indeed cover everything, but symbols of it, however exquisite, are not enough. Pope is with Shakespeare and Byron as poets of actual human affairs who only occasionally indulge in such symbolisms; and even more than they, he is, as Byron urged, a poet of morality. That is why he was impelled from the depths to leave his goddess and her attendant symbolisms ambiguous.

After all, we have watched certain of the virtuous honoured precisely because they never looked for fame (366). Pope finally realizes that 'She comes unlook'd for if she comes at all' (514). Fame is one of those things that you may have, in New Testament phrase, to lose in order to find. In the poem's latter parts Pope is writing from a new viewpoint, taking his stand within the centre of his own personal engagements; it is rather like the contrast of Epistles II and III with Epistle I in the *Essay on Man*. That his noble conclusion had a very deep meaning for himself may be hinted by a biographical reminder. Poetic fame was with him a burning desire, and he knew the attendant temptations, and the dangers of spiritual pride. More, he built himself a little 'temple': his famous grotto. In this period, the great houses, grounds, statues and grottoes of noblemen were extensions of the personalities, as indeed are all possessions, of their owners. They were works of personal pride, of flamboyance. 'Vanity', wrote Dr. Johnson in his Life of Pope—and by 'vanity' he would have meant something like 'showiness'—'produced a grotto where necessity enforced a passage.' Bonamy Dobrée comments:

'Well, there may have been a touch of vanity at the beginning, but the celebrated grotto was a delirious fantasy in which Pope let himself go; for year after year it was his great toy, his unfailing release, and he kept on improving and enlarging it, lining the walls with different kinds of stone and crystals, ores and corals, arranging mirrors to enhance the effect, placing a thin alabaster lamp to strengthen the glooms, and contriving the most cunning water-works, little cascades and rills, which twisting about made gurgles and splashes, and "a little dripping murmur".

(Alexander Pope, v, 70)

There you have his own, personal, little temple; his little temple of fame. It was, if you like, his 'ivory tower', and, like all ivory towers, it had its dangers. The conclusion to *The Temple of Fame* acknowledges the danger: that is all.

To return to our symbolisms. We point to: (i) the exquisite miniatures of sculptured action, which are at once action, sculpture and poetry; (ii) the mountain-based temple with its living architecture and music; (iii) the use of sounds, dulcet or harsh, the peculiar preserve of Milton and Wordsworth, together with an exciting attempt, following Chaucer, to give sound a spatial definition. All these, and other related, effects are exactly ordered with details meticulously fitted to the general meanings, and all are, through the Goddess's ambiguity and the poem's conclusion, pointed beyond themselves and honestly placed, as far as the poet's personal experience at this early period could place them, in direct relation to the duties of actual life. Their relevance should be clear. From the start the 'dome' was Pope's symbol for the perfect poetic 'whole' (*Essay on Criticism*, 247–52; for other domes, see pp. 25, 33, 60, 95–6, 101). It, and architecture in general, may, here and elsewhere, be felt as balanced against 'nature' as is the great 'whole' of the *Essay on Man*, which all such structures symbolize.

I do not contend that this is Pope's greatest poem, nor that all our poets are entering a competition with regard to this particular province of their art. But I do contend that this is a province of central importance, and that Pope has mastered it with a peculiar felicity and exactitude. Each poet in turn has his own excellences unmatched elsewhere; but if we want, within a single poem, not merely a peculiarly fine poetic handling of 'the beauteous works of peace',[1] but a deliberate use of them as symbols of profound metaphysical importance, together with a grouping and compacting of such, and other, basic symbolisms in just relationship to each other and to wider issues, we shall find that in Pope's *Temple of Fame*, and there alone.

[1] *Windsor Forest*, 378.

IV

THE BOOK OF LIFE:

On Byron's Adulation of Pope

IV. THE BOOK OF LIFE

I N this section I quote from Byron's *Letters and Journals* (LJ),
edited by R. E. Prothero (Lord Ernle); and from *Byron: A Self-
Portrait* (SP), edited by Peter Quennell. For the two lengthy
sections which I call here and elsewhere the '*Blackwood's* Defence'
and the 'Bowles Controversy', see pp. 131, 137 below.

I

In the preceding essays I have tried to do justice to the total meaning of Pope's poetry. His doctrinal challenge has hitherto been, in the
main, resisted, not by open opposition, but by the far subtler and
more effective means of pretending that it does not exist. Great
poetry offers to distend our minds, but since few appear willing
to risk 'the awful daring of a moment's surrender' which it asks
of us, some form of defence mechanism is generally set up to avoid
labour or embarrassment. Hence arises the tendency to reduce
poetry to an appreciation of its manner, according it a purely
technical, at the best a verbal, response, while ignoring those
'thousand charms' on which Pope himself, in his *Essay on Criticism*,
so strongly insisted (pp. 42, 136); or we find scholars dissolving the
various art-forms into their supposed 'sources' and crediting first the
author, and next the art itself, with no more than an inorganic
residue; or, again, as a last resort, the poetry is ignored and replaced
by a concentration, generally to his severe disadvantage, on the poet's
life. All this has happened to Pope. While such methods persist, the
voice of poetry remains muffled; and when at last it is allowed to
speak, the first reaction is likely to be one of incredulity or annoyance.

Nevertheless, the attempt must be made. Nor is our own attempt
the first, since the gist of the argument has already been stated by a

great man in a number of passages which together constitute a land-
mark in literary criticism; and anyone inclined to question the claims
I have been making for Pope's poetic doctrine should consider the
yet greater claims made for it by Lord Byron. There is a development, or tradition, still in process of formulation and reformulation,
of which the first three figures are Shakespeare, Pope, and Byron;
and the closer the attention which we give to them, both in themselves and in their inter-relationship, the more clearly shall we
understand where we are today. We shall now discuss what Byron
had to say of Pope, and also try to discover why it fell to him, alone
among the great critics of our literature, to say it.

We have seen how Pope appears to preserve intact the quintessence
of New Testament teaching whilst simultaneously re-establishing
and consolidating a tradition of human powers and politics, at once
classical and aristocratic, sinking its foundations to the ancient world;
and in so doing he makes a statement of imperishable worth to
Renaissance man. Now Byron, writing after a period of more
revolution, including the French Revolution and the literary revolution inaugurated by Wordsworth and Coleridge, reasserted the
values for which Pope stood. But his stage was far wider. In both his
life and his poetry he reflected the European soul, the world-
soul; and faced, as we are faced today, by a tumultuous anarchy of
powers and passions, he rejected the theories of romanticism whilst
looking back to Pope as an ideal and an exemplar; for there lay, in
his view, the magic key. The scale was small, but it was the real
thing. Though he himself in certain moods deplored his own con-
cessions to romanticism, we can nevertheless regard his diction and
style as a flowering from that same soil of traditional nobility that we
recognize in the words of Pope. There is the same verbal solidity and
rondure, the same surface lustre witnessing the vigour and the virtue
within, the same incorporation of heroic energies and values,
together with the same interpenetration of these with themes of
liberalism, Christian ethic, civic righteousness, and all that constitutes, in general, the great 'campaign of peace' (p. 13 above). In
both poets, as the message matures, the reliance on a poetic diction
decreases; the diction has been dissolved into the message. Byron's
problem was, briefly, Pope's. Political disruption he knew to be
inevitable, and in part good; but in poetry, whose proper function
he took to be the safeguard of those powers through which alone a
new harmonization might be glimpsed, he was uncompromising in

his reiterated assertion that the more individualistic extravagances of his day were pointing to disaster.

His admiration of Dryden and Pope, but especially of Pope, was clear from the start. Both *English Bards and Scotch Reviewers* (1809–11) and *Hints from Horace* (1811) show affinities of conception and treatment to the work of Pope: their tone is 'Augustan'.

English Bards and Scotch Reviewers is a remarkable achievement for a young poet. Within its light summary and critical review of current poetry, Crabbe alone, 'though nature's sternest painter, yet the best' (858), receives unqualified approval. Scott is both castigated and admired, being urged to leave absurd romances for subjects worthier of his genius (153–88, 911–48). Southey, Wordsworth and Coleridge get a series of knocks. Southey's prolific output in narrative is contrasted with the past, when one expected an epic once in a thousand years (189–234); Wordsworth, a 'dull disciple' of Southey, is called a 'mild apostate from poetic rule' (235–54); and 'gentle' Coleridge, 'the bard who soars to elegize an ass' (255–64). In contrast, honours are paid to Homer and Virgil (189–98), Shakespeare (592), Milton (187), 'great Dryden' (113, 187), Pope's 'pure strain' (109, 187), and also Massinger (592), Otway (115, 592), Congreve (115) and Sheridan (580–5). Shakespearian quotations are, as elsewhere in Byron, embedded in the verse: 'But managers for once cried, "Hold, enough!"' (735); 'hang a calf-skin on those recreant lines' (740); 'our men in buckram', and 'penetrable stuff' (1049–50). Byron's main literary standards of reference were fixed thus early. He stood for sound sense as opposed to 'strain'd invention' (851) and the general itch to newness and personal excitement impelling contemporary letters. Fear of being 'trite' had ruined poetry:

> Yet Truth sometimes will lend her noblest fires,
> And decorate the verse herself inspires . . .
>
> (855)

The desire is for a more solid, more practical, more ethical, poetry.

Objections rise to our minds. Among his contemporaries, Byron attacks Wordsworth, Coleridge and Southey, and approves of Crabbe (857), Scott's 'hallow'd harp' (934), 'melodious Rogers' (803), Campbell (801), and Gifford (819–30). Surely he has chosen wrong? Can the work of Scott, Rogers, Campbell and Gifford be said to have survived? Is even Crabbe a deeply important writer to us? Conversely, are not Wordsworth and Coleridge at least as well

known as Byron himself? Yes. But we must observe that Byron is
not satisfied with his favourites, and is concerned to rouse them to do
better justice to their abilities (Scott, 931–2; Campbell, 801; Rogers,
803; Gifford, 819, 829; Sheridan, 582–3; Moore, 294). Moreover,
since it is clear that Byron's own work has been under-rated, it may
be that some of these lesser figures have suffered an injustice in their
degree. For the rest, we may best read this first statement less as a
judgement on individuals than as the definition of a critical standpoint. Certain objections regarding Byron's dislike of the 'Lakers'
we shall discuss later: he certainly recognized the genius of Coleridge
and Wordsworth (pp. 122, 127 below).

What is important is Byron's extraordinary desire, at this youthful
age, for a more traditional poetry. He was deeply anxious. He
deplores 'the degradation of our vaunted stage', and asks, 'is all sense
of shame and talent gone?' (575–6). He writes, moreover, in a
strangely avuncular fashion, encouraging and urging on established
writers many years his senior, as though they were school-boys;
praising, but asking them to mend their ways. What must Scott
and the others have thought of this youthful moralist? For moralist
he is, not alone in his will to reawaken a past nobility in letters, but
in a more strict sense also. Though admiring Moore as the 'young
Catullus of his day', he deplores his licentiousness, calling his verses
'melodious advocates of lust' (287–90). And if his own failings be
adduced:

> Altho' some kind, censorious friend will say,
> 'What, art thou better, meddling fool, than they?'
> And every brother rake will smile to see
> That miracle, a moralist in me.
> No matter—when some bard in virtue strong,
> Gifford perchance, shall raise the chastening song,
> Then sleep my pen for ever!
>
> (697)

The lines condense Byron's continual and reiterated views on his
own attacks. Again and again he admitted his own failings, both in
morals and in being untrue to the Augustan tradition—the two,
converging under the name of Pope, were to him almost the same
—whilst remaining uncompromising in the general, the impersonal,
statement. Nor did he rate his own statement high, but was genuinely
ready, indeed anxious, to give place to one more worthy than him-

self to chastise the age. He was, from the start, half-willing, or more, to stop writing, and asserts that he intended to publish no record of the travels on which he was shortly to embark:

> But should I back return, no tempting press
> Shall drag my journal from the desk's recess.
>
> (1023) [1]

He often later talked of retiring from authorship. We could say that he wrote, and published, in his own despite.

We may observe Byron's natural assumption of what might be called a civic, or patriotic, responsibility, indicating a certain humility such as you find in Pope, but scarcely in Blake, Wordsworth, or Shelley. Pope and Byron claim less, in a way, for themselves; they speak as mouthpieces of a living, yet traditional, order, not as lonely, self-inspired or God-inspired, prophets. You see it in such a phrase as Pope's 'My Country's Ruin makes me grave'.[2] You have it in Byron's:

> For me, who, thus unask'd, have dared to tell
> My country what her sons should know too well,
> Zeal for her honour bade me here engage
> The host of idiots that infest her age;
> No just applause her honour'd name shall lose,
> As first in freedom, dearest to the Muse.
> Oh! would thy bards but emulate thy fame,
> And rise more worthy, Albion, of thy name!
> What Athens was in science, Rome in power,
> What Tyre appeared in her meridian hour,
> 'Tis thine at once, fair Albion! to have been—
> Earth's chief Dictatress, Ocean's lovely Queen:
> But Rome decay'd, and Athens strewed the plain,
> And Tyre's proud piers lie shattered in the main;
> Like these, thy strength may sink, in ruin hurled,
> And Britain fall, the bulwark of the world.
>
> (991)

He is thinking, and feeling, nationally, as a patriot, before assuming his satiric mantle. Byron is to be sternly dissociated from the more

---

[1] This couplet is an improved version of the original, composed after Byron's return. See Hartley Coleridge's note.

[2] *Sat.*, *Epilogue*, II, 207.

obviously 'national' poets, Shakespeare, Milton, Tennyson; he was, or soon became, international, and therein lies much of his importance; but it is worth noting that, whatever his later attacks on Britain, his was an internationalism based on a preliminary patriotism.

No sensitive reader of this poem, and certainly no one attuned to the rest of Byron's work, will waste time on any suspicion of the poet's emotional integrity. Though it is sometimes said that these catapults of criticism were motivated by the review of his own *Hours of Idleness*, yet an early version, entitled *British Bards*, had been composed, and publication intended, before ever the review appeared (*Works, Poetry*, ed. Hartley Coleridge, I, 293); and in any case *Hours of Idleness* was itself pregnant with the values we are discussing, and what was done in its cause was done also for the tradition; and so we need not be surprised to recognize in the later poem, throughout all its more important passages, the impersonal anger of great satire. These themselves constitute an honourable part of the tradition which they defend. So pregnant of wit and wisdom, and technically so excellent in point and balance, in choice of word and compactness of line, in swinging, speeding couplets, in paragraph control, they inevitably recall Pope in both manner and statement, though Byron's manner is never quite Pope's, and his vaster genius, together with the complexities and tumult of his time, drew him to wider fields.

With *English Bards and Scotch Reviewers* we naturally group *Hints from Horace*, a work more purely academic in conception akin to Pope's *Essay on Criticism*. This poem was composed in Greece in 1811, but not published till 1831. In it astute comments are made on the literary situation in general and drama in particular, Shakespeare and Milton being used as prototypes as Pope uses Homer and Virgil. Byron himself regarded *Hints from Horace* as more important than *Childe Harold*, and his respect for it was maintained.[1] We need not subscribe to his judgement; but, though its artistic merit falls below his first satire, its interest for the student of Byron's literary theory remains considerable, and, were that, rather than Pope, our present concern, we should give it an extended hearing.

More relevant to our immediate purpose are Byron's literary relations with Leigh Hunt. He admired Hunt's work in conception, but was dubious of his style: of one of his odes he told Murray that its thoughts were good 'but the expressions *buckram*'.[2] He was

---

[1] Murray, 11 Jan., 1821: LJ, V, 221. [2] April, 1814: LJ, III, 69.

excited about *Rimini*, and wrote to Hunt on 22 October, 1815,[1] urging him to complete it whilst the inspiration was active, but offered certain criticisms, which he called merely 'verbal', with regard to an 'occasional quaintness and obscurity, and a kind of a harsh and yet colloquial compounding of epithets, as if to avoid saying common things in a common way.' Hunt's reply (30 Oct., 1815) is interesting. He defended himself

'in vindication of a theory which I have got on the subject, and by which it appears to me that the original part of my style—if the attempt to bring back an idiomatic spirit in verse can be so called —must stand or fall.'

(LJ, III, 418)

He did, however, admit a horror of the 'prosaic' and the 'eccentric', and invited further discussion, and in his turn offered some criticisms of Byron, who, he says, had 'the complete thing in point of feeling and character—why not, always, in point of words?' He continues:

'The plain matter is this: it appears to me that we often hurt the effect, in modern poetry, of very true feelings and descriptions by putting them in false language, that is to say, we accommodate our-selves to certain habitual, sophisticated phrases of *written* language, and thus take away from real feeling of any sort, the only language it *ever actually uses*, which is the *spoken* language.'

(LJ, III, 418)

The two were clearly at cross-purposes: each admired the other's substance, whilst rejecting his style, or diction. Each thought the other's style *artificial*. Byron's reply (about Nov., 1815) ran:

'I have not had time to attack your *system*, which ought to be done, were it only because it is a *system*. So, by and by, have at you.'

(LJ, III, 248)

To Byron, Hunt's style was a vulgarity. He recalled later how, though admiring *Rimini*, he had from the start remonstrated against its 'vulgarisms', and when Hunt referred to his 'system', then, says Byron, he 'said no more'.[2]

The argument is confusing. Byron himself, in both his dramas and *Don Juan*, was to use an informal, at times a colloquial, manner. Of

[1] LJ, III, 226.
[2] The Bowles Controversy, LJ, v, 588.

his dramatic style, he wrote to Murray on 14 July, 1821: 'It has been my object to be as simple and severe as Alfieri, and I have broken down the *poetry* as nearly as I could to common language'.[1] But notice that the aim is simplicity and that the 'poetry' exists first, to be 'broken down'; the result is to be attained not by working up a colloquial idiom into poetry, but by whittling down an established diction to make a style both literary and colloquial which draws no attention to itself as either. That, anyway, was what Byron wanted: it was to be transparent, like a 'clear spring, bubbling in the sun'.[2] He was in this following Pope, whose poetic story shows a similar development, and the difference from what Hunt was doing will be clear.

It is also clear that Byron, too, could appear to subscribe to a system. But, though so much of a classicist, both in his life-long support of Pope and in his later theories of composition, that his natural tendency was to repudiate any systemization may be seen from his comment on Bowles' *Invariable Principles of Poetry* (1819):

'I do hate that word "*invariable*". What is there of *human*, be it poetry, philosophy, wit, wisdom, science, power, glory, mind, matter, life, or death, which is "*invariable*"? Of course, I put things divine out of the question.'

(The Bowles Controversy, LJ, v, 543)

Whatever Byron, or his diction, or literary theories, stood for, it was not really definable as a system: it was not thought out, not invented. However 'literary' it may appear to us, to him it was already an authentic part and parcel of life, and in supporting what he felt to be a dying tradition, he was trying to preserve what was to him, quite simply, an accepted sovereignty. Above all, he was trying to preserve the *dignity* of poetry. In contrast, Hunt, in both theory and practice, appeared to represent a deliberate vulgarization and a debasing of coinage; and it is the more necessary to labour the point, since we naturally, after a long period of romantic influence and democratic acceptance, tend to believe that such theories as those of Wordsworth and Hunt, since in this they were at one, are the

---

[1] LJ, v, 323.

[2] Murray, 4 July, 1821; LJ, v, 218. See my article in *The Times Literary Supplement*, 3 Feb., 1950. Extended studies of Byron's dramatic work by Patricia Ball and B. Taborski await publication.

final and only wisdom. It is important to realize that they are not.[1]

Byron's considered views on Hunt are given in a remarkable and fascinating letter to Moore on 1 June, 1818:

'*Hunt's* letter is probably the exact piece of vulgar coxcombry you might expect from his situation. He is a good man, with some poetical elements in his chaos; but spoilt by the Christ-Church Hospital and a Sunday Newspaper—to say nothing of the Surrey gaol, which conceited him into a martyr. But he is a good man. When I saw *Rimini* in MS, I told him that I deemed it good poetry at bottom, disfigured only by a strange style. His answer was, that his style was a system, or *upon system*, or some such cant; and when a man talks of system, his case is hopeless: so I said no more to him, and very little to anyone else.

'He believes his trash of vulgar phrases tortured into compound barbarisms to be *old* English; and we may say of it as Aimwell says of Captain Gibbet's regiment, when the Captain calls it an "old corps" —"the oldest in Europe if I may judge by your uniform". He sent out his *Foliage* by Percy Shelley . . . and, of all the ineffable Centaurs that were ever begotten by Self-love upon a Night-mare, I think "this monstrous Sagittary" the most prodigious. *He* (Leigh Hunt) is an honest charlatan, who has persuaded himself into a belief of his own impostures, and talks Punch in pure simplicity of heart, taking himself (as poor Fitzgerald said of *himself* in the *Morning Post*) for *Vates* in both senses, or nonsenses, of the word. Did you look at the translations of his own which he prefers to Pope or Cowper, and says so?—Did you read his skimble-skamble about Wordsworth being at the head of his own *profession*, in the *eyes* of *those* who followed it? I thought that poetry was an *art*, or an *attribute*, and not a *profession*;—but be it one, is that . . . at the head of *your* profession in *your* eyes? I'll be curst if he is of *mine*, or ever shall be. He is the only one of us (but of us he is not) whose coronation I would oppose. Let them take Scott, Campbell, Crabbe, or you, or me, or any of the living, and throne him;—but not this new Jacob Behmen, this . . . whose pride might have kept him true, even had his principles turned as perverted as his *soi-disant* poetry.

[1] In this connection it may be worth noting that Middleton Murry observes 'how different is Keats' conception of naturalness in poetry from that of a Wordsworth or a Leigh Hunt, intent on "the real language of real people" ' (*Keats and Shakespeare*, v, 59).

'But Leigh Hunt is a good man, and a good father—see his Odes to all the Masters Hunt;—a good husband—see his Sonnet to Mrs. Hunt; a good friend—see his Epistles to different people;—and a great coxcomb and a very vulgar person in every thing about him. But that is not his fault, but of circumstances.'

(LJ, IV, 237)

Elsewhere Byron limits the charge of vulgarity to Hunt's literary style, saying that he is 'anything but a vulgar man', and again: 'Of my friend Hunt, I have already said, that he is anything but vulgar in his manners.'[1] As for our letter, to which we shall return, observe particularly the references to 'self-love' and 'nightmare'; and also the humorous capital made from Hunt's more personal poems. The attack is levelled against a certain kind of presumptuous individualism, and is not without relevance to the artistic confusions of our own century.

Hunt's poetry cannot be said to have survived, but Byron's complaint is basically the same with, variously, Wordsworth and Keats, though he acquits Wordsworth and Southey of 'vulgarity'.[2] We must not forget that Byron knew nothing of *The Prelude*, as yet unpublished, and had only Wordsworth's shorter poems and *The Excursion* on which to base his judgements. Nor are all his comments derogatory. On 7 September, 1814, he told Murray:

'There must be many "fine things" in Wordsworth, but I should think it difficult to make *six* quartos (the amount of the whole) all fine, particularly the Pedlar's portion of the poem; but there can be no doubt of his powers to do almost any thing.'

(LJ, III, 131)

To Leigh Hunt on 30 October, 1815, he wrote:

'I take leave to differ with you on Wordsworth, as freely as I once agreed with you; at that time I gave him credit for a promise which is unfulfilled. I still think his capacity warrants all you say of *it* only, but that his performances since *Lyrical Ballads* are miserably inadequate to the ability which lurks within him: there is undoubtedly much natural talent spilt over the *Excursion*; but it is rain upon rocks —where it stands and stagnates; or rain upon sands—where it falls without fertilizing.'

(LJ, III, 238)

[1] The Bowles Controversy, LJ, v, 588, 591.   [2] Ibid., 591.

It is a matter of 'natural talent'; that is, individual, personal, ability; but without any contacts with what Byron felt to be the organic body of traditional poetry; and hence infertile, 'rain upon rocks'. He does not, however, deny the 'rain', the personal ability. His attention was mainly on

> *A drowsy-frowsy poem, call'd the 'Excursion',*
> *Writ in a manner which is my aversion.*
>
> (*Don Juan*, III, 94)

In this matter we must be honest with ourselves. We have all read Wordsworth's *Excursion* through once, and can point to our favourite passages, but how often have we returned to it, as a whole?

With Keats, the problem was different. Byron's antipathy was roused in part by what he considered the tawdry excesses of Hunt's 'Cockney' school: 'it is in their *finery*', he says, that they 'are *most* vulgar'.[1] The excess of decoration in *Endymion* is a good example of the kind of poetry Pope decried in his *Essay on Criticism* as 'false eloquence', spreading its 'gaudy colours' too thick (311–12), though it is of course true that such a fecundity in a young writer may be a sign of genius. There was much in *Endymion* to repel Byron. The heavily enjambed couplets may have appeared almost as an *attack* on a medium about which he felt, as we shall see (p. 134), strongly; and indeed, this may be, in its way, some sort of justification for what is otherwise an unaccountable phenomenon, since the poetry is always labouring to produce rhymes which the enjambments simultaneously kill. One feels a semi-conscious revulsion from the couplet at work, though this same tendency becomes elsewhere a carefree and buoyant freedom, which is inoffensive enough.

There was, however, a more cogent reason for Byron's annoyance. He deeply resented Keats' strictures on the Augustans in *Sleep and Poetry*, which he saw as a piece of unwarrantable *hubris* from 'a young person learning to write poetry and beginning by teaching the art'.[2] Keats was one of those who 'decry Pope', having 'written some lines against him, of which it were better to be the subject than the author'; one who, as a young man, had 'set out with assailing the Poet whom of all others a young aspirant ought to respect and honour and study'; who regarded the succession of great names from

---

[1] Ibid., 591.
[2] *Blackwood's* Defence, LJ, IV, 491.

Dryden to Johnson as 'a School of dolts'; [1] and who was accordingly labouring under a 'distortion of intellect'.[2] Keats was, of course, fighting for his own poetry, and we may compare T. S. Eliot's statement that when a poet writes as a critic, we must be prepared to find him 'trying to defend the kind of poetry he is writing, or to formulate the kind that he wants to write'.[3] But we must not allow our appreciation of Keats to cloud our understanding, nor regard Byron's private letters, though neither the *Blackwood's* Defence nor the Bowles Controversy come under this heading, on this, or any other subject, as a public unkindness. He always spoke out with force and vigour. He noted in the letter to Hunt which we have already (p. 122) quoted for its remarks on Wordsworth that: 'I write in great haste and, I doubt, *not* much to the purpose; but you have it hot and hot, just as it comes, and so let it go.' [4] That is true, too, of certain more heated utterances on Keats in the letters. We must recognize that his anger was directly proportional to his love of Pope and irritation at the contemporary denigrations.

He was, however, saddened by the news of Keats' death. On 26 April, 1821, he wrote to Shelley with reference to the second of his two public letters to Bowles [5] which he had recently sent off for publication: 'Had I known that Keats was dead—or that he was alive and so sensitive—I should have omitted some remarks upon his poetry, to which I was provoked by his *attack* upon *Pope*, and my disapprobation of *his own* style of writing.' [6] He next arranged to cut out—and the action was characteristic of his behaviour in such matters [7]—his more incisive criticisms, among them some of those which we have just used, together with a number of quotations from Keats' work that told strongly in favour of his own argument. Here is the opening of one of them:

> *The hearty grasp that sends a pleasant sonnet*
> *Into the brain ere one can think upon it;*
> *The silence when some rhymes are coming out;*
> *And when they're come the very pleasant rout . . .*
>
> (LJ, v, 588, note)

---

[1] The phrase occurs in Keats' *Sleep and Poetry*, 196–7. Pope is not specifically mentioned. The attack is on 'the school'.

[2] The Bowles Controversy, LJ, v, 588; 589, note.

[3] *The Music of Poetry*, W. P. Ker Memorial Lecture, Glasgow, 1942.

[4] LJ, III, 241.   [5] Dated 25 March, 1821; LJ, v, 567.

[6] LJ, v, 268.   [7] See *Lord Byron: Christian Virtues*, III, 122–3.

The lines occur at *Sleep and Poetry* (319). The underlinings appear to be Byron's. His arguments cannot be followed without an honest facing of such lines. Even so, he had very freely admitted Keats' powers of 'imagination', which he saw as having been misdirected by false guides who should feel remorse at having perverted a young man of promise.[1] It must be remembered that Byron is not writing of Keats' 1820 volume, which contained *Hyperion* and the great odes. Of *Hyperion*, he wrote later, after Keats' death, in a manuscript note to his *Blackwood's* Defence dated 12 November, 1821:

'My indignation at Mr. Keats' depreciation of Pope has hardly permitted me to do justice to his own genius, which, malgré all the fantastic fopperies of his style, was undoubtedly of great promise. His fragment of *Hyperion* seems actually inspired by the Titans, and is as sublime as Aeschylus. He is a loss to our literature; and the more so, as he himself, before his death, is said to have been persuaded that he had not taken the right line, and was reforming his style upon the more classical models of the language.'

(LJ, IV, 491, note)

The thought recurs in *Don Juan* (XI, 60), where Keats is said to have died 'just as he really promised something great'. Byron's position is clear. He would naturally have liked the austere diction and comparative reserve of *Hyperion*, and would have approved the poet's submission of himself to the telling of an objective story whose contours are unblurred by any overplus of decoration; while the change to blank verse left the couplet in peace. Had both lived, and most assuredly had they met, there might have been little to quarrel over.

We can say nothing like that of his relations with Wordsworth and Southey. To them Byron's opposition was not merely literary. In literature Wordsworth and Coleridge had broken with tradition; but it was not just the break, but rather *the will to break*, the will to revolution, that so clearly distinguishes them from Byron. They were men of extremes: Wordsworth's *Borderers* and Coleridge's *Remorse* studiously elaborate through their darker, but not wholly unsympathetic, persons a daring Satanism beside which the Byronic heroes and Nietzsche's Zarathustra appear like Victorian moralists; and there may have been good reason to leave *The Borderers* unpublished. Wordsworth's passionate delight in the French Revolution

[1] The Bowles Controversy, LJ, v, 589, note.

and the Coleridge-Southey scheme of Pantisocracy witnessed a youthful will to revolution and a throwing over of traditional forms, customs and values which may be related to the philosophy of Godwin and the poetic idealism of Shelley, but corresponded to nothing in Byron. Byron held strong revolutionary convictions, but only in so far as revolution fulfilled the traditions of civilization as he saw them and served to guard its basic values. He had, like Pope, or Burke, both sides of the opposition steadily in mind; and this was so at all periods of his life; and, since there was nothing superficial about his revolutionary ardour, it persisted undimmed. He himself could never have become a political reactionary. So, when he saw Wordsworth and Southey reacting from their early heterodoxies to a conformation as extreme as their youthful fantasies, he regarded them as little better than a pair of unprincipled time-servers:

'Wordsworth's place may be in the Customs—it is, I think, in that or the Excise—besides another at Lord Lonsdale's table, where this poetical charlatan and political parasite licks up the crumbs with a hardened alacrity; the converted Jacobin having long subsided into the clownish sycophant of the worst prejudices of the aristocracy.'

(Note to *Don Juan*, I, Dedication, 6)

Whether or not Byron did Wordsworth and Southey an injustice does not here concern us. He could admit their poetic powers:

> You're shabby fellows—true—but poets still,
> And duly seated on the immortal hill.
>
> (*Don Juan*, I, Dedication, 6)

But the rest he could not forgive. He himself had never known, at least in politics, what it was to be either young or irresponsible, as his early notes to the second canto of *Childe Harold* witness, and he could not himself understand the waverings of lesser minds—lesser, I mean, on such issues as these—than his own. It is important that we recognize all that was involved in his general distaste for 'the Lakers', and meanwhile we must never forget that he had neither *The Prelude* nor Wordsworth's later, more impersonal, poetry, the poetry of the *Ecclesiastical Sonnets*,[1] under survey. He himself thought naturally in terms of a unity involving both poetry and politics,

---

[1] That I do not underrate Wordsworth's later poetry should be clear from my account of his life's work in *The Starlit Dome*.

though the poetry and the politics are beyond party.[1] To Pope and Byron poetry and state-affairs were indissolubly related, while the poetry, in subject, diction, and technique, contains and subsumes, from start to finish, all those party tensions it is to resolve.

Such poetry will be at once traditional and liberal, aristocratic and simple. The poetry of Pope and Byron, at least where style is concerned and complexities involved, is certainly simpler and more readily to be understood by the less educated than are the major works of a Blake, Wordsworth, or Coleridge; and as for subject, there is, in Byron anyway, nearly always enough of objective reference to myth or history to make communication the easier. Though throughout deeply engaged in the eternal dimension, his higher flights, with the possible exception of *Manfred*, are close pinned to earth; and even *Manfred* relies on a well-known pattern of remorse, devils, and damnation, though the hero is not damned. We can see why Byron wrote off Wordsworth as 'this arch-apostle of mystery and mysticism',[2] and made fun of Coleridge

> *Explaining metaphysics to the nation—*
> *I wish he would explain his explanation.*
> (*Don Juan*, I, Dedication, 2)

Byron's own handling of the ultimate mysteries, as I have shown in *Byron's Dramatic Prose* (see p. 150, note, below), tended to avoid metaphysical speculation. But it would be an error to suppose that he was lacking in metaphysical insight. Despite his avowed opposition to romanticism, he understood Coleridge's poetry better than any one of his period, once coupling him with Crabbe as one of the two first of contemporary poets, praising the *Ancient Mariner* with fervour, encouraging him to complete *Christabel*, and being alone responsible for the survival of *Kubla Khan*, in which the author himself saw no significance, and probably of *Christabel* too.[3] These presumably won his acceptance by their firmly realized, and indeed objective, use of symbolism and atmosphere. What Byron disliked in poetry was anything too vague or personal, too far removed from the concrete solidities of poetic creation, regarding all such individualistic and abstract excursions as the direct way to a romantic agony,

---

[1] For Byron's political thinking, see D. N. Raymond's *Political Career of Lord Byron* (1924); V. de S. Pinto's *Byron and Liberty* (Nottingham, 1944); and *Lord Byron: Christian Virtues*, III.

[2] Hunt, 30 Oct., 1815: LJ, III, 239. [3] *Lord Byron: Christian Virtues*, II, 59–60.

as when his criticism of Hunt's poetry is couched in terms of 'self-love' and 'nightmare' (p. 121), or when he observes in Keats 'a sort of mental masturbation', together with a 'soliciting his own ideas into a state which is neither poetry nor any thing else', leading direct to 'Bedlam'.[1] All this follows closely the criticism which Swift in *The Battle of the Books* levelled at the moderns, when he contrasted their self-exuded poisons with the objective, bee-like activities of the ancients, making from this or that flower 'honey and wax' as a means to 'sweetness and light'.

We, in our day, are even more deeply self-centred; we, too, hanker after a colloquial idiom, like Wordsworth and Hunt; we, too, have seen in every field of art works which appear to be 'begotten by self-love upon a nightmare' (p. 121). And yet we have also watched T. S. Eliot rather tentatively asserting the aristocratic values and directly insisting on tradition; though the tradition he means is not Pope's or Byron's. His 'classic' principles, however, are not far from those on which Byron constructed his plays. Byron's later diction, as surely as Pope's, aimed at lucidity and simplicity, and both he and Eliot steer clear of those fantastic originalities to which a too personal theory or 'system' may lead the devotee, even though the system may derive from a search for the colloquial.

Byron was not, of course, out to attempt any such transcendental flights as those of a Blake or a Wordsworth. But here again we only see how closely he is with Pope in his steady will to inject poetry into the human situation, psychological and political, before reaching out beyond man's natural sphere; though, as in Pope too, the trans-cendencies are never denied, continually suggested, and at choice moments colour the human drama with a moving splendour.

II

We shall next discuss more exactly Byron's reverence for Pope. He regularly regarded his own work as miserably inadequate in comparison, without apparently recognizing how far its manner and diction preserved, in all its variations, the values he believed were being lost. Nor did he recognize how much more tumultuous a world he was himself labouring to master, but, with a characteristic integrity, refused excuses, while keeping his eye steadily on the ideal.

[1] Murray, 9 Nov., 1820: SP, ed. Peter Quennell, II, 536; LJ, V, 117, omitting 'masturbation'.

That was to be found in Pope, whom he regarded as the universal poet of mankind.

Writing to Murray on 15 September, 1817, we find him regarding *Childe Harold* as the best he would ever do, and suggesting, as so often, retirement from composition. Then, after an astute comment on Moore's *Lalla Rookh*, he continues:

'With regard to poetry in general, I am convinced, the more I think of it, that he and *all* of us—Scott, Southey, Wordsworth, Moore, Campbell, I,—are all in the wrong, one as much as another; that we are upon a wrong revolutionary poetical system, or systems, not worth a damn in itself, and from which none but Rogers and Crabbe are free; and that the present and next generations will finally be of this opinion. I am the more confirmed in this by having lately gone over some of our classics, particularly *Pope*, whom I tried in this way —I took Moore's poems and my own and some others, and went over them side by side with Pope's, and I was really astonished (I ought not to have been so) and mortified at the ineffable distance in point of sense, harmony, effect and even *Imagination*, passion, and *Invention*, between the little Queen Anne's man, and us of the Lower Empire. Depend upon it, it is all Horace then, and Claudian now, among us; and if I had to begin again, I would model myself accordingly.'

(LJ, IV, 169)

On 2 February, 1818, he addressed Moore on the subject:

'I don't know what Murray may have been saying or quoting. I called Crabbe and Sam the fathers of present Poesy, and said, that I thought—except them—*all* of "*us youth*" were on a wrong tack. But I never said that we did not sail well. Our fame will be hurt by *admiration* and *imitation*. When I say *our*, I mean *all* (Lakers included), except the postscript of the Augustans. The next generation (from the quantity and facility of imitation) will tumble and break their necks off our Pegasus, who runs away with us; but we keep the *saddle*, because we broke the rascal and can ride. But though easy to mount, he is the devil to guide; and the next fellows must go back to the riding-school and the manège, and learn to ride the "great horse".

'Talking of horses . . .'

(LJ, IV, 196)

It is admitted that Crabbe and Rogers are merely a 'postscript'; and he is perfectly well aware of the greatness of romantic poetry. His point was, simply, that the 'romantic' manner had little permanent value, whereas the other had. His anger at the misvaluing of Pope grew fiercer. He would defend him 'against the world'. He attacks 'the new School of Critics and Scribblers, who think themselves poets because they do *not* write like Pope'. He feels personally about it, continually returning to the subject in his letters to Murray:

'I have no patience with such cursed humbug and bad taste; your whole generation are not worth a canto of *The Rape of the Lock*, or the *Essay on Man*, or the *Dunciad*, or "anything that is his".'

(12 April, 1818; LJ, IV, 225)

Again:

'*Read him*—most of you *don't*—but *do*—and I will forgive you: though the inevitable consequence would be that you would burn all I have ever written, and all your other wretched Claudians of the day (except Scott and Crabbe) into the bargain.'

(25 Jan., 1819; LJ, IV, 278)

Again, with reference to Francis Hodgson:

'He is right in defending *Pope* against the bastard Pelicans of the poetical winter day, who add insult to their parricide by sucking the blood of the parent of English *real* poetry—poetry without fault— and then spurning the bosoms which fed them.'

(18 May, 1819; LJ, IV, 304)

And, last:

'Herewith you will receive a note (enclosed) on Pope, which you will find tally with a part of the text of last Post. I have at last lost all patience with the atrocious cant and nonsense about Pope, with which our present blackguards are overflowing, and am determined to make such head against it as an Individual can, by prose or verse; and I will at least do it with good will. There is no bearing it any longer; and if it goes on, it will destroy what little good writing or taste remains amongst us. I hope there are still a few men of taste to second me; but if not, I'll battle it alone, convinced that it is in the best cause of English literature.'

(29 March, 1820; LJ, IV, 425)

In thus championing the tradition Byron was paradoxically acting as an individualist.

But his solitary battle gave him no pleasure. He was deeply pained, and far more truly concerned than about his own work or his friends'. His peculiarly objective concern for literary matters is obvious always, but this goes deeper. Pope stood for something which he regarded as all-important: it was no mere question of 'style'. As one of our quotations (p. 129) shows, Pope's poetry meant to him 'sense', 'harmony', 'effect', 'imagination', 'passion', 'invention': he was thinking of the whole rich, pulsing, solid achievement in all its human wisdom and excelling powers; of Pope's created world. Moreover, as we shall see, politics were involved too, and also ethic. Pope had occupied that specifically liberal yet classical-traditional territory, at once heroic and pacific, which Byron himself inherited.

Before passing to his more elaborated praise of Pope in the Bowles Controversy, we must notice Byron's lengthy statement on the literary situation, from his answer, dated 15 March, 1820,[1] to an attack in Blackwood's Magazine, which I call, here and elsewhere, his 'Blackwood's Defence'. This is the 'note' referred to in Byron's letter to Murray of 29 March, 1820, from which we have just quoted.

He starts by charging his age with the corruption of poetry and continues:

'The great cause of the present deplorable state of English poetry is to be attributed to that absurd and systematic depreciation of Pope, in which, for the last few years, there has been a kind of epidemical concurrence. Men of the most opposite opinions have united upon this topic. Warton and Churchill began it, having borrowed the hint probably from the heroes of the *Dunciad*, and their own internal conviction that their proper reputation can be as nothing till the most perfect and harmonious of poets—he who, having no fault, has had REASON made his reproach—was reduced to what they conceived to be his level; but even *they* dared not degrade him below Dryden.'

(LJ, IV, 485)

Byron himself, naturally, intends no slight against Dryden.

We pass to some aspersions on the works of Southey and Wordsworth with a thrust at Wordsworth's prefaces 'couched in such prose

[1] LJ, IV, 474.

131

as must give peculiar delight to those who have read the prefaces of Pope and Dryden, scarcely less celebrated for the beauty of their prose than for the charms of their verse'. Coleridge is, as elsewhere, let off more lightly and his poetry respected. But all three are guilty on the main charge, involving Pope:

'These three personages, Southey, Wordsworth, and Coleridge, had all of them a very natural antipathy to Pope; and I respect them for it, as the only original feeling or principle which they have contrived to preserve. But they have been joined in it by those who have joined them in nothing else: by the Edinburgh Reviewers, by the whole heterogeneous mass of living English poets, excepting Crabbe, Rogers, Gifford and Campbell, who, both by precept and practice, have proved their adherence; and by me, who have shamefully deviated in practice, but have ever loved and honoured Pope's poetry with my whole soul, and hope to do so till my dying day. I would rather see all I have ever written lining the same trunk in which I actually read the eleventh book of a modern epic poem at Malta, in 1811 (I opened it to take out a change after the paroxysm of a tertian, in the absence of my servant, and found it lined with the name of the maker, Eyre, Cockspur Street, and with the epic poetry alluded to) than sacrifice what I firmly believe in as the Christianity of English poetry, the poetry of Pope.'

(LJ, IV, 486)

There cannot be many examples of a major poet so slighting his own life's work in order to safeguard the reputation of an earlier master.

Then follow more thrusts at the poetry of Wordsworth and Southey and a sharp denial, with evidence drawn from the past, that contemporary popularity argues a lack of poetic genius. Here is the rest:

'It may be asked, why, having this opinion of the present state of poetry in England and having had it long, as my friends and others well knew—possessing, or having possessed too, as a writer, the ear of the public for the time being—I have not adopted a different plan in my own compositions, and endeavoured to correct rather than encourage the taste of the day. To this I would answer, that it is easier to perceive the wrong than to pursue the right, and that I have never contemplated the prospect "of filling (with *Peter Bell*, see its Preface) permanently a station in the literature of the country".

Those who know me best, know this, and that I have been considerably astonished at the temporary success of my works, having flattered no person and no party, and expressed opinions which are not those of the general reader. Could I have anticipated the degree of attention which has been accorded me, assuredly I would have studied more to deserve it. But I have lived in far countries abroad, or in the agitating world at home, which was not favourable to study or reflection; so that almost all I have written has been mere passion —passion, it is true, of different kinds, but always passion: for in me (if it be not an Irishism to say so) my *indifference* was a kind of passion, the result of experience, and not the philosophy of nature. Writing grows a habit, like a woman's gallantry: there are women who have had no intrigue, but few who have had but one only: so there are millions of men who have never written a book, but few who have written only one. And thus, having written once, I wrote on; encouraged no doubt by the success of the moment, yet by no means anticipating its duration, and I will venture to say, scarcely even wishing it. But then I did other things besides write, which by no means contributed either to improve my writings or my prosperity.

'I have thus expressed publicly upon the poetry of the day the opinion I have long entertained and expressed of it to all who have asked it, and to some who would rather not have heard it: as I told Moore not very long ago, "we are all wrong except Rogers, Crabbe, and Campbell." Without being old in years, I am old in days, and do not feel the adequate spirit within me to attempt a work which should show what I think right in poetry, and must content myself with having denounced what is wrong. There are, I trust, younger spirits rising up in England, who, escaping the contagion which has swept away poetry from our literature, will recall it to their country, such as it once was and may still be.

'In the mean time, the best sign of amendment will be repentance, and new and frequent editions of Pope and Dryden.

'There will be found as comfortable metaphysics, and ten times more poetry in the *Essay on Man*, than in the *Excursion*. If you search for passion, where is it to be found stronger than in the epistle from Eloisa to Abelard, or in *Palamon and Arcite*? Do you wish for invention, imagination, sublimity, character? seek them in the *Rape of the Lock*, the *Fables* of Dryden, the *Ode of Saint Cecilia's Day*, and *Absalom and Achitophel*: you will discover, in these two poets only, *all* for which you must ransack innumerable metres, and God only knows how many *writers* of the day, without finding a tittle of the same qualities—with the addition, too, of wit, of which the latter have none. I have not, however, forgotten *Thomas Brown the Younger* nor the *Fudge Family*, nor Whistlecraft; but that is not wit—it is humour. I will say nothing of the harmony of Pope and Dryden in comparison, for there is not a living poet (except Rogers, Gifford, Campbell, and Crabbe) who can write an heroic couplet. The fact is, that the exquisite beauty of their versification has withdrawn the public attention from their other excellences, as the vulgar eye will rest more upon the splendour of the uniform than the quality of the troops. It is this very harmony, particularly in Pope, which has raised the vulgar and atrocious cant against him:—because his versification is perfect, it is assumed that it is his only perfection; because his truths are so clear, it is asserted that he has no invention; and because he is always intelligible, it is taken for granted that he has no genius. We are sneeringly told that he is the "Poet of Reason", as if this was a reason for his being no poet. Taking passage for passage, I will undertake to cite more lines teeming with *imagination* from Pope than from any *two* living poets, be they who they may. To take an instance at random from a species of composition not very favourable to imagination—Satire: set down the character of Sporus, with all the wonderful play of fancy which is scattered over it, and place by its side an equal number of verses, from any two existing poets, of the same power and the same variety—where will you find them?

'I merely mention one instance of many, in reply to the injustice done to the memory of him who harmonized our poetical language. The attorneys' clerks, and other self-educated genii, found it easier to distort themselves to the new models, than to toil after the symmetry of him who had enchanted their fathers. They were besides smitten by being told that the new school were to revive the language of Queen Elizabeth, the true English: as every body in the reign of Queen Anne wrote no better than French, by a species of literary treason.

'Blank verse, which, unless in the drama, no one except Milton ever wrote who could rhyme, became the order of the day—or else such rhyme as looked still blanker than the verse without it. I am aware that Johnson has said, after some hesitation, that he could not "prevail upon himself to wish that Milton had been a rhymer." The opinions of that truly great man, whom it is also the present fashion to decry, will ever be received by me with that deference which time will restore to him from all; but, with all humility, I am not persuaded that the *Paradise Lost* would not have been more nobly conveyed to posterity, not perhaps in heroic couplets, although even *they* could sustain the subject if well balanced, but in the stanza of Spenser or of Tasso, or in the terza rima of Dante, which the powers of Milton could easily have grafted on our language. The *Seasons* of Thomson would have been better in rhyme, although still inferior to his *Castle of Indolence*; and Mr. Southey's *Joan of Arc* no worse, although it might have taken up six months instead of weeks in the composition. I recommend also to the lovers of lyrics the perusal of the present laureate's *Odes* by the side of Dryden's on Saint Cecilia, but let him be sure to read *first* those of Mr. Southey.

'To the heaven-born genii and inspired young scriveners of the day much of this will appear paradox: it will appear so even to the higher order of our critics; but it was a truism twenty years ago, and it will be a reacknowledged truth in ten more.'

(LJ, IV, 488)

Byron's 'ten' years is an understatement; had he said a couple of hundred he would have been nearer the truth. Such over-optimism appears to be a regular constituent of prophetic talk, from the New Testament on: an eternal truth grasped, its flashing power forces a more rapid interpretation in temporal terms than temporal terms allow.

Our first reaction to this uncompromising statement is likely enough to be hostile. Byron's convictions register with such smashing, yet effortless, force, that we are always in danger of blaming him for his superlative manner. Observe that he at least claims to respect *any* sincerely held opinion, even against Pope. For the rest, there is certainly much sound sense. Coleridge's poetry is respected, but the aspersions on Southey's metrical experiments and fantastic tales are probably just, and the general level of Wordsworth's prose merits much, if not all, of Byron's strictures; compare his famous prefaces with Byron's prose, and the difference in precision and power will be evident. The assessment of the relative merits of the *Essay on Man* and *The Excursion* is not unreasonable, nor is the praise of *Eloisa to Abelard*, to the powers of which Byron was finely sensitive (see pp. 140–1, 151). Moreover, he rates his own work as nothing in comparison with Pope's, admitting himself to be guilty of many of the faults he criticizes. The consideration of Italian as our first, and only *poetical*, language was so deeply held that he modelled his later style on the Italian and even planned to compose his greatest work in the language,[1] and his own plays were modelled, in both language and structure, on classic principles. Most important of all, he sees and states clearly, with a diagnosis which is one of general critical interest quite apart from our present concern, how and why Pope had been misrepresented, suffering for his technical virtuosity and rational clarity, so that such comparatively minor elements had been allowed, as so often happens in literary criticism, to fog the contours of his major achievement. Finally, observe the respect accorded Johnson, whom he elsewhere calls 'the noblest critical mind which our country has produced',[2] and the high valuation placed upon the couplet.

We shall not, naturally, subscribe to all his judgements in point of detail and emphasis, but we can get the general tenour of his contention and recognize a core of truth. Pope was 'the Christianity of English poetry'; far more than 'taste', as usually understood, was involved; the question was, whether our literature 'shall or shall not relapse into the Barbarism from which it has scarcely emerged for above a century and a half'.[3] The word 'barbarism' is indicative: the Augustan manner is regarded as the voice of civilization.

But we must not remain content with the 'manner'. We have for too long shrivelled the appreciation of Pope, and not Pope only, into talk of style and language in dissociation from the subject-matter; all good enough, and necessary to a specialist enquiry, but not the main thing. Pope himself in his *Essay on Criticism* has carefully warned us of those critics who, 'fond' of some subsidiary interest, 'make the Whole depend upon a Part', some looking merely for 'conceit', and others for 'language', 'sense' being slurred by a concentration on 'style' (263–308):

> *But most by Numbers judge a Poet's song;*
> *And smooth or rough, with them is right or wrong:*
> *In the bright Muse though thousand charms conspire,*
> *Her voice is all these tuneful fools admire . . .*

(337)

They are like those going to church not for the 'doctrine', but for

[1] Murray, 6 April, 1819: LJ, IV, 284. [2] The Bowles Controversy, LJ, V, 564.
[3] Gilchrist, 5 Sept., 1821: SP, II, 666.

the 'music' (343); and the charge would be just as valid were they
to be found going to church, as they do today, for discord rather
than music. Byron (p. 134) levels a similar indictment against Pope's
critics: what he saw in Pope was no mere technical virtuosity but,
as one of the letters (p. 129) shows and his *Blackwood's* Defence makes
clear, qualities far richer. He was concerned to advertise all the
'thousand charms' of Pope's muse; his close texture of impressions,
his play of fancy, his rounded and choice vocabulary, his richly
inlaid perceptions; above all, his fine, vigorous, and essentially poetic
philosophy, aiming to penetrate and redirect not so much man's
thinking as his instincts, whereby he became in Byron's mind the
greatest ethical poet of the world.

III

We shall now pass to consider Byron's more expanded arguments
on Pope's importance. These occur in the section entitled *Controversy
between Byron and Bowles as to the poetry and character of Pope* given
in Appendix III (522–92) to the fifth volume of the *Letters and
Journals*.[1] Byron composed two extended letters in answer to the
Rev. W. L. Bowles' *Invariable Principles of Poetry* (1819). The first
was published in 1821; [2] the second, which did not appear in print
until 1835, Byron withheld in view of his adversary's good-natured
acceptance of his strictures. He asked Murray to thank Bowles for
his 'candour and kindness', adding: 'You will of course *not* publish
my defence of Gilchrist, as, after Bowles' good humour upon the
subject, it would be too savage.'[3] In these letters Byron defends
Pope variously against the implications of the *Principles* and the
criticisms made upon his life in Bowles' edition of Pope's works
(1806), which Byron had already attacked in *English Bards and Scotch
Reviewers*:

> *If Pope, whose fame and genius, from the first,*
> *Have foiled the best of critics, needs the worst,*

[1] Tillotson ('Nature', 18, note) refers to the 'early nineteenth-century controversy on Pope's status as poet', which he describes as 'a muddle of vituperation,
pedantry, and vital aesthetics'. He notes that 'the history of the controversy
has been set out by J. J. van Rennes in *Bowles, Byron and the Pope–Controversy*
(1927)'.
[2] Completed 10 Feb., 1821; LJ, v, 201.
[3] Murray, 14 May, 1821; LJ, v, 285–6.

Do thou essay: each fault, each failing scan;
The first of poets was, alas! but man.
Rake from each ancient dunghill every pearl,
Consult Lord Fanny and confide in Curll;
Let all the scandals of a former age
Perch on thy pen, and flutter o'er thy page.

(367)

The disagreement was of some standing, and when Bowles' *Principles* drove home the attack from a new angle, Byron was roused to a reply.

Briefly, Bowles was arguing from a romantic view that nature was in itself a more poetical subject than things made by man. His key statement runs: 'Images drawn from what is beautiful or sublime in nature are *more poetical* than images drawn from art'.[1] The Pyramids and the Great Wall of China, he says, though impressive enough, derive their appeal from natural or moral, and by this he means human and historical, associations: the point is, they are not *in themselves* so poetical.[2] Byron's reply urges the limitations of pure nature. He is not, perhaps, altogether true to his own experiences, which, in prose and poetry alike, record a quivering susceptibility to natural phenomena of certain more titanic kinds; sun, tempests, the ocean, mountains.[3] In engaging in the rather unprofitable argument as to whether a ship is or is not more poetical than the sea, he at least leaves us some good descriptions of actual seas and fleets.[4] But when he urges that the Parthenon is a finer thing than the rock it stands on, and questions the aesthetic value of the desert without its pyramids,[5] he is perhaps not quite fair to Bowles, who was supporting primarily that in nature which was peculiarly 'beautiful' or 'sublime'. Byron develops [6] some interesting appreciations of the arts, architectural and sculptural, of Italy, which, being alive with 'mind', are considered finer than Mont Blanc; and Westminster Abbey and St. Paul's are, as objects, said to hold poetry, apart from all human purposes and associations. The pictorial artist, it is argued, always

[1] LJ, v, 531.   [2] LJ, v, 527.
[3] In her *Goethe and Byron* (Byron Foundation Lecture, Nottingham, 1949–50), E. M. Butler makes some interesting comparisons between the mountains, cataracts and sea of *Childe Harold* and the nature-poetry of Goethe's *Faust*. Goethe, she writes, tends 'to contract rather than expand before nature's immensities', whereas 'the diametrically opposite tendency was innate in Byron'.
[4] LJ, v, 543–6.   [5] LJ, v, 546–7.   [6] LJ, v, 547–52.

improves on nature, if only by choice of view, distance, light: 'Nature, exactly, simply, barely, Nature, will make no great artist of any kind, and least of all a poet.'[1]

The issues are fairly clear and need little discussion. Byron never embraced a poetic pantheism and, though he remains our greatest poet of sun and sea, regarded both rather as symbols of divinity than as themselves divine, as at *Manfred*, III, ii (sun); *Sardanapalus*, II, i (sun; and, later, stars); and *Childe Harold*, IV, 183 (ocean); and in *Manfred* he realizes his part-Alpine and part-spiritual atmosphere through various mythological personifications. He certainly never allowed nature a central, protagonist, importance as rival to divinity or man. It is, however, true that his heavy emphasis here on arts of design does not correspond to their relative importance in his own poetic universe, though they are (see pp. 84, 87) more important than has been properly recognized. He is, of course, thinking not of his own poetry, but of Pope's, and we may, for simplicity, regard as the crux of the matter the game of cards in *The Rape of the Lock*, which Bowles had compared derogatarily with a forest walk as a poetic theme. Byron's answer is important:

'To the question, "whether the description of a game of cards be as poetical, supposing the execution of the artists equal, as a description of a walk in a forest?" it may be answered, that the *materials* are certainly not equal; but that "the *artist*", who has rendered the "game of cards poetical", is *by far the greater* of the two. But all this "ordering" of poets is purely arbitrary on the part of Mr. B. There may or may not be, in fact, different "orders" of poetry, but the poet is always ranked according to his execution, and not according to his branch of the art.'

(LJ, V, 552-3)

Again,

'Away, then, with this cant about nature, and "invariable principles of poetry!" A great artist will make a block of stone as sublime as a mountain, and a good poet can imbue a pack of cards with more poetry than inhabits the forests of America.'

(LJ, V, 557)

Byron is simply out to defend Pope against those who find in him a dearth of nature poetry.

[1] LJ, V, 550.

That Pope's feeling for nature was powerful enough we have already amply demonstrated, and that it should most often be approached in terms of collaboration with man is surely no just criticism. The desire of Pope's century to make friends with nature is witnessed by their attainments in landscape gardening; and Pope, says Byron, 'was the *first* who ridiculed the "formal French, Dutch, false and unnatural taste in gardening", both in *prose* and verse'. He notes his up-bringing at Windsor and frequent visits to country seats, among them Stowe; that he made 'his own little "five acres" a model to princes'; and that Warton thought that one of the best works of Kent, whom Byron calls 'the first of our artists who imitated nature', was modelled after Pope's example. As for the poetry, Byron asserts that it would be easy by quotation to show that 'no poet ever admired Nature more, or used her better, than Pope has done'; and as for 'schools of poetry', such things are never talked of 'till the decay of the art has increased with the number of its professors'.[1]

Byron is anxious to drive home to his readers the wealth and substance of Pope's imaginative creation. 'His various excellence', he writes, 'is really wonderful: architecture, painting, *gardening*, all are alike subject to his genius';[2] 'architecture' referring to *The Temple of Fame*, from which Byron quotes in his *Blackwood's* Defence. In a letter to Murray written in March, 1821 *apropos* of his answer to Bowles, he wrote: 'I will show more *imagery* in twenty lines of Pope than in any equal length of quotation in English poesy', and, after listing twenty-three images from the lines on Sporus in the *Epistle to Dr. Arbuthnot*, continues:

'Now, is there a line of all the passage without the most *forcible* imagery (for his purpose)? Look at the *variety*, at the *poetry*, of the passage—at the *imagination*: there is hardly a line from which a *painting* might not be made, and *is*. But this is nothing in comparison with his higher passages in the *Essay on Man*, and many of his other poems, serious and comic.

(LJ, v, 259–60)

Or again, he turns—we are back at the Controversy again—to *Eloisa to Abelard*, praising its consummate artistry and delicacy of feeling:

'The "licentiousness" of the story was *not* Pope's—it was a fact. All that it had of gross, he has softened;—all that it had of indelicate, he has purified—all that it had of passionate, he has beautified;—all that it had of holy, he has hallowed. Mr. Campbell has admirably marked this in a few words (I quote from memory), in drawing the distinction between Pope and Dryden, and pointing out where Dryden was wanting. "I fear," says he, "that had the subject of Eloisa fallen into his (Dryden's) hands, that he would have given us but a *coarse* draft of her passion." Never was the delicacy of Pope so much shown as in this poem. With the facts and the letters of Eloisa he has done what no other mind but that of the best and purest of poets could have accomplished with such materials. Ovid, Sappho (in the Ode called hers)—all that we have of ancient, all that we have of modern poetry, sinks into nothing compared with him in this production.'

(LJ, v, 581)

It is indeed strange that so little attention should have been accorded this supremely beautiful and powerful work, surely among the first treasures of its kind; if, indeed, it does not rather stand alone, a kind apart.

Our last quotation shows that Byron does not rate Dryden level with Pope; his was not merely an admiration for the neo-classic manner, though that was a constituent; it was, pre-eminently, a fervour inspired by recognition of Pope's status as a man of genius with a message and a meaning of first importance. That is why Bowles' criticism of Pope's character, based mainly on scandal and innuendo, so infuriated him: for, after all, he asked, what do all these 'accumulated hints' amount to? [1] We, in our day of 'debunking', have watched many such attempts, conscious or unconscious, to let biography make small what we deeply know to be great, and it will do us, as literary commentators, no harm to consider Byron's uncompromising condemnation. After answering certain of Bowles' criticisms as to Pope's character, he continues:

'But there is something a little more serious in Mr. Bowles' declaration, that he "*would* have spoken" of his "noble generosity to the outcast Richard Savage", and other instances of a compassionate and generous heart, "*had they occurred to his recollection when he wrote*". What! is it come to this? Does Mr. B. sit down to write a minute and laboured life and edition of a great poet? Does he

[1] LJ, v, 541.

anatomize his character, moral and poetical? Does he present us with his faults and with his foibles? Does he sneer at his feelings, and doubt of his sincerity? Does he unfold his vanity and duplicity? and then omit the good qualities which might, in part, have "covered this multitude of sins"? and then plead that *they did not occur to his recollection*"? Is this the frame of mind and of memory with which the illustrious dead are to be approached? If Mr. Bowles, who must have had access to all the means of refreshing his memory, did not recollect these facts, he is unfit for his task; but if he *did* recollect and omit them, I know not what he is fit for, but I know what would be fit for him. Is the plea of "not recollecting" such prominent facts to be admitted? Mr. B. has been at a public school, and, as I have been publicly educated also, I can sympathize with his predilection. When we were in the third form even, had we pleaded on the Monday morning that we had not brought up the Saturday's exercise, because "we had forgotten it", what would have been the reply? And is an excuse, which would not be pardoned to a schoolboy, to pass current in a matter which so nearly concerns the fame of the first poet of his age, if not of his country? If Mr. B. so readily forgets the virtues of others, why complain so grievously that others have a better memory for his own faults? They are but the faults of an author; while the virtues he omitted from his catalogue are essential to the justice due to a man.'

(LJ, v, 562)

Again:

'A fulsome editor is pardonable though tiresome, like a panegyrical son whose pious sincerity would demi-deify his father. But a detracting editor is a parricide. He sins against the nature of his office and connection—he murders the life to come of his victim. If his author is not worthy to be remembered, do not edit at all: if he be, edit honestly, and even flatteringly. The reader will forgive the weakness in favour of mortality, and correct your adulation with a smile.'

(LJ, v, 586)

That is a statement of general application, never more needed than today. But Byron solaces himself with the Shakespearian thought that his hero lies beyond such criticism:

'Pope himself "sleeps well"—nothing can touch him further; but those who love the honour of their country, the perfection of her literature, the glory of her language—are not to be expected to permit an atom of his dust to be stirred in his tomb, or a leaf to be stripped from the laurel which grows over it.'

(LJ, v, 568)

Observe the phraseology: 'honour', 'country', 'glory', 'dust', 'laurel'. The diction is poetic, heroic, patriotic; a diction which many of Byron's contemporaries would have been too proud, too self-centred, to use.

Byron speaks a language similar to Pope's, and in both it is the sign of a certain spiritualized aristocracy, a certain fervour, a certain message. It springs from the aristocratic, that is, the civilized, tradition of Renaissance Europe which, in its turn, derives authority from the ancients. There is in it an ethic, however hard to define: to Byron Pope was 'the greatest moral poet of any age, or in any language'; [1] he was not merely a poet wealthy in all the normal resources of the art, but, pre-eminently, a guide to man, as well in his manner as in his matter; virtue was felt to permeate his work. In contrast to Pope's nobility of manner lay what Byron regarded as the vulgarity of the Cockney school:

'The grand distinction of the under forms of the new school of poets is their *vulgarity*. By this I do not mean that they are *coarse*, but "shabby-genteel", as it is termed. A man may be *coarse* and yet not *vulgar*, and the reverse. Burns is often coarse, but never *vulgar*.'

(LJ, v, 591)

The Lake School are, for once, exonerated; it is in their 'finery' that the new school, by which Byron means certain London writers, are 'most vulgar', and

'they may be known by this at once; as what we called at Harrow "a Sunday Blood" might be easily distinguished from a gentleman, although his cloathes might be the better cut, and his boots the best blackened, of the two:—probably because he made the one, or cleaned the other, with his own hands.'

(LJ, v, 591)

There is a sting in that; not, of course, a social sting, but an attack on the writer who has no humility before convention or tradition, as when T. S. Eliot, in our time, compares Blake's philosophy to

[1] LJ, v, 568.

143

home-made furniture. This London school, followers of Hunt, might well be in themselves 'honourable' and 'gentlemanly', but, if so, such qualities were 'studiously excluded from their publications'. He continues:

'Far be it from me to presume that there ever was, or can be, such a thing as an *aristocracy* of *poets*; but there *is* a nobility of thought and of style, open to all stations, and derived partly from talent, and partly from education—which is to be found in Shakespeare, and Pope, and Burns, no less than in Dante and Alfieri, but which is nowhere to be perceived in the mock birds and bards of Mr. Hunt's little chorus.'

(LJ, v, 591)

He admits that this 'gentlemanliness' is hard to define except by concrete examples, and proceeds to suggest the professions, which may be high or low in social status, which do, and those which do not, appear to have it, with the interesting conclusion that women have more of it than men. It is a poetic necessity:

'In poetry, as well as writing in general, it will never *make* entirely a poet or a poem; but neither poet nor poem will ever be good for anything without it. It is the *salt* of society, and the seasoning of composition. *Vulgarity* is far worse than downright *blackguardism*; for the latter comprehends wit, humour, and strong sense at times; while the former is a sad abortive attempt at all things, "signifying nothing". It does not depend upon low themes, or even low language, for Fielding revels in both;—but is he ever *vulgar*? No. You see the man of education, the gentleman, and the scholar, sporting with his subject—its master, not its slave. Your vulgar writer is always most vulgar the higher his subject, as the man who showed the menagerie at Pidcock's was wont to say—"This, gentlemen, is the *eagle* of the *sun*, from Archangel, in Russia; the *otterer* it is the *igherer* he flies". But to the proof. It is a thing to be felt more than explained. Let any man take up a volume of Mr. Hunt's subordinate writers, read (if possible) a couple of pages, and pronounce for himself, if they contain not the kind of writing which may be likened to "shabby-genteel" in actual life. When he has done this, let him take up Pope; and when he has laid him down, take up the cockneys again—if he can.'

(LJ, v, 591)

The comparison with 'blackguardism' is revealing. We are close to an ethic, but the ethic is not quite a matter of good and evil as normally understood, while even 'blackguardism' may be in part redeemed by 'wit', 'humour' and good 'sense'. With these quotations we may group Byron's well-known letter to Murray of 12 September, 1821:

'The pity of these men is, that they never lived either in *high life*, nor in *solitude*: there is no medium for the knowledge of the *busy* or the *still* world. If admitted into high life for a season, it is merely as *spectators*—they form no part of the Mechanism thereof. Now Moore and I, the one by circumstance, and the other by birth, happened to be free of the corporation, and to have entered into its pulses and passions, *quarum partes fuimus*. Both of us have learnt by this much which nothing else could have taught us.'

(LJ, v, 362)

We are pointed to a balance of humanism and religion. 'Solitude' suggests religion, or its equivalent of meditation and, in general, spirituality; 'high life' suggests the real forces at play among leaders, political or social, who are presumably being distinguished, with a direct reference to 'passions', from a middle-class overlaying the 'pulses' and energies of life with a second-rate and second-hand morality. Whatever our social views, we must be clear as to Byron's meaning. It is something you do not get in sermons or tracts, but you will find it in Castiglione's *Il Cortegiano* and in Nietzsche's *Thus Spake Zarathustra*.

Pope and Byron were torch-bearers of a certain truth, or way of life, a nobility at once personal and civic, humanistic and spiritual, heroic and yet Christian, most hard to characterize, since none of these exists by itself, and each is involved in the rest. We may call them upholders of a tradition, but the term is misleading since this tradition only exists in so far as it is recreated from the centre. Poetic diction may or may not accompany the expression of this 'truth', or way; both Pope and Byron use a less literary speech in their later work. But it remains valuable as a symbol and symptom of the wisdom implied, consisting, as at its best it does, in a choice and use of words which have become through the winnowing of centuries bearers of certain traditional, yet not specifically religious, verities and virtues. Such a diction burns in the noble humility of Byron's acceptance of a possible oblivion when he writes that if destiny bar

My name from out the temple where the dead
Are honour'd by the nations—let it be—
And light the laurels on a loftier head!
And be the Spartan's epitaph on me—
'Sparta hath many a worthier son than he'.
(*Childe Harold*, IV, 10)

It is doubtful whether the exact kind of humility and nobility carried by those lines, whether their exact wave-length, as it were, could be transmitted in a less traditionally heroic, a less aristocratic, diction. The diction is itself constituent to the virtue in question: to use a paradox, the lines are *superbly* humble.

In this period, classical influence bulks large; at other periods other choices might function better. Fine language is a repository of living values, and by acceptance of certain already formed, compact, units of poetry in word or phrase, and beyond that, of certain established areas of thought and emotion, a poet may get to work in a more valuable way than he who despises them, since he is not always melting everything down to remould it nearer to his own heart's desire. He is not starting from scratch and neglecting the twenty or more centuries that have forged his tools. It may, indeed, be sometimes necessary to do that; we seem to be doing it today. But we are also very clearly over-doing it, and Byron's peculiar value and challenge to us lies precisely in his refusal, in his will to preserve, and as it were hurl against the centuries to come, the poetic achievement of Pope.

He does not, however, remain content with vague attempts to characterize a nobility of manner; he claims that Pope is a moral force in a far more precise sense, though we must be on our guard against the dangers inherent in the word 'moral'. His life-long craving was, in every sphere, a craving for moral, including sexual, purity. His youthful lyrics show it; so does his *English Bards and Scotch Reviewers*; his satire *The Waltz* was written from a loathing of public embraces; and the Doge's final denunciation in *Marino Faliero* is barbed with as fierce a puritanical fervour as you will find in English literature. As Hobhouse, long after his death, witnessed, his natural poetic tendency was to deny wrongdoing any attractive quality: 'It will be the eternal praise of his writings, as it was one of the merits of his conversation, that he threw no lustre on any exploit, however brilliant, any character, however exalted, which had not contributed to the happiness or welfare of mankind.'[1] According to Lady Blessington, he felt that, had his genius not been thwarted by opposition, it might have developed into 'one unbroken blaze of light';[2] and by this he would have meant a kind of teaching, or poetic doctrine, a Promethean illumination. In this, he had, in his own eyes, failed; even so, as far as sexual morality was concerned, his poetry was long known as 'the chaste muse of Albion', and the title was correct enough, at least up to the composition of *Beppo*, *Don Juan* and *Sardanapalus*, when he made an advance with full understanding of what he was doing, and why. Of *Don Juan* he wrote:

'If they had told me the poetry was bad, I would have acquiesced; but they say the contrary, and then talk to me about morality—the first time I ever heard the word from anybody who was not a rascal that used it for a purpose. I maintain that it is the most moral of poems; but if people won't discern the moral, that is their fault, not mine.'

(Murray, 1 Feb., 1819; LJ, IV, 279)

We may say that the 'moral' of *Don Juan* exists in terms of (i) its emphasis, in the Juan and Haidée episode, on the innate purity of young love, even without the marriage bond, an emphasis which we may relate to the illicit love of the hero in the deeply considered pattern of *Sardanapalus*; and (ii) the sunny humour shining over a number of episodes where a conventional veneer is stripped from human instincts, showing them, without bitterness, exactly as they are. The critical implications are too complex to discuss here, but we can agree that the 'moral' of *Don Juan* has much to do with its attack on convention, insincerity and 'cant'; and this is what Byron means.

We have accordingly two antithetical but complementary principles active throughout Byron's life and writings. They are: (i) a craving for moral purity, and (ii) a detestation of cant, which was driven to an almost perverted extreme of self-accusation, and in general a refusal to forget, or deny the rights of, all basic passions and compulsions, sexual, social, and political. What he demanded was a righteousness that *left nothing out*; a comprehensive righteousness

---

[1] *Travels in Albania and other Provinces of Turkey*, J. C. Hobhouse, Lord Broughton; 2nd ed., 1858; vol. I, App. 542; quoted *Lord Byron: Christian Virtues*, II, 95.
[2] *Conversations*, 304.

with, to use Pope's indispensable line, 'wild Nature's vigor working at the root';[1] at the limit, a sexually-impelled asceticism or purity. He hoped that marriage might give it him, but it could not. In one place only he found what he wanted: in the work of Pope. Pope offered a classic purity in strong contrast to what appeared to him the fungoid growths of those contemporary sects, schools and schisms which he scorned, and this exquisite temple of art contained all that could be desired of passion, ethic and reality. Our cluster of values is well illustrated in a fine passage:

'The attempt of the poetical populace of the present day to obtain an ostracism against Pope is as easily accounted for as the Athenian's shell against Aristides; they are tired of hearing him always called "the Just". They are also fighting for life; for, if he maintains his station, they will reach their own—by falling. They have raised a mosque by the side of a Grecian temple of the purest architecture; and, more barbarous than the barbarians from whose practice I have borrowed the figure, they are not contented with their own grotesque edifice, unless they destroy the prior, and purely beautiful fabric which preceded, and which shames them and theirs for ever and ever. I shall be told that amongst those I *have* been (or it may be still *am*) conspicuous—true, and I am ashamed of it. I *have* been amongst the builders of this Babel, attended by a confusion of tongues, but *never* amongst the envious destroyers of the classic temple of our predecessor. I have loved and honoured the fame and name of that illustrious and unrivalled man, far more than my own paltry renown, and the trashy jingle of the crowd of "Schools" and upstarts, who pretend to rival, or even surpass him. Sooner than a single leaf should be torn from his laurel, it were better that all which these men, and that I, as one of their set, have ever written, should

> *Line trunks, clothe spice, or, fluttering in a row,*
> *Befringe the rails of Bedlam, or Soho!*[2]

There are those who will believe this, and those who will not. You, sir, know how far I am sincere, and whether my opinion, not only in the short work intended for publication,[3] and in private letters which can never be published, has or has not been the same. I look

---

[1] *Essay on Man*, II, 184.   [2] *Horace, Ep.* II, i, 418 (the quotation is inexact).
[3] The work is *Hints from Horace* which had not as yet been published: see Murray, 11 January, 1821; LJ, v, 221.

upon this as the declining age of English poetry; no regard for others, no selfish feeling, can prevent me from seeing this, and expressing the truth. There can be no worse sign for the taste of the times than the depreciation of Pope. It would be better to receive for proof Mr. Cobbett's rough but strong attack upon Shakespeare and Milton, than to allow this smooth and "candid" undermining of the reputation of the most *perfect* of our poets, and the purest of our moralists. Of his power in the *passions*, in description, in the mock heroic, I leave others to descant. I take him on his strong ground as an *ethical* poet: in the former, none excel; in the mock heroic and the ethical, none equal him; and, in my mind, the latter is the highest of all poetry, because it does that in *verse*, which the greatest of men have wished to accomplish in prose. If the essence of poetry must be a *lie*, throw it to the dogs, or banish it from your republic, as Plato would have done. He who can reconcile poetry with truth and wisdom, is the only true "*poet*" in its real sense, "the *maker*", "the *creator*"—why must this mean the "liar", the "feigner", the "tale-teller"? A man may make and create better things than these.'

(LJ, V, 559)

This serves to explain Byron's passionate concern for an art which he often appeared to scorn as merely, to use a telling line from *English Bards and Scotch Reviewers* (10), 'that mighty instrument of little men'. Unless poetry held relevance to life's actualities and transcended itself into ethic, it was of secondary importance; and with Pope it had so transcended itself.

Throughout his life Byron scorned fiction and steadily laboured to attune his own genius to historical exactitude. From the start, his poetry was deeply concerned with the actual, whether through his own experiences or those of nations, with a close regard for peoples and politics and almost, we might say, a journalist's interest in historic places. His greater plays, *Marino Faliero*, *The Two Foscari* and *Sardanapalus*, were undertaken as strictly historical studies to which he devoted a close research. Writing to Murray of *Marino Faliero*, he once remarked that he hated 'things all fiction', and even found *Othello* and *The Merchant of Venice* the less satisfying on that account: 'There should always be some foundation for the most airy fabric, and pure invention is but the talent of a liar'.[1] Byron shows no

---

[1] 2 April, 1817; LJ, IV, 93.

explicit recognition of the sense in which Shakespeare's work was more than a decorated fiction; and in his age, since interpretative theory has been slow to evolve, this was inevitable. But what his critical mind could not be expected to recognize, his prose and poetry, with their clustering Shakespearian reminiscences and quotations, themselves witness, illustrating how closely Shakespeare was involved in his own deepest and most urgent convictions and purposes; more, his whole life, as I hope in due course to show, may be defined directly in terms of Shakespearian drama.[1] The truth is, Shakespeare, whom he regarded as 'the *worst* of models, though the most extraordinary of writers',[2] was too close to him in point of passion and energy to serve as an ideal; the ideal must be set beyond the world of Shakespearian and Byronic passion, and all those sexual and political upheavals of which such passion may be variously the cause or the reflection. What he searched for was something of classic purity. We have already seen (p. 148) how Pope's work compared to the moderns was said to bear the relation of 'a Grecian temple of the purest architecture' to a mosque. Again, writing to Moore, 3 May, 1821:

'As to Pope, I have always regarded him as the greatest name in our poetry. Depend upon it, the rest are barbarians. He is a Greek Temple, with a Gothic Cathedral on one hand, and a Turkish Mosque and all sorts of fantastic pagodas and conventicles about him. You may call Shakespeare and Milton pyramids, if you please, but I prefer the Temple of Theseus, or the Parthenon, to a mountain of burnt brick-work.'

(LJ, v, 274)

That is a neat definition. The Gothic Cathedral symbolizes medieval art, while the oriental references are exactly applicable to the poetry of romanticism, which reaches its typifying crystallization, as I have shown throughout *The Starlit Dome*, in picture-symbols of domes and other oriental structures; in *Kubla Khan* pre-eminently, but also elsewhere, with the peculiarly significant repudiation in Wordsworth's *Prelude* (VIII, 70–120). Shakespeare and Milton, being hard to place, are at least given a symbol of huge size and starry-pointing aspiration. But all this was to Byron no mere matter of artistic

---

[1] A preliminary sketch of Byron's Shakespearian relationship is given in my *Byron's Dramatic Prose* (University of Nottingham Press, 1954).
[2] To Murray, 14 July, 1821; LJ, v, 323.

technique, or rather that and the greater realities were with him in-distinguishable. The central definition of the perfect political order as 'a fair free Commonwealth' in *Marino Faliero* takes the form of a Grecian temple, whose pillars are exactly proportional to the main structure, 'giving and taking strength reciprocal' to compose the 'grace and beauty' of the whole.[1] The classic ideal was to permeate life, through and through. This meant both the full use and the perfected mastery of passion; it meant at once freedom and control; it meant poise, and it meant peace, for mankind.

We cannot too strongly emphasize that in his insistence on Pope's ethic, Byron was not supporting a conventional didacticism. Of that there was not, and never had been, in any age, a lack. We have just seen how to him 'morality' was the preserve of 'rascals'. His own life-long battle against hypocrisy and cant leaves no room for doubt here. His defence of Pope is throughout robust and broad-minded, with scant mercy shown to 'this immaculate period, this moral millenium of expurgated editions in books, manners, and royal trials of divorce'.[2] He praises *Eloisa to Abelard* for treating its subject 'with so much delicacy, mingled, at the same time, with such true and intense passion'; [3] the ethic lies in the subtlety and sympathy of the handling. As for the poem's supposed 'licentiousness':

'Licentiousness!—there is more real mischief and sapping licentious-ness in a single French prose novel, in a Moravian hymn, or a German comedy, than in all the actual poetry that ever was penned or poured forth, since the rhapsodies of Orpheus. The sentimental anatomy of Rousseau and Mad^e de S. are far more formidable than any quantity of verse. They are so, because they sap the principles, by *reasoning* upon the *passions*; whereas poetry is in itself passion, and does not systematize. It assails, but does not argue; it may be wrong, but it does not assume pretensions to Optimism.'

(LJ, v, 582)

This might apply well enough to *Don Juan*. Poetry throws up the basic energies and substances for our inspection and experience, but reasoning must be used with caution. To 'reason upon the passions' may, by stating a static, superficial and specious morality ('pre-tensions') without contact with the vitalities, 'sap' the inmost 'prin-ciples', the vital energies, of true virtue. Poetry is largely 'passion'

---

[1] *Marino Faliero*, III, ii.   [2] LJ, v, 575.
[3] LJ, v, 581.

and avoids—Byron has already, in another context, said as much
(p. 119)—systemization: it attacks by revealing.

So much may be said of all poetry, of the poetry Byron writes off
as 'fiction', the poetry of Homer and Shakespeare. But Byron was
also out to differentiate Pope as ethical poet from such great predecessors. It is, however, clear that he was being admired not for any
intellectual system—Pope once himself repudiated the thought,
claiming to move freely among all systems with no ultimate allegiance other than righteousness [1]—but for his passionate awareness of
energies, and will to relate them through poetic expression to highest
virtue. That is why Byron emphasized his supremacy in (i) the
mock heroic and (ii) ethical poetry (p. 149), these two together
signifying an incorporation of old energies into a new virtue. This
is all very different from a simple didacticism. Pope distinguished his
satiric use of real persons from 'general propositions' and 'precepts'
which, being merely rational, or mental, could not be supposed to
affect the 'passions', the strongest 'motive' of 'reformation'.[2] Now,
though he finally achieved this peculiar excellence of ethical poetry,
yet from the start his technique and diction had themselves been
pointing the way. We may, indeed, say that the morality of all
poetry exists in its compression and pointing, through diction,
rhyme, metre, or stanza, of emotional essences; and we can observe
that Byron in our last quotation distinguishes poetry from the im-
moralities of novel and drama. It has a discipline which they lack;
and yet, if it departs too far from the required technique, it becomes
a vulgarity, and that is, in Byron's thinking, an immorality, the
terms being to him all but identical, and hence his violent antipathy
to the Cockneys. We may, indeed, recall that Pope's Inferno, The
Dunciad, was not filled with seducers, murderers, or oppressors, for
of those he has little to say beyond placing them snugly among the
harmonies of the Essay on Man, but with failings more subtle and,
granted a millennial view, more important: it is filled with dealers
in dull, that is dead, literature.

If we transfer, point by point, the thoughts of the Essay on
Criticism from the art of poetry to the art of life, we shall get some
idea of the poetic morality which Pope and Byron are offering. It
cannot really be defined in moral terms; it is rather a harmonization

[1] Horace, Ep. I, i, 23-34.
[2] To Arbuthnot, 26 July, 1734; quoted Tillotson, Conclusion, 163; and see p. 72
above.

of essences with a resultant poise such as that defined in Nietzsche's *Thus Spake Zarathustra*, which may, and perhaps must, be, at least in description, associated with the aristocratic, and that means the civilized, traditions of Europe, rooting back to ancient Greece. Such 'poise' is not specifically religious; indeed, it will mature rather from a just balancing of religious and secular compulsions. Man's instincts are respected, even honoured; his civic and political compulsions, which may well conflict with his personal religious intuitions, have their place. The humanistic is fully involved and contained, and there is accordingly a peculiar point in the exquisite balancing of statesmanship and poetry in the following tribute to Pope's 'moral wisdom':

'If they had said nothing of *Pope*, they might have remained "alone with their glory", for aught I should have said or thought about them or their nonsense. But if they interfere with the "little Nightingale" of Twickenham, they may find others who will bear it—*I* won't. Neither time, nor distance, nor grief, nor age, can ever diminish my veneration for him, who is the great moral poet of all times, of all climes, of all feelings, and of all stages of existence. The delight of my boyhood, the study of my manhood, perhaps (if allowed to me to attain it), he may be the consolation of my age. His poetry is the Book of Life. Without canting, and yet without neglecting religion, he has assembled all that a good and great man can gather together of moral wisdom cloathed in consummate beauty. Sir William Temple observes "that of all the numbers of mankind that live within the compass of a thousand years, for one man that is born capable of making a *great poet*, there may be a *thousand* born capable of making as great generals and ministers of state as any in story". Here is a statesman's opinion of poetry: it is honourable to him, and to the art. Such a "poet of a thousand years" was *Pope*. A thousand years will roll away before such another can be hoped for in our literature. But it can *want* them—he himself is a literature.'

(LJ, V, 590)

Observe carefully our central passage:

'Without canting, and yet without neglecting religion, he has assembled all that a good and great man can gather together of moral wisdom cloathed in consummate beauty.'

Surely no sentence was ever more packed with value. Insincerity is ruled out, but religion, though it does not dictate, is nevertheless contained; the 'wisdom' has been gradually 'assembled' from a life-time of varied experience by one who is not merely 'good', for that is not enough, but also 'great', a term hinting a full incorporation of basic energies. The phrase 'moral wisdom' itself suggests a depth beyond morality as generally received; and it is endued with poetic 'beauty', thus approaching the Greek ideal of actions not merely good, but beautiful. This is the heart of Byron's faith.

What shall we say of these remarkable passages, written by a man who consistently rated poetry as inferior to action and statesmanship? Byron despised poetry-as-fiction or poetry-as-self-expression; what he wanted was poetry-as-ethic or poetry-as-civic-power. The ethic here acclaimed is an ethic taking full count of passions and politics; it is no limited, specifically religious, didacticism, yet religion is somehow housed and contained: 'without canting, and yet without neglecting religion'. To Byron, morality was, normally, cant, and religion, if directly preached, would generally appear so too, since, as he often observed, the principles preached were lived neither by their exponents, nor by the society they upheld. Statesmanship he regularly respected, and its graceful interplay with poetry in our last passage is peculiarly interesting, each honouring the other. Because he has offered a living wisdom making no distinction of church from state, Pope's work is rated as the 'Book of Life'. We are, indeed, close to religion. Byron himself respected the Christian Church, and had an especial feeling for Catholicism; and his love for Pope was entwined with this very feeling. In opposing the rating of Cowper's *Homer* above Pope's, he wrote: 'And now that we have heard the Catholic reproached with envy, duplicity, licentiousness, avarice—what was the Calvinist?' [1] And yet the wisdom and reverence sur-veyed by Pope and Byron are not quite those of the Christian Church; the wisdom is an incarnate wisdom, and the reverence includes a reverence for all that is secular in human life.

Byron makes no attack on 'religion'; on the contrary, he honours and reverences it in a manner worthy of a Dr. Johnson or a T. S. Eliot; but his positive valuations are none the less a challenge. He is driven at least to *associate* Pope, 'the greatest moral poet of any age or in any language', [2] with the New Testament itself:

'The depreciation of Pope is partly founded upon a false idea of the

[1] LJ, v, 558.   [2] LJ, v, 568.

dignity of his order of poetry, to which he has partly contributed by the ingenious boast,

> *That not in Fancy's maze he wander'd long,*
> *But* stoop'd *to Truth, and moralized his song.*[1]

He should have written "rose to truth". In my mind, the highest of all poetry is ethical poetry, as the highest of all earthly objects must be moral truth. Religion does not make a part of my subject; it is something beyond human powers, and has failed in all human hands except Milton's and Dante's, and even Dante's powers are involved in his delineation of human passions, though in supernatural circumstances. What made Socrates the greatest of men? His moral truth —his ethics. What proved Jesus Christ the Son of God hardly less than his miracles? His moral precepts. And if ethics have made a philosopher the first of men, and have not been disdained as an adjunct to his Gospel by the Deity himself, are we to be told that ethical poetry, or didactic poetry, or by whatever name you term it, whose object is to make men better and wiser, is not the *very first order* of poetry; and are we to be told this too by one of the priesthood? It requires more mind, more wisdom, more power, than all the "forests" that ever were "walked for their description", and all the epics that ever were founded upon fields of battle. The *Georgics* are indisputably, and, I believe, *undisputedly*, even a finer poem than the *Aeneid*. Virgil knew this; he did not order *them* to be burnt:

> *The proper study of Mankind is Man.*[2]

'It is the fashion of the day to lay great stress upon what they call "imagination" and "invention", the two commonest of qualities: an Irish peasant with a little whisky in his head will imagine and invent more than would furnish forth a modern poem. If Lucretius had not been spoiled by the Epicurean system, we should have had a far superior poem to any now in existence. As mere poetry, it is the first of Latin poems. What then has ruined it? His ethics. Pope has not this defect; his moral is as pure as his poetry is glorious.'

(v, 554)

---

[1] *Epistle to Dr. Arbuthnot*, 340.
[2] *Essay on Man*, II, 2.

Our warning must be repeated: Byron's use of the word 'precepts' must not mislead us. The New Testament does not, strictly speaking, offer 'precepts' at all; its two positive commandments are vague and general; its teaching is illustrated mainly through parable, or poetry, and so felt as an outflowering from life itself; the righteousness of the Pharisees is repudiated; and Christ himself is, not the preceptor, but 'the way'. All this, of course, Byron knew well enough, though the phrasing of it in a pre-Nietzschean era was perhaps impossible. What held him in both the New Testament and in Pope was less a doctrine than a power, the power St. Paul spoke of, for good; the poetry of the *Essay on Man*, *Moral Essays* and *Imitations of Horace* being less an obvious teaching than a diagnosis of falsities and doctrine of sublimation, aiming to set 'the *Passions* on the side of Truth',[1] with a will to human and social wholeness, or integrity. Byron admired Pope for his Nietzschean affinities, and it is because he found in Pope this higher teaching, which was to flower so purely in *Thus Spake Zarathustra*, that he was warmed by him as by no other writer of modern times.

IV

Pope as a poet of peace follows Shakespeare and Milton rather as the New Testament follows the old. In both the earlier conflicts are incorporated; the relation of Pope to Shakespeare is often exact (pp. 43–6), and the conflict of religion and humanism in Milton is, with comparatively little left out, resolved in Pope. In both the New Testament and Pope we find a certain quiescence, at least as far as outward action is concerned, with a new emphasis on personal, and in Pope civic, regeneration. The old conflicts are resolved not by any static proposition or propositions, but by a living incarnation, in the 'here' and 'now': what could not be thought out, is lived into. More, in both there is a transference from a limited nationalism, for Shakespeare and Milton were nationalist poets or prophets as surely as the writers of the Old Testament, to an emphasis on (i) the individual, and (ii) the greater whole, or God. So Pope, who, unlike the New Testament, includes also the civic, political, and aristocratic virtues, is really less national than specifically, as was Byron later, international, with an internationalism which may be said to reflect the political implications of St. Paul's epistles.

[1] *Horace, Ep.* II, i, 218.

Byron's phrase 'the Christianity of English poetry' (p. 132) should be carefully studied. 'Literature', or 'poetry', contains, as divine inspiration does not, a human element; that is, it is in part secular; it surveys and incorporates the animal energies and the political energies; in it body and soul, state and church, may be felt in conflict or in resolution, but at least they are both there. The New Testament, as we are taught to understand it, does not directly survey this territory, except by off-hand comment; it represents the delivery of a great, perhaps the greatest, message man has ever received *under conditions of immediate stability assured by the secular rule of Rome*. Its descendant, the Christian Church, has existed beside, and often in tension with, the secular state. But poetry in the Renaissance world has steadily tried to assimilate the one to the other. Dante was on the side of Emperor as against Pope, and his great vision was a vision of world-order centred in Rome. Poets from Aeschylus, Sophocles and Virgil to Wordsworth, Tennyson and Francis Berry aim to sanctify the secular and secularize, without diluting, the sacred; or may sometimes, as are Hardy and Eliot, be found expressing a sense of acute discomfort at what appears a final incompatibility. You can therefore see why Byron, who of all great poets was most deeply involved in matters national, political, and international, was drawn to Pope instead of to the New Testament. If you look through his works, prose and poetry, you will find very few references to Christ, but you will find continual evidence that he was saturated, as poet, thinker, and in the widest sense as man, in the Old Testament. The two books he loved best throughout his life were, without any question, the Old Testament and the works of Pope; the one completed the other; he was personally drawn less to the Prince of Peace than to the Poet of Peace; and that is why he called Pope 'the Christianity of English poetry'.

We have heard, in our time, much about 'tradition'. But there are two main traditions for us to consider. There is the tradition descending from medieval Christianity and the Church of Rome, through the more specifically religious implications of Dante and the more medieval aspects of Shakespeare to the prose and poetry of the seventeenth century; and thence to the Dantesque affinities of Byron, and on to T. S. Eliot. But there is also the other, more humanist, and dramatic, tradition, descending from ancient Greece, through Virgil and Dante as prophets of world-order, to Renaissance Italy and Shakespeare, to Pope and Byron; and thence to Ibsen, Nietzsche, and Bernard Shaw.[1] Both have their rights, and both can today claim to serve the cause of the New Testament, of Christ Himself. And, though we can, surely, agree that the desired end is a synthesis, disagreement will necessarily arise as soon as we start talking of the future, since each will clearly assert that it has room for the other, if only it be allowed to guide. We in England are always ready to be shocked at any suggestion of Crown rather than Church as prime mediator between Christ and man, too often forgetting that its connotations far outspace the secular, and that it still remains, in our national body, supreme.

Byron's ranging imagination was not limited to a secular humanism, but could imagine Italy, or Rome, as both 'Mother of Arts' and

> *Parent of our religion! whom the wide*
> *Nations have knelt to for the keys of Heaven!*
> (*Childe Harold*, IV, 47)

He could, through the person of Dante, survey St. Peter's as

> *a fane surpassing all before,*
> *Such as all flesh shall flock to kneel in: ne'er*
> *Such sight hath been unfolded by a door*
> *As this, to which all nations shall repair,*
> *And lay their sins at this huge gate of Heaven.*
> (*The Prophecy of Dante*, IV)

He does, indeed, as man, poet, and thinker, cover both traditions, as did Dante [2] and Shakespeare; and that is why the word 'nations' recurs when he thinks of Rome: the sins are the sins, not of individuals, but of nations. Byron is our pivot; looking back to the ancients, Dante, Shakespeare and Pope, he is also the precursor of Ibsen and Nietzsche, those great dramatic thinkers who were tormented by knowledge of the pressing need to achieve a new harmony of Church and State. The bonds of civilization were bursting asunder. Byron had felt it coming; much, in the French Revolution, had already come. Religion, as Europe knows it, is not enough. So he, Ibsen and Nietzsche, all three looked back to the

---

[1] I am thinking of *Emperor and Galilean* (*Christ and Nietzsche*, II, 56, 65–7; V, 216, and note; VI, 235, 237), and Shaw's deep concern with the psychology of government; e.g. in *Caesar and Cleopatra* and *Back to Methuselah*.

[2] A good account of Dante as political prophet and of his relation to Byron may be found in Joseph Mazzini's essays *On the Minor Works of Dante* and *Byron and Goethe*.

ancient world; each tried to preserve the best of the Renaissance and aristocratic values; each had dreams of a greater humanity to be; each after his own fashion laboured to bring Church and State together. The task was bitter: each in turn had to shock those who thought contemporary Christianity was a real religion; each fought against cant and was accused of devilish wickedness; and we need not deny that, with his blinding clarity of sight, and his greater experience of the developing disruption, Nietzsche was led to speak out, at times, 'not wisely, but too well'. But what would we have? Do not our quotations from Byron in this essay themselves, in all their riot and wealth, witness the growing complexity, the inroads of chaos? Those who carried the torch yet deeper into the night of the great 'anarch' whose advent Pope had foreseen at the conclusion to *The Dunciad*, carried it through buffeting winds. It was often near enough, as it is today, to extinction; and whenever it flares momentarily in the darkness, it gilds its bearer's face with a satanic hue. But it remains our torch, our beacon, none the less; and it will be fatal to leave that truth unrecognized.

To compose the great conflicts tearing our world we cannot remain content with secular politics. But neither can we expect our Church, as a Church, to guide, or lead; in matters psychological, social or political, it shows no sign of being able or willing to attempt such a task; it acts as a leaven, as an auxiliary, in no sense a master. And it is perhaps right that it should do so. We do not, indeed, want a new religion; what we want is something for which we have no name, something forecast by Nietzsche's intuition of a 'Roman Caesar with the soul of Christ',[1] the 'third empire' of Ibsen's *Emperor and Galilean*, in which Church and State will have been dissolved, with, nevertheless, victory for neither, and fullest blessings maintained of both; in which each will indeed be themselves for the first time in history within what Tennyson foresaw as those 'new majesties of mighty states',[2] that 'Parliament of man' and 'Federation of the world'[3] to be ushered in by the new nobility of those greater men who are to compose 'the Christ that is to be'.[4]

It cannot be exactly defined; it is for us, for our world, to create the definition.[5] But to Byron at least it was forecast by the life-work

[1] *The Will to Power*, IV, vi, 983. [2] *Love Thou Thy Land.*
[3] *Locksley Hall.* [4] *In Memoriam*, CVI.
[5] We are, indeed, already trying to do so; and our interest in the poetic styles of Shakespeare and Donne can be related to the attempt. In *The Shakespearean*

of Pope as a, or rather *the*, universal poet, of mankind, of peace. Pope, a Catholic by upbringing, was in effect a deist (p. 6 above); Byron, whose explicit religious beliefs were deistic, was imaginatively drawn to Catholicism; but for neither could any religion, as such, exist apart from that greater catholicism, including all basic energies and all political purposes, to which their lives were similarly dedicated.[1] The politics were more than national. Byron, banished by ostracism from his native land, could the more naturally take a cosmopolitan, an international, view. He writes home from Italy to England as to a nation of strangers, unwilling to insult their national idols:

'I shall not presume to say that Pope is as high a poet as Shakespeare and Milton, though his enemy, Warton, places him immediately under them. I would no more say this than I would assert in the mosque (once Saint Sophia's), that Socrates was a greater than Mahomet.'

(LJ, v, 560)

But, he says,

'If any great national or natural convulsion could or should overwhelm your country in such sort as to sweep Great Britain from the kingdoms of the earth, and leave only that, after all, the most living of human things, a *dead language*, to be studied and read, and imitated, by the wise of future and far generations, upon foreign shores; if your literature should become the learning of mankind, divested of party cabals, temporary fashions, and national pride and prejudice; —an Englishman, anxious that the posterity of strangers should know that there had been such a thing as a British Epic and Tragedy, might wish for the preservation of Shakespeare and Milton; but the surviving World would snatch Pope from the wreck, and let the rest sink with the people. He is the moral poet of all civilization; and as such, let us hope that he will one day be the national poet of mankind.'

(LJ, v, 560)

Moment (1954) Patrick Cruttwell has recently defined the social *milieu* of the early seventeenth century as a society trying to realize in England the medieval dream of Emperor and Pope in unison (IV, 109). See my review of Mr. Cruttwell's book to appear in *The Universities Quarterly*.

[1] For a more precise relation of Pope's doctrine to 'religion' see p. 178 below.

We are not ourselves making these claims for Pope; we are merely expounding Byron's views. His phrases make an amazing cluster: 'the greatest moral poet of any age or in any language' (p. 143), the 'poet of a thousand years' (p. 153), 'himself a literature' (p. 153), the 'Christianity of English poetry' (p. 132) and 'Book of Life' (p. 153); and now, 'the moral poet of all civilization' and 'national poet of mankind'. With these phrases, it is true, we need not agree, but, even so, we shall not forget them. For whether or not they be true of Pope is of less importance than *the reasons that led Byron to make them.*

We may well ask—has not Byron's own poetic universe a richness and variety, a dimension of action, far in excess of Pope's? And can we agree that all this is outweighed by Pope's perfection of execution and precision of ethical psychology? Surely Byron's emphasis on the supremity of poetic doctrine, which is *not* the doctrine of intellectual ethics, has its limitations? Yes. But only for one reason. Pope's universe, in its way perfect, is yet the reflection of a single class in one nation at a certain point of time; and even so, much polished for the purpose, and indeed itself an attack on contemporary society for its unrealized virtue. It reflects a peaceful society; it speaks in terms of the arts and the compulsions of peace, its sweetness and its dangers; but such peace, to us, can only be known in a limited context. Byron's world is far greater; nor is it peaceful; it is a world labouring for peace. If ever a perfect world-order is established on earth, then perhaps such works as *Marino Faliero* and *Sardanapalus* may grow out of date. We cannot say, and the discussion is perhaps profitless. But, were they to do so, we may yet suggest that the New Testament itself and *Thus Spake Zarathustra* would still be confronting man with a spiritual challenge; and, with them, the works of Pope. What Shakespeare did for Elizabethan England and Pope for Augustan London, Byron attempted for Europe, for the world. And he was right in taking the spiritualized humanism of Pope for his exemplar. Byron willed the good, not of Britain alone, but of all mankind, as one family; one brotherhood; and of that family, that brotherhood, Pope, the poet of peace *par excellence*, and therefore the chastiser of *the vices of peace*, is the star. But the works of Shakespeare and Byron, perhaps of many Shakespeares and many Byrons, must be lived through before the culture of Augustan aristocracy as sublimated and purified almost out of recognition by the genius of Pope becomes the universal lot of mankind.

V
AFTERTHOUGHTS

V. AFTERTHOUGHTS

PEACE is no idle business, for energies are the stuff of life. Pope is clearly not a poet of conflict and war, as are Shakespeare, Milton and, with reservations, since his work is pointed, even more explicitly than Shakespeare's, towards peace, Byron; but his world is tinglingly alive and active. Its aim is the just ordering of energies in man and society. Balanced opposition replaces conflict to compose a harmony which becomes ethic. He seems to say, as did Castiglione before him and Nietzsche's Zarathustra after, that best action can only mature from a blend of energy with form to make the supreme 'way' and only living virtue.

Pope's early poetic instincts were pastoral, his *Pastorals* being published in 1709 and the *Messiah* in 1712. Such a start marks in itself no lack of energy or purpose. For what *is* pastoral? Pastoral normally envisages man in a sunny climate at work which appears to be limited to the comparatively easy business of guarding and caring for one's flock: life is, or appears, simple. But is this necessarily a release? No. For now we are faced only the more clearly by the basic torments of life: love and death, unreachable desire and irreparable loss. The pastoral—you feel it in Lyly's plays—defines the problems and tensions awaiting man when, if ever, all other turmoils are stilled. Of Pope's four early pastorals, the two best, Summer and Winter, are concerned respectively with love and death. Here is the conclusion to *Summer*:

> *But see, the shepherds shun the noonday heat,*
> *The lowing herds to murm'ring brooks retreat,*
> *To closer shades the panting flocks remove;*
> *Ye Gods! and is there no relief for Love?*

But soon the sun with milder rays descends
To the cool ocean, where his journey ends.
On me love's fiercer flames for ever prey,
By night he scorches, as he burns by day.

(85)

In poetry of a nearly equal poignancy *Winter* mourns the loss of a
loved one, with exquisite references of human death to nature's
winter:

Behold the groves that shine with silver frost,
Their beauty wither'd, and their verdure lost . . .

(9)

The poetry would relate the human wound to natural process, and
so integrate man's soul into his natural setting. Hence the contrast in our first passage of nature's kindly rhythms with man's
enduring pain; the very contrast grows from the will towards its
surmounting.

Nature is one solution; poetry the other. In pastoral there is not
only the obvious poetry. The *dramatis personae* are themselves poets,
and engage in poetic competitions. In balancing man against nature,
love against death, season with season, in the antiphonal speeches of
the persons, and the technique of the poetry itself, in all this we can
say that pastoral is attempting to create a balance, or poise, in despite
of, indeed composed of, man's most ultimate pains and problems.
It holds, in small compass, the essentials of all literary composition.

It is, moreover, clear, as E. K. Chambers long ago pointed out in
an admirable essay,[1] that the English pastoral tradition descending
from Theocritus and Virgil blends, as in *Lycidas*, with the religious
pastoralism descending from the Old and New Testaments and incorporated into the Christian church (e.g. David as shepherd-boy,
the shepherds visited by the Angel of the Lord, such phrases as 'feed
my sheep' and 'the good shepherd', the Bishop's crook, the word
'pastor'). The two are necessarily akin, since pastoral suggests peace,
and Christianity worships the Prince of Peace. It is not, therefore,
surprising that Pope should have composed a poem called *Messiah*
(1712) blending the prophecy of Isaiah with Virgil's Messianic
Eclogue, which he took to derive, through the Sibylline books, from
the Hebrew. In the *Messiah* a golden age is prophesied. The Saviour

[1] *English Pastorals*, Introduction to Selections (no date).

crushes Death and Hell and tends man as a loving 'shepherd'. Wars are gone:

> *No more shall nation against nation rise,*
> *Nor ardent warriors meet with hateful eyes,*
> *Nor fields with gleaming steel be cover'd o'er,*
> *The brazen trumpets kindle rage no more.*
>
> (57)

All nature is transmuted, while 'boys in flow'ry bands the tiger lead' (78), a pretty image of what Pope is always himself doing, as, with his exquisite harmonies, he tames and guides man's tigerish passions.

Such is the soil from which *Windsor Forest* (1713), *The Rape of the Lock* (1712–14), *Eloisa to Abelard* (1717), and the *Elegy to the Memory of an Unfortunate Lady* (1717), grow. Before passing on, a word or two on these may be offered: they are poems respectively of (i) pastoral peace, (ii) aristocratic society, (iii) unsatisfied love and (iv) death. All spring from the pastoral.

Of *Windsor Forest* we have treated already. In its completed, 1713, form, it develops a neat reference of idyllic pastoral to Britain, and of Britain to peace. The first *Pastorals* with their references to Windsor and the Cam were careful to keep contemporary Britain in mind; here those gestures are expanded. Britain is regarded as the enemy of oppression, and peace invoked by Father Thames:

> *Hail, sacred peace! hail, long-expected days,*
> *That Thames's glory to the stars shall raise!*
> *Tho' Tiber's streams immortal Rome behold,*
> *Tho' foaming Hermus swells with tides of gold,*
> *From heav'n itself though sev'n-fold Nilus flows,*
> *And harvests on a hundred realms bestows;*
> *These now no more shall be the Muse's themes,*
> *Lost in my fame, as in the sea their streams.*
> *Let Volga's banks with iron squadrons shine,*
> *And groves of lances glitter on the Rhine,*
> *Let barb'rous Ganges arm a servile train;*
> *Be mine the blessings of a peaceful reign.*
>
> (355)

Observe Pope's antipathy to 'iron squadrons', an impression in direct descent from the 'brazen trumpets' of his *Messiah*: he is by nature hostile to such metallic and Miltonic impressions. Noble or sacred structures are of a different category, so 'Temples rise, the beauteous works of Peace', and London is crowned by 'a new Whitehall' (378–80). For the rest, the poem's main emphasis falls on nature and the softer emotions, and he would like these to involve each other. It is 'Albion's', or Britain's, task to assure that happy consummation.[1]

Next, *The Rape of the Lock*, which belongs here more precisely than may at first appear. Its setting is society, its theme a social quarrel, its moral, the futility of ill-temper. An aristocratic and peaceful society is assumed, and wars, politics, and social injustice not really relevant, as may appear from the jarring nature of the couplet:

> The hungry Judges soon the sentence sign,
> And wretches hang that jurymen may dine.

> (III, 21)

The satiric point is in itself worth making, but its implications so appallingly awful that it rings discordant in the context and risks shattering our poem. Neither here nor even in his later satires is Pope opposing such obvious wrongs; he speaks normally only of the subtler evils of an aristocratic society in full enjoyment of place and peace, of man removed, as in pastoral poetry, from natural hardship, strenuous labour, and social unrest. The aristocratic *milieu* of the last few centuries corresponds directly to the pastoral, and that is why we find so many pastoral, or otherwise Greek mythological, elements in the interior decorations and templed gardens, such as those at Stowe, of the aristocracy of Pope's day.

Of *Eloisa to Abelard* little more need be said: it is a full dramatic exploitation of the love-torment less powerfully present in pastoral, and here most beautifully balanced with divine love. The poem's statement is in the careful weighing and balancing, not just in the conclusion, and it recalls the balancing of human and divine love and beauty in Spenser's four *Hymns*: both Lyly and Spenser write from a world-view close to Pope's. With *Eloisa to Abelard* we may group the *Elegy to the Memory of an Unfortunate Lady*, a poem of considerable pathos and power, offering a fine treatment of unrestful ambition as 'the glorious fault of Angels and of Gods' (14), balanced against a denunciation of 'steel'd' sympathies, unyielding hearts, and

[1] See also my short essay on Pope entitled 'The New Whitehall' in *Hiroshima* (1946).

the short-lived and brittle pageantry of the mighty 'proud', and concluding:

> *So perish all, whose breast ne'er learn'd to glow*
> *For others good, or melt at others woe.*

$$(41-6)$$

This is our first sample of that satiric anger that is to burn so powerfully later. Patriotism is constituent to the emphasized pathos of the lady's death abroad, and among foreigners. The only comfort is in nature, idyllically presented.

There is clearly nothing placid about Pope. As his work develops it becomes vitriolic in attack, but the attack, like that of the New Testament or *Thus Spake Zarathustra*, which both presuppose a peaceful society, is levelled less against obvious wrong-doing than against the subtler evils of insincerity, false reason, mentalized education, pride, avarice, and ambition. On the other side, his positives are instinct, the voice of God, nature, kindness to men and animals, peace, the cosmic whole. His final purpose is to set 'the Passions on the side of Truth'; [1] to deliver morality from her 'false guardians'; [2] to establish, as Byron saw (p. 153), a virtue which is not cant; and to charge with a newly enlightened significance the traditional values of patriotism and fame. Death and love are, it is true, not emphasized in his later work, but Pope's function as a poet of peace may be said to fall in line with his pastoral beginnings.

The 'campaign of peace' is naturally strenuous, since, the more obvious outlets of competition removed, man is thrown back on himself and endures the severest of all possible tests. He cannot remain static. He is, whether we like it or not, a dynamo; and he is this for a purpose which, in its turn, cannot be understood without due regard to his dynamic nature. That is the subject of the *Essay on Man*.

This crowning work has already been discussed. Here I would merely add a few afterthoughts. The interpretation already given provides a peculiarly interesting example of 'spatial' analysis. The *Essay on Man* is certainly philosophic, and yet its meaning can only be understood in terms of its artistic structure; it is, in its own way, one of our 'musical buildings'. Fundamental to all religion, art and philosophy lies the all but insoluble problem of assimilating the world of good and evil in man's experience to the divine powers.

[1] *Horace, Ep.* II, i, 218.   [2] *Dunciad,* IV, 27.

In the *Essay on Man* we have various epistles with their own, water-tight, approaches, at least two apparently incompatible philosophies being presented in balance, and yet we are not asked to choose one and reject the other, but rather to accept both, and build from them a new totality. The coherence is less logical than structural, though within the structure itself can be discovered, as we have seen (pp. 51–53, 82), the inmost secret of creative living, of virtue not merely in the moral, but also in the magical, sense of that time-honoured word. Once again we find Pope working with balance, since by using both of the two main life-views possible, he outlines a 'way' towards equipoise and harmony. We can thus watch the 'spatial' approach doing what logic could not do, and perhaps in no other work on record is its nature so clear; so that study of the *Essay* assists our understanding of the spatial, or rather space-time, nature of art in general. It is a grand-style example of the truth that a poet does not so much think thoughts as *make* them, though it may be for us to attempt to think the thoughts which he has made. As in a drama, where truth is shadowed by conflicting voices, so the *Essay* builds from opposition a unity. Christian symbolism is directly comparable. The Trinity itself is a sublime paradox involving dramatic interactivity within a triangular unity; and to understand it you have, in the mind's eye, to give it spatial formulation, since without such a triangular image you can scarcely receive the resolution of three-in-One and Ode-in-Three.

Though such an approach, based, as all sound interpretation must be, on the space-time nature of art, what had for generations been regarded as the second-hand versification of a second-rate philosophy took on significance as doctrine.[1] Once again, the old type of 'source' had been silenced. Scholars no longer limit the meaning of *Antony and Cleopatra* by consideration of Plutarch, nor will they in future regard Pope's *Essay on Man* as a pastiche of Bolingbrokian metaphysics; and in any case, as Carl van Doren remarked to me many years ago, the main substances of Pope's poem are not to be found in Bolingbroke. We must hope that, the ground now cleared, there will

---

[1] The nature of my divergence from the traditional reading will be clear from Geoffrey Tillotson's remark: 'Pope was at his weakest as a philosopher. The *Essay on Man* is beautifully planned on paper, but not as reason' ('Design', 48). My whole point is, that the planning, or structure, *is* the philosophy; and that by such a dynamic, or dramatic, method, Pope has come near to solving the enigma of good and evil.

not be any return, as in Shakespeare there has been, to an over-concentration on contemporary philosophies of 'order' to the neglect of the central achievement. After all, the philosophies concerned are, in both instances, the vast and general philosophies of order, hier-archy, and harmony. Such conceptions are not the preserve of any particular age or culture, though each in turn will naturally shape and colour them to taste: you find them variously in Indian, Greek, Medieval and Renaissance thought; and among the Incas of Peru. That admitted, what we have to do is to study not the official philosophies, but what our poet or dramatist does with them. The danger is more insidious than it at first appears, since there is always a tendency to weigh down the winged poetry, to clog its wings, with, to use Pope's impolite phrase, such 'learned lumber'.[1] We must sternly avoid the temptation to explain poetry in terms of secondary rather than final causes, to reduce it to something rooted backward rather than as something pointing on. For it cannot endure enslavement to any static scheme, however vast; it is a living organism, and as such must be understood. Our interpretative dis-coveries came not from learning, but from a plain inspection of the poetry of Shakespeare, Pope and others, and a reading of them 'with the same spirit'—and that means, as F. W. Bateson has reminded us, with the same vital and creative insight—'that its author writ'.[2]

Such was the reading of The Essay on Man first given in 'The Vital Flame' (1939) and, there is little doubt that it has come to stay. In his introduction to the fine Twickenham edition of the poem published in 1950, Professor Maynard Mack has followed this inter-pretation in accepting the 'conflict' of opposing philosophies as con-stituent to a dramatic whole transcending the separate approaches (lxxiii); agreeing that, though 'the presence of such ambivalences' supplies 'no answer to the logical problem', it nevertheless 'suggests that psychologically the combination of acceptance as a state of mind with moral effort as a rule of conduct is both possible and sound' (xlvi); and that poetry, while refusing judgement on the plane of logic, can 'take the argument to another plane altogether', where the problem is 'dissolved' in an 'enlarged' context (lxx). He, too, both observes Pope's Shakespearian affinities, and contrasts, in point of depth, his philosophic drama with the personified ritual-drama of Milton's Satan (see p. 48, note). Throughout he follows our spatial

[1] Essay on Criticism, 613. [2] Ibid., 234.

interpretation, getting the 'meaning' (lxx) not from the parts, but from their interaction within the dramatic whole, and so restating our central doctrine that man, through trust in the creation as harmony, may 'both support and help to realize' that harmony by 'disciplining' himself (lxxx). That is, man creates (p. 50) the harmony from faith in which his creation of it develops: the doctrine is statically paradoxical but dynamically coherent, and must be understood not within the factual, but within the actual; as a living, forward-thrusting, act in a living universe.

This is what the *Essay on Man*, as an artistic whole, says; what Byron intuitively recognized, and our interpretation first clearly revealed and formulated; and on it Professor Mack has now set the seal of his acceptance in the standard edition of the poem. We can accordingly regard this interpretation as established; and that being so, we must not be surprised to find its challenge still radiating lines of force, today. Which leads us on.

Since my first interpretation, my admiration of the *Essay on Man* has been, if anything, increased. Its relevance to other works of poetic or religious doctrine appears the greater the more closely you study it, and I would urge that the opinions here expressed be read in conjunction with their further developments in my references to the *Essay* throughout *Christ and Nietzsche*. The comparison with Nietzsche must, indeed, be driven home again and again:

> *The surest Virtues thus from Passions shoot,*
> *Wild Nature's vigor working at the root.*
>
> (II, 183)

The doctrine is, of course, the doctrine of modern psychology, and whenever we feel doubtful regarding the rights of instinct, we should remember that what we call 'sublimation' cannot be accomplished without establishing a friendly relation with the thing to be sublimated, any more than you can successfully civilize a child or train an animal without love. Sublimation in direct contact with the dynamic energies may, indeed, be called the core of the *Essay's* doctrine, as it is also of *Thus Spake Zarathustra*. In both we are concerned with the gradual transmutation of what is, in any case, right [1] to what is, all things considered, best. The 'best' is to be inwardly experienced and inwardly recognized, and it is the only

---

[1] 'Whatever is, is right'; I, 294.

true happiness, as Pope reminds us when *returning to the phrase* in Book IV:

> *Whatever is, is right—This world, 'tis true,*
> *Was made for Caesar—but for Titus too:*
> *And which more blest? who chain'd his country, say,*
> *Or he whose Virtue sigh'd to lose a day?*

(IV, 145)

The true virtue will not, however, be limited to a conventional morality. We are reminded of St. Paul's balancing of permission and expedience.

Though the good-and-evil antimony is, in the main, settled by the doctrine of creative psychology whereby every vice holds potentially a corresponding virtue (II, 185–94), Pope nevertheless uses also the more general thought of the two principles necessarily inter-shifting in every man (II, 231). Though firmly distinguishing vice from virtue (II, 211–12) and indeed regarding it as a 'monster' only to be seen to be hated (II, 217), he knows that in actual experience we find the two inextricably intertwisted and combining in 'a thousand ways' (II, 214). We have accordingly to recognize the presence of such 'extremes' joining in man 'to some mysterious use' (II, 206); we have to accept the mystery without what Byron calls 'cant' (p. 153); and somehow from this Shakespearian acceptance, this balancing of the positive and the negative within us, good matures through the grace of what Pope calls a 'mightier Pow'r' (II, 165), functioning as the 'Eternal Art' (II, 175).

That the *Essay on Man* outspaces its 'Augustan' period as normally understood we have sufficiently shown, but we need not limit its contacts to the Renaissance, widely considered, nor even to the Western tradition. In reading Sri Aurobindo's colossal work of mystical philosophy, *The Life Divine* (Calcutta, 1939), I was continually struck to find how much of his visionary structure was covered by the lucid couplets and fourfold plan of Pope's *Essay*.

I shall now intentionally select for comparison works superficially unlike Pope's *Essay*. Our obvious modern comparison would be that profound poem, so similar in scope and purpose (e.g. especially, on nature at the root of both crude instinct and spiritual illumination, III, 975–1057), Robert Bridges' *Testament of Beauty*; or that remarkable work of poetic philosophy and creative doctrine, whose very title hints its relevance to our story, Murray Hickey Ley's *A is All*

(San Francisco, 1953). Here I can only point to the many references to Bridges throughout my *Christ and Nietzsche*, and pass on to a recent work at first sight, in its wild Dionysian extravagance, the polar opposite of all that Pope, as artist, appears to stand for. I refer to John Custance's highly suggestive *Wisdom, Madness and Folly* (1951). Strange though it may seem, this work continually recalls Pope's scheme. It is, however, not nearly so wild as it at first appears. Though strongly inspirational in origin, it is well-buttressed by references to thinkers of status from Kant onwards, such as Herbert Spencer, William James, Freud, Jung, Bergson, D. H. Lawrence, Berdyaev and Toynbee. Most important of all, its two basic principles, which the author calls 'negative' and 'positive', are, as he himself reminds us, roughly correspondent to Nietzsche's 'Dionysian' and 'Apollonian'. Often he calls them 'instinct' and 'reason', like Pope; and, like Pope, refers to the great 'all' or 'whole' as his final reference. Custance's positive principle, 'reason', recalls those thinkers characterized by Pope as 'more studious to divide than to unite' (II, 82); it is a faculty 'whose very nature' it is 'to divide and cut off' (V, 146); 'a male, aggressive power' with, as phallic symbol, 'a flaming sword for analysis, division, destruction' (VI, 170).[1] But its era of supremacy is coming to an end, since 'the Negative is preparing a terrible revenge on modern civilization' (IV, 93), as Pope foresaw in his vision of our disrupted culture at the close of *The Dunciad* (p. 64). Somehow the lost 'balance' must be redressed 'through a victory of the Negative', the more female, Dionysian principle, 'after its long eclipse' (V, 147). The final aim is, however, no violent orgy of visions and emotions, but a just balance, 'reconciling the opposites and allowing power to flow freely and harmoniously' (IV, 97). This is what John Custance envisages as the 'brave new world', to use Aldous Huxley's Shakespearian adaptation, ahead of us, a reconciliation which he finds complete in (i) the personality of Jesus (IV, 97) and (ii) the culture of ancient Greece, his balance recalling Byron's view of Pope as 'the Christianity of English poetry' (p. 132):

'Again and again visions of Greece appeared to me, little though I knew of the classics and classical civilization. And always the Greeks

---

[1] This is roughly what 'reason' meant for Pope. To Milton 'reason' was the supreme faculty, the difference being in part a difference in doctrine and in part a shift in the word's meaning.

appeared to me quite unique. They alone of all peoples had achieved a Golden Mean between Positive and Negative, and it was to this perfect balance that their amazing achievements appeared to me to be due. In charts I drew at the time attempting to classify the peoples of history according to the Positive and Negative elements, the Greeks always came along a central line. Through the Golden Mean the Kingdom of God had very nearly been created on earth.'

(IV, 97)

That is, too, Nietzsche's reading of classical culture as, at its best, a fusion of Dionysian and Apollonian. Our quotation helps us to see why Byron so admired the 'Grecian temple' (pp. 148, 150) of Pope's poetry; his was an age of Dionysian upsurgings in literature and the challenge of the masses, and of a false Apollonianism in morals and religion; his own life was one long endeavour to harmonize his tumultuous passions with an ingrained, almost puritanical, moral idealism; and he saw in Pope's exquisite Apollonian projection of a Dionysian philosophy, and there alone, since Shakespeare was *too* Dionysian, the very fusion for which he longed. We can see, too, why Pope himself drew sustenance from the ancients, his very style recapturing in balance and poise the statue-poses of antiquity (pp. 91–2). But such thoughts do not leave us on the plane of 'psychology'; those very poses enjoy and transmit a breath of the eternal; and Custance writes throughout from a sense of the eternal categories.

His graded hierarchies make a delightful list:

'There are thus, I am impelled to postulate, positive and negative Gods, or Powers of God, positive and negative saints and martyrs, angels and archangels, godesses, devils, warlocks and witches, sirens, fauns, nymphs, sprites, gnomes, gremlins, poltergeists, fairies, ghosts, men and women, anthropoids and animals, birds and insects, fishes, reptiles and bacteria.'

(VI, 167)

'Negative' here holds no suggestion of 'evil'; indeed, it is for the negative that the author is arguing. But see how closely the intuition fits Pope's natural and divine hierarchies. So too, with 'chance': in Pope's purposeful universe 'chance' is directly equated with 'direction' (I, 290; p. 46), and Custance has a similar intuition, or sense, of 'guidance' (V, 142), devoting a whole section to 'Purpose and Chance' (VI, 160–8), quoting C. S. Myers' statement that 'accidents' are 'scientific impossibilities' (VI, 163), and constructing a neat myth to illustrate a possible blending of the powers of prayer with the rights of that natural law and cosmic balance on which Pope similarly insists.[1] The practical necessity Custance finds of dividing 'the personal and purposive aspect of things up into concepts of various Beings, endowed with personality and purpose, and fulfilling various functions' (VI, 163), may be compared with the impulse, in Pope and others, towards what is technically called 'personification'. The author of *Wisdom, Madness, and Folly* is one with Nietzsche, though here Pope offers no analogy, in looking for some sort of 'superman' (VI, 182).

This is a strikingly original book, but much of it is contained, and nearly all foreshadowed, in the lucid couplets of Pope's short *Essay*. Such thinking from the heart of life will always be original, but seldom new, and needs in every age driving home against the static concepts and lifeless clichés that pass for exact thought. Or again, we may say that it is, for the most part, just common-sense. If, says Mr. Custance, he could put into words what he has seen in periods of ecstasy, he would have gone near to solving the problem of the universe. Such a statement would be of general use:

'It would give everybody a logical, intelligible and satisfactory way of life for this world and the next. It would be an indispensable *vade mecum* for every sensible person.'

(VI, 150)

It would not be unreasonable to claim as much for *The Essay on Man*: indeed, I did so in my original essay (p. 46 above). All this Pope knew, and underlined the thought by composing his *Universal Prayer*.

The main purpose of both is to integrate man self-consciously into a vital, purposeful, and not less than personal, universe. Above all, vitality must be assured; and this involves a full assimilation of the Dionysian. Dionysus was an oriental god. *Thus Spake Zarathustra* uses an oriental setting, and our Renaissance poets may often be supposed as labouring to incorporate a more eastern, feminine and Dionysian, at once vital and spiritual, wisdom into the more masculine and mentalized culture of the West.[2] Pope's *Essay* lies within this movement, and its affinities to Aurobindo's *Life Divine* need not surprise us. Or we may turn to another great seer of our

[1] VI, 161-2; *Essay on Man*, IV, 111-30.
[2] The relevant references are given in my *Christ and Nietzsche*, IV, 138-9.

day, at first sight poles apart from Pope, John Cowper Powys. Here
he is, writing, in one of the truly great pieces of contemporary
criticism and perhaps *the* greatest analysis of humour in existence,
on Rabelais:

'Now the way Rabelais opens up the path in which, for one
reader at least, he is, after his favourite Saint Paul, the supreme
Pioneer, may be roughly styled, following Plato's method through
the mouth of the cautious Timaeus, as a fair speculative "likelihood",
the way of the transference of reverence from static symbols to dynamic
realities. In the case before us this way of Rabelaisian thought may
be hinted at as follows and the form it takes is a new reconciliation
of reason and instinct, a reconciliation according to which both
religion and morality, those opposite emotional impulses, are fused
and subsumed in a larger and more integral creative energy, an
energy which is nothing less than the concentrated action of the
individual soul as it deals with the Multiverse of unfathomable
dimensions around it.

'I will put the situation as clearly and plainly as I can. Jesus said:
"*I* am the way, the truth and the life." Now this saying Saint Paul
transferred to the individual soul by his profound and original concept
of: "Not I, but Christ in me." What Rabelais suggests, according to
my "likelihood", is our right to carry this great Pauline advance a
step still further and to merge the concept "Christ in us" in the less
objective, less symbolic, and much simpler concept of the *deeper
soul in us*, that is to say, of the inexhaustible creative energy in the
depths of our own individual being. By this bold transference of
reverence from the *positive* awe and propitiation and sanctity of
Religion, as well as from the *negative* puritanism of Rational Morality, to an unfathomable well-spring of creative force in our own
soul, both the unreal systematizations of reason and the too real
propitiations of religion are shaken off, and in their place there arises
out of the depths the energy that destroys and creates all that exists.'

(*Rabelais*, 1948; IV, ix, 385)

Powys' contention is summed up as follows:

'The "Jesus Christ" who is "the same yesterday, today, and forever"
became through the genius of Saint Paul "the Christ in me", that
is to say "the Christ in us all".'

(*Rabelais*; IV, ix, 385)

Much, and perhaps all, of that applies to Pope. Powys' 'Christ in us all' blends instinct with Pope's 'God within the mind' (II, 204). Both contend that true virtue is not in danger: Pope's 'God within the mind' acts as a distinguishing faculty, or check, and vice has only to be seen to be hated (II, 218); and Powys quotes Rabelais' statement in the fifty-seventh chapter of *Gargantua* regarding 'an instinct and spur which always drives them on to virtuous deeds and makes them draw back from vice which they call honour'.[1]

It is abundantly clear that such a gospel holds danger: it is as though the only way to the best is just as likely to prove the way to the worst. As Pope neatly puts it, 'our greatest evil' lies disconcertingly close to 'our greatest good' (II, 92). We may, indeed, agree on the importance of channelling the deeper forces, but surely we want more direction as to *how* this is to be done? That direction Pope does not offer, and this may well appear a weak link, or shaky buttress, in his building; but it is, strangely enough, *at once the poem's central weakness and greatest strength*. For here we can *insert whatever religious beliefs and practices may best suit our particular needs*.[2] The *Essay* has ample room for them. Pope lays, as we have seen, explicit and primary emphasis on 'a mightier Pow'r' than passion (II, 165), and on 'the God within the mind' (II, 204). Such phrases may be supposed to cover much that is usually meant by 'religion'. Here we shall all have different approaches, and for these the *Essay* certainly provides no substitute. It must nevertheless be regarded as not less, but more, comprehensive than any one set of beliefs, roughly corresponding to what we have in mind when we say that the British Empire or Commonwealth finds room for various religions with a creative tolerance suiting the nature of man, the limitations of dogma, and the egotism of personal belief. But such a world-wide system enfolding various religions is itself a super-religion, corresponding to Pope's *Universal Prayer*, and if it be argued that all this is statesmanship and not religion, we can point to our earlier arguments regarding the relative powers of crown and church within the British order (p. 158). Pope himself was never content with anything less than the whole of life, and intended to expand the

---

[1] IV, ix, 385–6; compare Milton's doctrine of a certain innate 'abstinence' in his *Reason of Church Government*, II, iii; quoted *Christ and Nietzsche*, V, 215, note.

[2] For a discussion of the central importance of the Crucifixion symbol in Christianity with respect to the sublimation of dangerous instincts, see *Christ and Nietzsche*, III, 104–5.

Essay on Man into a greater work involving society, politics, and the nation. His reach is vast, and inclusive. Man's inevitable religious controversies are taken in his stride, and allowed for:

> *But still this world (so fitted for the knave)*
> *Contents us not. A better shall we have?*
> *A kingdom of the Just then let it be:*
> *But first consider how those Just agree.*
> *The good must merit God's peculiar care;*
> *But who, but God, can tell us who they are?*
> *One thinks on Calvin Heav'n's own spirit fell;*
> *Another deems him instrument of hell;*
> *If Calvin feel Heav'n's blessing, or its rod,*
> *This cries there is, and that, there is no God.*
> *What shocks one part will edify the rest,*
> *Nor with one system can they all be blest.*
> *The very best will variously incline,*
> *And what rewards your Virtue, punish mine.*
>
> (IV, 131)

Nevertheless, virtue to Pope remains virtue, whatever the difficulties of assessment. This very indecision, this vacuum at its heart, as it were, is necessary to the *Essay's* whole conception; and in that it commits itself to no dogma, whilst nevertheless presupposing dogma, or some equivalent, at its heart, it corresponds neatly to the British Crown properly understood as a symbol above, and yet containing, all conflicts of party or religion. We, today, expect a world-state, a world-order; and if that new order is to be one of religious tolerance and inclusion, if, as Mr. Custance argues (p. 175), it is to balance correctly the positive and negative, masculine and feminine, principles, in exact descent from Hellenic culture and the New Testament; then we can scarcely do better than take the *Essay on Man* as our guide. Here we draw close to a new understanding of Byron's powerful intuition of Pope as 'the national poet of mankind' (p. 160).

Pope has, however, left us certain pregnant religious assertions of his own. His seraphs and angels are impregnated with a burning conviction that somehow stops short of any dogmatic limitation; you feel that if you don't like those terms, you can call them something else, but you do not question their reality. As for the lovely passage starting 'Submit—in this or any other sphere' (I, 285–94;

179

quoted p. 46), it is surely as good a practical definition of faith as any you will discover, expanding the New Testament assertion that the hairs of our heads are all numbered and that no sparrow falls to the ground without God's knowledge. Pope's lines, perhaps especially his exquisite equating of 'chance' with 'direction', give lucid and memorable expression to a *living* truth, existing in the order not of thought, but of life. The more you live with them, the truer they become; the more you accept the harmony, the more of it you find, and create, around you. They are creatively, dynamically, true.

Such is the basis of Pope's *Essay*, and here is, as surely, its heart:

> *So Man, who here seems principal alone,*
> *Perhaps acts second to some sphere unknown,*
> *Touches some wheel, or verges to some goal;*
> *'Tis but a part we see, and not a whole.*

(I, 57)

That 'sphere' or 'wheel' symbolizes those higher dimensions elsewhere in poetry expressed by temples, domes, urns, circles of various sorts; and without some such intuition, we shall drop to the level of those whose clouded thinking cannot conceive that the supernatural machinery of those spirits of the dead (I, 47–66) called 'sylphs', which Pope added to the first version of *The Rape of the Lock* and regarded as the greatest proof of judgement he had ever shown,[1] may indeed correspond to what actually goes on around us as surely as the card game and coffee-pots of that richly devised poem. Nor must we forget that other guardian spirit, the sainted maid of *Eloisa to Abelard*. Pope's poetic meaning will never be received without fullest honours accorded to the sovereignty of such intuitions. Through them he labours to integrate human existence within the higher dimensions, as a space-time concern blending impulse with value in tune with the eternal: he is trying to see life as art.

The two driving forces in Pope's work are: (i) his devotion to poetry, and (ii) his passion for a genuine ethic. These are twin aspects of a single ideal. If, in reading his early *Essay on Criticism*, you make, as I have made in lectures now for twenty years, point by point transferences to the art of life, you get some interesting results that may serve to supplement and interpret the *Essay on Man*; and the complexities of the later essay force us continually to speak in terms of drama. In both art and ethic Pope stresses the need for vitality:

[1] Spence, 142; quoted Tillotson, 'Design', 56.

his *Inferno*, *The Dunciad*, is full of dull writers; but he is not thinking of entertainment.

Vitality conditions penetration, insight and virtue. The business of poetry is involved closely with what we mean by 'eternity', and so is the business of man. In the great campaign of peace, when the old problems are gone, man must advance. He is, and will remain, dynamic, for good or for ill. The *Essay on Man* prepares for this, without fully succeeding in illustration of what must follow; for, after most admirably defining man's task of integration, it leaves us, in the later sections, with little more than a fine counsel of vital contentment and goodness, together, it must be admitted, with some slackening of poetic vigour. There are exquisite passages, there is wisdom and brilliance, but some of the sap has gone. Now this is just where Nietzsche so strongly diverges. We have talked much of 'sublimation', but, were the positive powers in man truly captured and released, and no one is more anxious for a full incorporation of all our most *secret* impulses than Pope, something very strange might come of it. The sublimation that merely results in morality as norm-ally understood may be, at least where genius is concerned, a specious sublimation, veiling poisons, and that is what all our denunciatory satirists are trying to say, from the New Testament onwards. What they are driving at is, whether they know it or not, a consummation greater, and rather frightening. Pope himself knew that he struck fear into his contemporaries.[1] Exactly what the new virtue, or greatness, is to be, we cannot say, except that it will hold traffic with higher dimensions of existence. Now, though Pope insists strongly on the reality of the superhuman powers, he strikes out no such ambitious programme for man himself. He insists that humanity should keep its station. But that very concentration on man which he counsels, involving, as it does, a realization of his physical and mental limita-tions, becomes, by forcing an acceptance of man's passions and their 'mysterious use' (*Essays on Man*, II, 206), a valuable advance; that very intellectual humility on which he insists itself throws open the way to an infinitude of super-rational possibilities. Pope's emphasis on man as man's proper study is at once humility and pride since, though the honest facing of instinct demands humility, the natural results of that honesty may, with God's help, be expected to flower in self-transcendence. Indeed, his very counsel of contentment with man's lot on earth may be said to feed that inmost Promethean spark

[1] IV, 266; also *Satires, Epilogue*, II, 209; see pp. 55, 76.

which cannot remain content. Pope has sown the seed; the rest has been, and is being, carried on by others. Here we touch the paradox of his personal studies, Sir Plume, Atossa, Sporus, presented statically, yet each a dynamo; poetically still, yet swirling with energies; creatures of art, of space-time.

And indeed, what Pope's explicit thinking does not formulate, his symbolisms and phraseology continually suggest:

> *Th' Eternal Art educing good from ill,*
> *Grafts on this Passion our best principle:*
> *'Tis thus the Mercury of Man is fix'd,*
> *Strong grows the Virtue with his nature mix'd.*

(II, 175)

There is a great adventure, maybe a great experiment, afoot, far beyond our comprehension; there is an injunction on man to *make* something of himself, though what exactly we cannot easily say. The New Testament is our guide, and *Thus Spake Zarathustra*, pointing to a righteousness beyond the righteousness of Scribe and Pharisee, and to a life of balance, poise and power. The exact destination, whether on this plane or another, we shall not visualize: we only know that we are invited to collaborate with the Eternal Artist.

POSTSCRIPT

THOSE to whom the lines of approach suggested throughout this book appear interesting would do well to read two valuable contributions on 'eternity' and the modern mind: *A Crisis in Human Affairs*, by J. G. Bennett (1948), and *Release from Time*, by C. Conway Plumbe (1950).

It is, I think, significant that the space-time and sense-blending qualities of poetic symbolism discussed on pp. 80-91 above correspond closely to reports received by trance-communication purporting to come from higher planes: a good recent example is A. Borgia's *Life in the World Unseen* (1954).

Relevant thoughts occur also in Joanna Field's *A Life of One's Own* (1934; *Pelican Books*, 1952), and Aldous Huxley's *The Doors of Perception* (1954). To these I might add that religious classic of the last century, Henry Drummond's *Natural Law in the Spiritual World*.

The time has surely passed when great poetry can be profitably discussed without attention to such advances.

INDEX

Fictional persons, quotations, etc., are indexed under the works to which they belong.

INDEX

encounter with

the new testament

encounter with
the new testament

an initiation

by INGO HERMANN

*translated from the German
by Raymond Meyerpeter, O.S.B.*

p. j. kenedy & sons · new york

Encounter with the New Testament
is a translation of *Begegnung mit der Bibel*
published in 1962 by
Patmos-Verlag of Düsseldorf, Germany

Nihil obstat: Myles M. Bourke, S.S.L., S.T.D.
            Censor Librorum
Imprimatur: ✠ Francis Cardinal Spellman
            Archbishop of New York
New York, December 3, 1964

The nihil obstat and imprimatur are official declarations that a book or pamphlet is free of doctrinal or moral error. No implication is contained therein that those who have granted the nihil obstat and imprimatur agree with the contents, opinions or statements expressed.

For my parents

Preface

Bold outlines and broad areas of color arise from the records of the past. They may be weak; they may be imperfect; but they are definite.

John Henry Newman

THIS BOOK was written for all those who want to read the New Testament with profit and joy, and without anxiety. An initiation, such as this book proposes to be, must stimulate study. For that reason it must introduce readers to the questions to be treated, even though the answers cannot yet be given with complete finality. Love of the Bible can grow only if the problems regarding its origin, its transmission, and its interpretation are seen. Therefore we shall not deal with old objections but with realistic questions.

Questions of interpretation, of distinguishing fact from myth, and of form criticism, for example, will not be dealt with from the standpoint of their power to edify, or of the degree to which discussion has already led to a satisfying result; rather, we shall consider the extent to which knowledge of them will be helpful in the encounter with the New Testament and exegetical science. This encounter may involve a measure of danger to quite a few persons. Whether it pays to run the risk is a matter for each individual to decide for himself.

The present work was completed in February, 1961, but adverse circumstances delayed its publication. Despite the fact that literature appearing since then could not be taken into account, the thoughts presented here seem not to have lost anything of their relevancy.

7

Contents

encounter with

the new testament

INTRODUCTION

Why an Initiation?

IN OUR DAY, many people are trying to grasp the meaning of Christianity. Some of these are Christians simply striving for a deeper understanding of their faith; others are looking in from the outside with a desire to obtain knowledge of something that somehow appeals to them. Both of these groups will very soon encounter the difficulty that Goethe expressed when he spoke of "religion complicated by all kinds of dogmas." [1]

It is true that fully developed Christian doctrine is complicated, despite the simplicity of its fundamental message, viz., that God wants men to be saved and therefore communicated Himself to His creatures. Every doctrine is complicated and necessarily strives to formulate itself into a system and thus present an over-all view. To do this, it employs a speculative formula. However, the separate elements of such a formula may be difficult to recognize and place in their proper setting. Therefore, anyone who is endeavoring to capture the essence of Christianity by beginning with full-blown *doctrine* may quickly become discouraged. Yes, he may even conceive a suspicion that religion is a matter of intelligence: that only a highly gifted person can understand Christianity.

But Christian faith is not the same thing as Christian doctrine. First comes preaching or proclaiming; only later is the doctrine of the preacher organized into a system. It is true that Jesus of Nazareth was a rabbi by profession, that is, a teacher. But the exciting thing about His teaching was that He did not preach the Jewish doctrines; rather, it was the message of the approaching Kingdom

13

of God that He proclaimed. His preaching was proclamation. It was not meant to present doctrines but to appeal directly to the nature of man. In the gospel the message is stated quite simply: Be converted, for the Kingdom of God is at hand (Matt. 4:17).

The preaching of Jesus continues to exist as proclamation. His preaching is a historical fact, and as such it is the historical source of the New Testament. In every generation this beginning has to be interpreted and penetrated anew; it requires systematic comprehension and orientation. The result of this procedure is what we call Christian theology. But the preaching of Jesus does not become doctrine because of its form, even though, considering its content, the elements of doctrine are present. After all, His preaching is the source of doctrine.

Since Christian preaching is a historical event, it can be made present only insofar as it is evaluated as a past event, and its historical individuality and relevance are perceived. In our day anyone who inquires about the essence of Christianity may not limit his search to a timeless, superhistorical set of doctrines or even to a modern statement of Christian truth. Rather, it is fundamental to an understanding of the historicity of Christianity that one should be familiar with the era of its origin. One must consider this origin for its own sake in order to be initiated into the manner of thinking and speaking proper to that time. There is no other way.

We therefore do not need to modernize the Bible in order to undertake the task of our initiation. Rather, the contrary is true: we must adapt our manner of thinking to the standards of the Bible. We are saying nothing new when we admit that our present religious thinking is very far removed from the kind of thinking that prevailed when the Bible was written. We think along the lines of recent Occidental philosophy or we expect the Bible to give us answers in accordance with the hypotheses of so-called sound reason. We think nothing of garnishing our preconceived thoughts with biblical phrases (e.g., by adding to our own ideas, "as even Scripture quite correctly states, . . ."). Relying on our theological opinions or even on nothing more than the beliefs of our childhood, we become highly indignant if the history of religion or exegetical theology calls our hypotheses into question and compels us to change our thinking.

In view of this fact, if we wish to accustom ourselves to the thinking of the Bible, we should approach the task with the understanding that we are not to accuse the Bible of being out of touch with our times, but to accuse ourselves of unbiblical thinking. In our effort to adapt ourselves, it is not so much a matter of considering *what* the Bible says as of noting *how* it says a given thing. Above all, we must become initiated into the mode of biblical thinking. What the Bible says and how it says it, are unique and not subject to simple duplication, either in content or manner.

Thus, for example, the Christological dogma of the Church cannot be, and was not intended to be, the "adequate condensation of biblical teaching" about Christ.[2] Anyone, therefore, who wishes to encounter the Christ of the living faith—anyone who wishes to be stamped with His features—cannot limit himself simply to accepting as true the systematic formulas of the Church's teaching about Christ. One's recognition of the doctrinal formulas does not implicitly give one the biblical source. The essence of ecclesiastical tradition consists exactly in the fact that it retains apostolic proclamation as its source through the centuries; it can never make that preaching superfluous. Apostolic teaching remains the permanent criterion because it will always be the irreplaceable source and because it was unique in the mode of its occurrence in history.

It would therefore be a misunderstanding to believe that, in view of the didactic development of biblical utterances, the "imperfect beginning" today possessed only historical value and that a Christian's Bible-reading could serve at best to produce an edifying sketch of the personal picture of Christ. This would mean that a consideration of Scripture along the lines of historico-critical exegesis would only hinder edification.

Corresponding to the misunderstanding that tries to lean on "long-established" tradition, there is a second which is frequently connected with it. This is the misunderstanding of the expression "healthy human intellect." It is the error of not appreciating the problem of understanding historical texts. It maintains that dogma has sufficiently established who Christ is. It maintains that what this Christ, exhaustively characterized by the doctrine of the hypostatic union, has said and done, can easily be read in the biographies which we call the gospels. It further maintains that His words and deeds are narrated only to fill the abstractness of dogma with life for the sake of pious meditation, and thus to combine clearness of understanding with warmth of feeling. This conception continues to be current because it does not carefully observe *how* the Bible has handed down the apostolic teaching. Our present "initiation" will make that clear.

In the considerations that follow, no material introduction into the theological contents of the Bible will be given; it will be our endeavor to present a formal initiation into the manner of thought and speech common to the Bible. But our efforts cannot provide a substitute for further study of the biblical message or the study of "biblical theologies" and the commentaries on individual books of the Bible. Our analysis is intended, rather, to lay the groundwork for an understanding of the Bible and to clarify the conditions under which the reading of the Bible and of writings about it will be fruitful.

Again, an "initiation" must not speak *about* the Bible or biblical thinking; it must not be an "introduction"; it should keep as closely as possible to the texts. The reader should acquire a facility in the private reading of the Bible so that he will be able to interpret difficult texts unaided. He should see how the keys to writings on the Christian faith are made. For that reason we shall repeatedly look into the workshop of the exegetical experts and observe them at the task that will eventually result in a theological interpretation of New Testament teaching. In this process, for the sake of simplifying the explanation, different passages of the New Testament will be placed side by side, regardless of their relationship in time, so that that characteristic which is so important for the first encounter—formal uniqueness —will become apparent.

This procedure may sometimes be tedious, but in the end it will result in great, gratifying simplicity. The path is a difficult one, not because the original setting is so hard to comprehend, but because we have wandered so far away from it. The Bible is as simple as our Lord's sermons to the poor. Anyone who follows our procedure to the end will come to experience and to realize this fact.

He will perhaps also see what a great prospect the study of the Bible has opened up to our generation. Its historical origin is common to all Christians. Consequently, the differences between individual Christian denominations must stem entirely from the fact that theological and historical development has followed different lines.[3] No one should object to theological and historical development as such; it would be an unhistorical approach to look upon all development in Christianity since the days of Jesus as abortive or even sinful. The source can be kept flowing only by active development, that is to say, of course, only by a development which is faithful to the source and does not distort its meaning. It must continue to draw from the source according to its innate logic, thus keeping it alive and operative. How far this is the case in the details of the various courses of development; where development is in accord with origin and where it is not; where it is true to the origin and where it is in error—these significant questions need not be discussed here. The important thing for us is that the divergence of development, a perennial issue for Christianity, can be overcome not so much by discussion of this development as by consideration of the common origin. At any rate, all endeavors to overcome the divergent development must begin with this consideration. If Pope John saw "mutual acquaintance" [4] as the first step toward reunion in faith, then the question arises, whether efforts to become better acquainted can progress in mutual fidelity to truth only if they are at the same time efforts to become more familiar with the thought and speech of the common origin. St. Paul's words are even more relevant to the Christians of the twentieth century than to those of the first: "You have become sluggish at listening. You should by this time be teachers, but it has become necessary for you to be initiated all over again in the fundamental principles of God's words" (Heb. 5:11–12).

There is also a second consideration that takes us back to the "fundamental principles of the words of God." The difficulty of the Christian mission—one that we in our day can no longer overlook—lies in the fact that Christ can apparently be presented only in the garb of Western theology. The more vividly a truth of faith is comprehended, the more strongly is it bound up with a specific culture. The more exactly and completely the message of the New Testament was learned from the Graeco-Occidental language, the more powerfully was all of Christianity affected by European culture.

But are we not thus compelling the Asiatics and Africans to become Occidentals in order to become Christians? Who gives us the right to make our ideology and imagery a condition for reception of the faith by other cultures (not in principle but in fact)? Naturally, we do not have to condemn what the centuries of European ascendency accomplished; our doctrine is not in error. But we must avoid confusing doctrine and proclamation, our interpretation of the source with that source itself. Missionary preaching characterized by simplicity, originality, and realistic biblical thinking would surely more readily find its way into the heart of nations.

Therefore, it is not the purpose of Bible study to substitute the historical Semitic-Oriental form of Christian teaching for historically true, progressive development. The concern expressed here does not demand a historical narrowing. Rather, it envisions something that is emphatically taken for granted in the Christian religion, viz., that its historical origin, as origin, should continue to be alive and thus always be the stimulus for theological thinking to prevent its becoming a rigid system.

This vitality of the source has become possible, above all because of the fact that living tradition was committed to writing at a very early date. True, there is also unwritten tradition which possesses such admirable continuity that through it, or better, in it, anyone can make contact with past epochs. But consideration of the written manifestation of life in any age best provides that fruitful long-range view of the whole of tradition which can lead to a new encounter with origins. Only in the written word does a historical epoch come into its own to create the possibility of transmitting itself to a later epoch in such a way that its inner truth can become an object of consciousness (not only the content of it) for succeeding generations. Only when a tradition has been accepted as such and been written down does it make possible a later renascence.

Therein lies the inner necessity with which all significant religions have produced their sacred documents. Therein also lies, in a Christian and theological sense, the inner law by which the historical revelation of God has committed itself to the words of the Bible, so that rebirth from the source might be possible even though the historical life of the source has come to an end. And therein, too, lies the basic reason why apostolic origin and its written crystallization in the New Testament remain for Christian theology the incontestable foundation for all that follows, no matter how post-apostolic times may understand their relationship to their apostolic origin. The Catholic and the Evangelical understanding of tradition and Scripture may well agree on this point.[5]

Our endeavor, then, will be to provide an initiation into the origin of the Christianity that we encounter in the Scripture of the New Testament. Because the New Testament is a historical text, our first task will be to inquire into the conditions for understanding and interpreting historical witnesses to language in general.

CHAPTER ONE

What Does "Understanding"
Mean?

ANYONE WHO WISHES to understand the Bible as a document must note that it bears witness to three things: (1) to human language, (2) to a definite historical epoch, and (3) to a consciousness of religious faith.

Since the Bible bears witness to human speech, the question arises as to what we understand by human utterances altogether. Since the Bible is also the expression of a definite historical era and of a consciousness of religious faith that bears the imprint of the tradition of a particular nation, we shall inquire into the historical factors conditioning the Bible with respect to its view of the world and its style of expression. Therefore, it will surely not shock even the Christian reader to examine the Bible as a historical document and to inquire into the rules governing human speech. This procedure should prove appealing not merely as an unavoidable duty of honesty, but really as an obvious demand of faith, precisely to the person who sees that his privilege of living in the world by faith is grounded in the fact that God has had a hand in the shaping of history.[1]

What does it mean to understand? For a first, general answer, we shall make our point of departure the observation of historians that individual words may take on different meanings in the course of the history of a language. One who possesses some knowledge of classical Greek and undertakes to read the New

Testament will very quickly find that this knowledge is often a hindrance rather than a help. Many a word in common Greek (*Koine*), and even more in the language of the Bible (Septuagint and New Testament), influenced as it is by the Hebrew language, differs so much in meaning from the language of Homer and Plato that one is almost convinced that "the intended sense of the word is not directly identical with that of the word chosen to express it." [2] This fact is fundamental. It is essential to all understanding and interpreting: it preserves the reader from the naïve opinion that understanding words correctly is the most natural thing in the world.

Understanding is the process by which the hearer grasps the sense, or the meaning, of a statement. He interprets the ideas and "realizes" its meaning. But this result is not to be taken for granted. To take cognizance of a statement does not yet mean to understand it. In order to understand, for example, the words of St. Paul: "The Lord is the spirit" (2 Cor. 3:17), one must in the first place recognize the fact that between an individual word and its meaning, between an utterance and its sense, between a linguistic expression and the sense it is intended to convey, there exists no logical identity but only a unity of reference that is full of tension. It is necessary to unite the two poles in order to make an understanding possible. This is the process by which, as W. Dilthey says, we "recognize an inner relationship from external sense signs." [3]

The phenomenon of understanding then has a twofold aspect. First, the direct meaning of words and the complete sense of a statement are not simply identical; rather, they are mutually related, and understanding consists precisely in comprehending in the word its meaning.

Secondly, it is evident that if understanding is possible at all, it must be because the words are not accidental nor arbitrarily conventional, external signs. In the word, its signification becomes fundamentally accessible. In the utterance its sense can be grasped, and only if it is grasped can we speak of understanding. Therefore, to understand the sense of an utterance means to comprehend it as a genuine symbol, a substantial symbol, and not merely as a label or a substitute symbol.[4] In a substantial symbol two distinguishable actualities (word and meaning) coincide in such a way that each becomes real in the other and only in the other.

"It is not the case, however, that the symbolic signs which we encounter in language, myth, and art first 'are' and then, beyond this 'being,' achieve a certain meaning; their being arises from their signification. Their content subsists purely and wholly in the function of signification."[5] This identity of word and meaning shows how, in the process of understanding, the word may come to be known as an actual symbol of its meaning. But to experience this means to reconstruct what has happened previously in the speaker's mind.

But herein lies the difficulty of understanding and interpreting, for the linguistic expression is certainly not a mechanical reproduction of the intended sense, but rather a creative process. It is comparable to artistic creativity, not to photographic representation. In view of the intended meaning, the linguistic expression selects and places definite stresses; but that means that it imposes limitations. Our language is characterized not only by what it stresses about the intended meaning, but also by what it necessarily omits.[6] It is therefore always concerned with meaning and for that reason also with interpretation. It is essentially transparent; it does not obstruct the clear view of its meaning, though at the same time it is a veil. This, again, because signification is its business. Every verbal expression, hence also every text, stakes off, as it were, an open area around its meaning, within which interpretation is made possible and is required.

This is the realm of historical text-interpretation. Here the work of biblical interpretation begins. And here begin also the difficulties for the reader of the Bible. He has before him a historical text whose thought pattern is separated from ours by centuries. The Bible-reader of today must go back a long way; as an interpreter of the Bible he must travel the roundabout way that alone will lead to his goal. He will employ grammatical analysis, investigate historical concepts, and examine the linguistic usages belonging to different authors, or to particular periods. Only in this way, will he be able to "regenerate living thought connections." [7]

This way is often inconvenient. Will it take one to the goal? The answer to this question depends on the assumptions under which one undertakes the quest, on whether one exercises that discretion in understanding which language demands, and on whether one admits what Goethe says at the conclusion of his *Farbenlehre*, namely, that one can never sufficiently "be mindful . . . that a language is really only symbolical, only graphic, and never expresses thoughts directly, but only in reflection" [8]—mirroring them, as it were.

We must not lose sight of this aspect of language when attempting to understand the individuality of biblical thought and expression. Not only what the word means but also the object of that meaning is broken up in the language and expressed only in reflection. This is true especially of speech about God—and so Scripture explicitly makes known that it speaks about God only analogically, in symbols. [9] But in the word "only" is expressed the "rank" of a given statement about God. A statement about God is certainly not assumed to "define" Him. Even if not all statements of theological tradition reveal knowledge, Christian theology still reveals by its language—better, by its silence—the biblical norm for speaking about God. Sometimes this appears as the "negative theology" of St. Thomas; again, as the "learned ignorance" of Nicholas of Cusa; or, finally, as the unpretentious admonition of St. Augustine that none should dare to say that he has already found the truth.[10] This echo of St. Paul's statement about the "fragmentary nature of our knowledge" and about "seeing as in a mirror" (1 Cor. 13:12; 2 Cor. 5:7) is the result of sincere thinking about God. St. Thomas speaks of this in Question Three of the First Part of his *Summa Theologica*: "Regarding God, we can, of course, not know *what* He is, but, at most, what He is *not*. Hence, also, we cannot investigate *how* He is, but only how He is not." [11]

In much the same words that St. Thomas uses, the Fourth Lateran Council says: "Regarding Creator and Creature, no similarity can be asserted but that a greater dissimilarity must be admitted." [12]

These testimonies from tradition indicate theological conclusions which are fundamental to the biblical pattern of thought and without which no understanding of the Bible is possible. In his study on the "Development and Structure of New Testament Teaching," H. Schürmann, New Testament expert of Erfurt, has this to say: "Since New Testament teaching is permeated with adoring confession, there prevails in it a negative theology, i.e., it says much by saying nothing. Where it is most completely silent, as in the earlier stages of instruction, it says most." [13] The following chapter will attempt to describe this phenomenon.

CHAPTER TWO

The Language of Mythological Symbolism in the Bible

1. Myth and the New Testament

THE BIBLE SPEAKS in metaphor with a striking frequency. In its central parts, especially, it is not an abstract revelation of divine truths. Rather, it places before our eyes images which at the same time both conceal and reveal its actual testimony about God and the salvation of man. The revelations of the Old Testament usually occur in the form of images: we see the powerful God who appears to Moses in the noise of windstorms and thunder, but to Elias in a gentle breeze; who concludes the covenant with Israel through the mediacy of Abraham; who goes before Israel in the desert as a pillar of cloud and refreshes the people with water from the rock. And when the Old Testament speaks of God as the Creator of heaven and earth, of the plant world, of animals, and of man, this truth, too, is expressed in the colorful pictures of Genesis or of the Psalms.

In the New Testament much the same thing is true. The central theme of the message of Jesus, i.e., the coming reign of God, is announced in picture words.[1] Even the great theologians of the New Testament, St. Paul and St. John, speak in picture language rather than in abstract terms when they proclaim the central thought of their preaching: that the salvation of all men reposes in Christ and in Him alone. Christ, the eternal one, the incarnate, suffering Redeemer of fallen mankind; Christ, the second Adam; Christ, who is to appear on the clouds of heaven to judge all men—all these are theological notions that are to be understood not as actual doctrines but as bearers of doctrine.

It is therefore our task to make intelligible the meaningfulness of biblical terminology. But we shall confine ourselves to the New Testament. It is, of course, understood that all its writings are imbedded in the historical milieu of the first century after Christ. It will be evident that the patterns of thought and expression in New Testament writings bear the stamp of the same surroundings as the other writings of this same period. Hence it is to be expected that the New Testament, like antiquity in general, thinks in mental images and speaks in pictures which can be labeled as forms of expression common to ancient Oriental literature. Pius XII says as much in his encyclical *Divino afflante Spiritu*. This thought seems obvious to us, but not so long ago it was considered less so.

The nineteenth century had compiled a great store of information about the religious history of the nations of the ancient Orient. Men found amazing similarity between the Bible and the Oriental religions, and they were very ready to believe that the Bible was nothing more than one of many ancient mythologies. On the other hand, there were basic differences which seemed to justify the opinion that Bible and mythology had no connection. Consequently, two fronts—one relying on history for its religion and the other still believing in the validity of revelation—stood in opposition and remained thus entrenched for decades. A number of obstacles still barred the way to the liberating realization that men did not have to artificially divorce myth and revelation to attain a clear concept of divine revelation. There were two obstacles that were especially responsible for confusion and anxiety

in men's minds: a superficial notion of myth and a one-sided concept of revelation.

To the average person, *myth* was a vague, general term for
some fictitious tale originated in the remote past: an artificial
product of fantasy as opposed to "actual" history or to what is real
and scientifically comprehensible. Myth was therefore the embodiment of an explanation of life that was not binding in character. On the other hand, the *Bible* was considered "binding" and
able to prove something that was not simply imagined—something
beyond the power of any human fashioning—but only because it
was designated as the "Word of God," as revelation; and divine
revelation was understood to operate after the fashion of a tele-
graphic recorder which "types" messages in heaven that are simply
received on earth as complete, previously unknown doctrines.
This notion is false: the Bible itself does not pretend otherwise.
To designate the Bible as the "Word of God," however, is ultimately true, and the Bible makes that claim. It is easy to see
that one gets nowhere with such notions as the teleprinter theory.
Only after we have taken pains to appreciate myth in such a way
that the relationship between mythical and scriptural thinking
appears to be intrinsically necessary—only then will the uniqueness of the Bible stand out vividly before our eyes.

What, then, is myth? What is the real signification of this
Greek word which can mean "thought," "word," "speech," "narrative," or "message"? And, above all, what do we mean when we
talk about mythical thinking and speaking in the Bible? Does not
this very phrase imply that in the Bible untrue and unhistorical
images of fantasy obscure the boundary between the true and the
probable, the actual and the possible, the important and the
unimportant? Must we, in the end, admit that the New Testament proclamation about Jesus of Nazareth is nothing more than
a "Christ-myth," the "self-portrait" of a belief in miracles after the
pattern of ancient myths about gods and heroes?

Let us attempt to answer by examining the characteristics that are common to all myths. For mythical thinking, whether in Babylon, Egypt, Israel, or Greece, points beyond itself to a common source, i.e., to man's search for understanding, and, as W. F. Otto [2] has shown, to his intellectual endowment.

Research on the history of religion cannot, it is true, produce a definition of myth, but it can describe the phenomenon. Myth is understood to deal with otherworldly powers in terms of human experience; it is a symbol constructed from elements of actuality to express what in the religious sphere is believed to be absolute or otherworldly; [3] it is a narrative about "significant actions of gods." [4] Myth, therefore, speaks of "the unworldly in terms of the mundane," of gods as though they were men; it describes the otherworldly powers "in terms derived from the visible world, with its tangible objects and forces, and from human life, with its feelings, motives, and potentialities." [5] Accordingly, mythical thinking is a sensual interpretation "in symbol" of what the gods have experienced, and hence it is a clairvoyant sketch picturing world and man. It always favors personifications.[6] The symbol-reality is the vehicle of meaning for man and his existence.

Naturally, there is such mythical thinking and speaking in the New Testament. To interpret it, the first requisite is to make critical distinctions; to understand a myth, one must not simply consider what it says "objectively." W. F. Otto writes: "We must not rely on the direct understanding of myths." [7] Rather, it is necessary to consider the difference between image and thing. For mythical thinking is characterized by its failure to recognize this distinction; it lumps the two into one nebulous reality. "Wherever we find a relationship of mere representation, there exists for the myth, rather, a relationship of substantial *identity*, provided it has not deviated from its fundamental, original form and has not yet degenerated from its originality. The image does not *represent* the thing; it *is* the thing. It does not merely substitute for the thing; it acts like the thing so that it replaces it in its immediate presence." E. Cassirer, in his *Philosophy of Symbolic Forms,*[8] discusses the peculiarity of this level of mythical consciousness and shows the necessity of interpreting myths and defining their real purpose. That requires dissociating the mythical symbol from the plane of simple existence and elevating it to its rightful place on the level of signification.

For example, the manner in which the Ascension of Jesus is described, or the framework employed in the story of His temptations and the homage of angels; the account of the Transfiguration, or of Christ's descent into Hades, or the portrayal of the Last Day—all these are vehicles of signification whose real import first has to be lifted into prominence. H. Fries gives the basic principles of a solution to this problem: "The content of revelation and the Bible's manner of description and narration do not constitute an obvious connection or identity, guaranteed by Scripture to be inspired; they must be kept apart; they must be basically separable." [9]

As will be shown, this does not warrant the foregone conclusion that biblical accounts have no basis in history. The accounts only make it clear that the reported occurrences "can hardly be narrated except by means of the traditional ideographs of human visions." [10] This is similarly, even more emphatically, true of the theological reflections in the Gospel of St. John and the letters of St. Paul.[11] Thus, for example, the Christ-hymn of Philippians (2:5ff.) is considered even in Catholic theology to be "a clear proof of the existence of a Christ-myth." [12] However, the term Christ-myth is highly susceptible to misunderstanding; it is really not useful. We must make a more precise distinction, for it is evident that the mythological language of the New Testament is always only the partial adoption of a style of presentation or of a mythical category of expressions.

But these parts are never fitted together to form a new myth, complete in itself. There is nowhere a fully developed, entirely finished myth, though in the case of the Redeemer-first-man myth, that could easily have come to pass. H. Schlier has shown that this fact provides evidence of a switch from myth to symbolic language.[13] He maintains that there is not a single myth in the New Testament that might be understood in the direct sense of his statement; that there are only "mythical codes" which "signalize" the incomprehensible divine, and most of these are intended merely to develop Old Testament revelation and interpret it as wisdom.[14] This is the only explanation for the fact that in the New Testament, mythical elements of various and even opposite kinds are assimilated. Thus, Christ is included in both categories: that of Messiah and that of the second Adam; His death is understood as both a sacrifice and a cosmic occurrence. Or, again, the clear belief in Creation does not hinder the New Testament from speaking also of "rulers of the world" (1 Cor. 2:6).[15]

But this free use of individual mythical motifs is nothing but a beginning of the process of eliminating myth. The New Testament surmounts myth by applying to the historical Jesus elements familiar at the time, in the sense of an extra mythical predication of intention. This does not, however, crush the myth as myth or deprive it of influence. For the identification of image and thing which characterizes the original myth is exploded at the moment when mythical codes come to serve only as "signs" and as representations. But depriving myth of its power in this way does not imply the absence of the mythical. New Testament writers think in terms of myth in describing many details. But the free and easy use of fragments of myth proves the fundamental liberation of practical religious knowledge from the magic influence of the naïve and pure myth. The language of myth and of the Bible may be the same; the interrelationship of the two may be ineradicable; but their respective attitudes toward the world of symbols are essentially different.

E. Cassirer finds this to be true, not only in the Bible but also in every religion. (The classic example is the prophetic battle against the worship of images.) He writes: "The new ideality, the new spiritual dimension, that is opened up through religion not only lends myth a new signification but actually introduces the opposition between 'meaning' and 'existence' into the realm of myth. Religion takes the decisive step that is essentially alien to myth: in its use of sensuous images and signs it recognizes them as such—a means of expression which, though they reveal a determinate meaning, must necessarily remain inadequate to it, which point to this meaning but never wholly exhaust it." [16]

What is said here simply about religion holds true particularly for biblical thinking which, above all in Old Testament times, continues to live precisely on the rejection of myth; and in this method of negative theology the Bible attains to the greatest possible loftiness of human language about God. In contrast to thinking on the level of mythical immanence stands the religion of revelation, which changes every merely existing thing, but especially every occurrence that appears only in the interior world as allusion to and *sign* for the *otherworldly*.[17]

The foregoing chain of thought makes it possible to draw an important distinction between myth (as a universal, essential signification complete in itself) and mythological language (as a language of symbols).[18] It is the latter that permits us, in spite of the fact that the New Testament is set in the historical limitations of antiquity, to determine that, as G. Bornkamm says, the Bible is "the rejection of myth." [19] J. Bernhart states the point in this paradox: "If myth occurs in the Bible, it is automatically 'unmythed.' " [20]

What remains is the language of mythical symbols. The Bible makes use of mythical prototypes to announce the Christian message. That Jesus' death on the cross was not just the execution of a Jewish teacher or prophet but an event affecting the salvation of every single man—this the Bible proclaims under the concept of "sacrifice" and "redemption." It is evident that the reality which the images suggest and are intended to express has found its fulfillment in the salvific effect of the death of Jesus, and that therefore the proclamation of Jesus' death on the cross as having happened "for us" could not be more effectively represented than was done by the images of "sacrifice" and "redemption." Only these images appear to be adequate for expressing the intrinsic importance of the saving event.[21]

Therein lies the timeless binding force of the biblical turn of speech which no other system of concepts can supplant. Therefore, too, systematic theology, quite evidently necessary, is the more relevant the more closely it clings to the Bible. For this reason, initiation into the language of the Bible is nothing but that initiation into the "rudiments of faith" of which the letter to the Hebrews speaks. Mythical thinking as intellectual content in symbol is the "primitive phenomenon of humanity" (J. Bernhart) and at the same time the expression of man's highest potentiality: to arrive at a practical knowledge of God through the Word. Hence the myth is a permanent form of thought. It stands as an independent manner of interpreting being, *alongside* the scientific view of life.[22]

Therefore, the Bible and myth are not easily separable entities. Any attempt to separate what history has united would result in an oversimplification that would make the problem insoluble. "One must bear in mind, first, that the biblical history of religion is intertwined with the symbolic language of myth but, secondly, that this history has nothing to do with myth as myth. It subjects myth to its own purpose, that is, to serve as a poetic garb for the record of its own incomparable experience of God."[23]

2. The Function of Mythological Symbols

THE APPLICATION of mythological symbols to Jesus and His story leads to the fundamental question of all biblical interpretation: What is the relationship between image and actuality? [1] In other words, how is the mythological element in the Bible to be interpreted?

This question immediately gives rise to the modern inquiry into the historicity of New Testament accounts of events that are narrated in mythological dress; but this problem is only a part of the broader question of the correct interpretation of the mythological mode of expression in general. Of course, the problem becomes more acute here, since the decisive question precisely for modern man may be whether he can find in the claims of the New Testament an approach to a rational faith. At present, biblical theology is at pains to answer the questioning of modern man about the Bible. Finding a valid answer means nothing less than developing a principle of interpretation (a hermeneutic principle) by which the real point at issue can be presented clearly after being divested of its cloak of mythological symbols. We have just seen that a critical interpretation of myth and of the mythological mode of speaking is necessary in order to make possible an understanding of its real, intended meaning. Still, we cannot be satisfied with this general demand. We must expect the science of biblical theology to devise a hermeneutic method which will make possible a scientifically established criticism of the mythological element in the Bible. There is no such method generally recognized today.[2]

The most significant attempt to develop a complete method of hermeneutics may be R. Bultmann's program of so-called "demythologization." It is impossible to offer a full presentation of it within the framework of our initiation into biblical thought.[3] And yet we must ask whether "demythologization" does not perhaps deserve our consideration as offering a possibility of a critical initiation into the Bible and the problems of its interpretation; perhaps the effort of initiation could thereby be stimulated and advanced. No matter what our attitude toward Bultmann's conclusions may be, in this inquiry *every* effort to arrive at an honest understanding and a reliable explanation of the New Testament will be motivated by the same concern: to free the Bible of the defect of mute literalness and make its message audible and intelligible also to our time.[4] Nothing less is involved here than a new effort to open up the potentialities of religious faith.

Therefore, we shall turn our attention to some of Bultmann's perennially valid questionings, without, however, expounding, discussing or criticizing his program in the context of all philosophical and theological hypotheses. We may do this the more impartially, since the Bultmann literature, almost too voluminous for one to review, has sufficiently provided explanation. Apologetics, therefore, need not enter into our considerations. Our appreciation of Bultmann, the exegete, by no means implies approval or acceptance of his philosophical or theological a priori arguments. Moreover, our knowledge of language and mythology puts into our hands, as will be shown, the definite possibility of seizing Bultmann's thesis, transforming it, and understanding it as an ingredient of a principle of interpretation which (in contrast to Bultmann) not only "saves," but also shows as necessary, the historicity of the facts of salvation basic to the New Testament.

What does demythologization mean? Its first purpose is to interpret, in accordance with their objective content, the mythical forms of expression occurring in the New Testament. It is not intended to eliminate myth from the Bible, but, as Bultmann says, to bring its actual purpose into prominence. For this reason, we consider the word "demythologization" as unfortunate and liable to misunderstanding. This criticism of the view of life inherent in myth is, to a certain extent, the negative side of the method.[5] A critical clarification of the mythological in the Bible has always belonged to the perfectly normal task of theology.[6] Even our everyday thinking furnishes criticism of myth. Bultmann says: "In many instances, without intention and reflection, we demythologize the mythological statements of the Bible by the mere fact that myths have become images which have long ago lost the mythical sense of their origin. This happens most readily, to be sure, in the poetical writings of the Bible, as in the psalms, where even the mythological language is often meant to be poetic language. In daily life, too, we use images which derive from mythical thinking, as, for example, when we say that our heart urges us to do this or that. No one would understand that in its original mythological sense any more." [7] On this basis, too, we understand Bultmann's sentence, important for our consideration: "Anyone who understands the mythological concepts and images as symbols, is really demythologizing." [8]

How can one extract meanings from signs? Bultmann's answer may be summarized in his demand for a so-called existential interpretation. It is in this that he sees the positive task of his method. But what is meant here? For Bultmann, too, human existence is characterized by the fact that it is historical, that is, that it finds fulfillment only by means of ever new decisions with respect to present circumstances. Historical existence actualizes itself as an intelligent being-in-the-world, as a definite attitude toward oneself, as an understanding of oneself. This self-understanding is present not merely *alongside* an understanding of the world as separated from it, but as the real focal point in which all the consequences of relationship with the world meet.

Therefore, there can be no "objective" essential truth which is unimportant for my existence. Every utterance of man is dependent on his historical position in the world and is hence a function of his existential self-comprehension. Also, the mythological language of the New Testament is an expression of a definite self-comprehension; to be able to return to this self-comprehension through all the trappings of objectivity—this is the potential of existential interpretation. It searches in the New Testament for concrete possibilities of existential self-comprehension,[9] and thus brings into play what the myth (or mythical symbol) really expresses, merely camouflaging it behind the objectifying form of its mode of expression.

What, then, is the person who wishes to understand the New Testament to think of this principle of interpretation? It is well to note that it is not simply a question of examining a statement of the New Testament with respect to its bearing on one's life, that is, of interpreting it existentially. Existential interpretation goes far beyond that. It asks about the conditions basic to the understanding of historical reality in general, and answers thus: Present matter is historical only when, as a phenomenon of human existence, it is actual. On the other hand, it may be said that human existence expresses and interprets itself in every *historical* actuality. Since every statement that concerns a person, thus becoming a historical assertion,[10] is always in itself self-interpretation of human existence, one must ask what it is that is interpreting itself here. One must ask what understanding of existence lies behind it and is operative in it. This, precisely, is what is called interpreting existentially.

It is easy to conceive the prospects for understanding biblical texts with such a rule. Every man, in whatever age he may be living, can make for himself a basic self-comprehension to suit his wishes. He does not have to cling to the word-form of any particular epoch. He is allowed to make an "original" inquiry.

But we must return to the question of what we are to think of Bultmann's approach. The interpreting historian must say that he can by no means forego the use of existential interpretation, at least in a general way. Going back to the underlying understanding of existence is *one* way, perhaps the best, or at any rate an unavoidable way to a realistic understanding of the New Testament, even though this way *alone cannot* lead to the goal.[11] The historical evidence of a historical experiencing of God (i.e., the kind that concerns men in their world), as well as the actuality (i.e., a saving God) which is the foundation of this religious experience and is signified under the veil of the symbol—these are not open to an inquiry which is prepared to view only mere historical reality or doctrinal quintessence. Up to this point, readers and interpreters of the Bible not bound to a "system" can agree with Bultmann, particularly because he does not undertake existential interpretation in any other way than that toward which the system-seeking Catholic scholar strives if he demands an "anthropological limitation" of theological science.[12]

Still, it is difficult to follow Bultmann, the interpreter, when he derives the contentual consequences of his system from the methodical demand of myth-critique (as the negative part) and from existential interpretation (as the positive part of his hermeneutical method). Let us consider the most important consequences: The proclamation of the New Testament is an exclusively mythological expression of man's self-comprehension before God, describable only existentially; it never concerns itself with historical facts.[13] As we have said before, it is here that the dispute over demythologization comes to a head. Since 1941, when the programmatic article, "The New Testament and Mythology," appeared, the discussion over Bultmann has viewed this as the core problem. Hence it is not surprising that the weightiest arguments against Bultmann have focused precisely on this point. Those who think in terms of the New Testament will reject a demythologization that is carried out radically (in Bultmann's sense).

The question of the historicity of proclamation through mythical symbols can be instructive and fruitful in an initiation such as we are attempting. Therefore, we will now pose this question with an eye to Bultmann; however, we will then relinquish our argument with him to search for a principle of understanding and interpretation that is better suited to scriptural purposes.

Let us consider the statements of the New Testament about Christ. He is spoken of as teacher and prophet, but also as Messiah, as Saviour, as authorized announcer of the dominion of God over all nations. He confirms His message with miracles. He is the Saviour and the Redeemer from sin and death; He was crucified but arose from the dead. He will come at the end of time as the all-powerful judge, as the ruler of the world endowed with the spirit of God. Consequently, throughout history, He will be the ever-present master of the living and the dead.

Bultmann's existential interpretation sees in these statements about the figure of Jesus Christ nothing but a paraphrasing for us of the significance of Christ for the salvation of men. Early Christian preaching proclaims this Christ of faith, but the historical Jesus did not fit that description. Jesus was simply a teacher and prophet who was executed for reasons that can no longer be historically determined. He "appeared as a mere human being, as a prophet and teacher. He did not proclaim any doctrine regarding His person." Neither did He consider Himself to be the Messiah. He only knew "that the fact of His activity is the decisive thing." [14]

For Bultmann, on the contrary, Christ is a mythical figure created through the faith of the disciples by clothing the historical figure of Jesus in the gnostic myth about the "redeemed saviour" who comes as a divine being, who is redeemed through suffering, and who then rises from earth to heaven. This teaching is not, as in the liberal Bible-criticism of the nineteenth century, a spontaneous invention (and therefore, historically considered, a deception). Rather, it is founded in an act of God. God Himself acts insofar as He awakens the faith of the early Church in a son of God made man and in His resurrection. It is not, therefore, in miraculous, historical facts that God certifies His activity of saving, but in kerygma, i.e., in proclamation, insofar as it addresses man and demands obedience.

Absolute obedience is owed to this proclamation. Its authority should not be questioned, for it is promulgated by God. Belief in Christ is not belief in the historical Jesus, who, as such, would also be the Christ of faith: it is, on the contrary, exclusively belief in the Christ-incident of the kerygma. The Christian's submission to faith is therefore never directed toward something that has been, but to the present Christ-event in the word of Scripture. The message objectified as historical fact must be divested of its mythological form by existential interpretation. Modern man is no longer preoccupied with a mythological world-picture; nothing is left for him but to turn to Christ, if he understands the objectifying assertions of myth as expressions of an existential self-knowledge. The Christ of faith, existentially interpreted, is thus simply the potentiality of a new self-understanding—and *only* that. The proclamation of His crucifixion and resurrection is not equivalent to saying that He actually arose from the dead (such an assertion, according to Bultmann, belongs to the mythological form); it is simply the summons of God to man to realize that he is fallen and sinful, deserving to be crucified with Christ. It is through faith that man will also rise with Christ.

This succinct presentation should suffice to indicate the direction of Bultmann's thinking. We shall now return to our own statement of the case and endeavor to elaborate upon Bultmann's problem in a broader context. We have taken cognizance of myth-fragments and mythological symbol-conception in the New Testament; we have also seen the need of an interpretation that is based on existential experience and will bring into focus the real message of the mythological language of symbols. But how is this world of symbols and the self-understanding it expresses related to the historical event about which Scripture reports?

Considering the differentiation between symbol and the thing symbolized, it would now seem to be permissible to set up a thesis which will apply the understanding of symbol as developed above also to mythological passages in the New Testament. We shall attempt to do so particularly with an eye to Bultmann's rejection of the idea of historical happenings. Simply stated, the thesis is: The mythologically worded proclamation of the primitive Church (of the New Testament) is based on actual fact. It attests to occurrences that took place in the historical world of man.

In explanation of this thesis, it must first of all be stated that the relationship of the proclamation to history is characterized by that same "disagreement" that exists between every word and its intended sense. Consider the report of an event in the life of the earthly Jesus, for example, the crucifixion, since it is admitted to be a fact even by extreme demythologizers. No matter how "exact" the report might be, it is nevertheless interpretation; and it would still be such, even if no kind of theological interest had helped to formulate the report (cf. the next chapter). It would be interpretation because of the simple fact that it is a linguistic expression. We have already explained how this difference between symbol and thing symbolized is to be understood; likewise, we have shown that this difference exists between two values which necessarily are in a relationship of analogous conformity. On the one hand, the sign does not stand in isolation as a mere metaphor or allegory: it designates something as a label for the thing symbolized in such a way that it authentically represents the thing meant, even if always only analogously, and it is therefore a genuine symbol.

One may assume that a historical report is based on an actual event. The report is not the "event itself." [15] Nevertheless, it is true that knowledge of the "event itself" is attainable in the symbol, for the application of both is "analogous," that is, the two values are diverse but related; in spite of a disagreement, one reveals enough about the other so that in grasping it we also make contact with the other. Concretely stated: In a report about a historical event, we actually "touch" the event itself, by analogy.

Does this also hold true for "historical" occurrences that are described in a mythological manner? Is it true for the New Testament? As we shall later show in detail, the New Testament is not intended to be a historical report in the modern sense of the word. It is not an eyewitness account (there will be more about this in the third chapter). Yet there are accounts in the New Testament which have as their theme the historical actuality of what is reported, for example, the accounts of the resurrection, and especially St. Paul's thoughts in 1 Corinthians 15 (which, according to Bultmann's own words, are "fatal" to radical demythologizing). The Apostle reminds the Corinthians above all of the resurrection kerygma of the early Church: "As something most important, I passed on to you what I also had received, that . . . Christ arose on the third day" (15:3f.). He calls attention to the appearances of Jesus after the resurrection. And then he pronounces those sentences which make all demythologizing of the resurrection of Jesus impossible (15:12–20):

> If, then, it is proclaimed that Christ arose from the dead how can some of you say that there is no rising from the dead? If there is no rising from the dead, then Christ did not rise. But if Christ did not rise, our proclaiming is senseless; senseless, too, your faith. Then we are false witnesses to God, having testified against God that He revived Christ, if the dead do not

rise. For if the dead do not rise, Christ did not rise. But if Christ did not rise, your faith is futile; you are still in your sins. Then, too, those who have fallen asleep in Christ are lost. If we place our faith in Christ only in this life, we are more pitiable than all other men. Now, however, Christ did rise as the first of the dead.

Here an event is described as historical, and not only that—the actuality is indeed the real theme of the statement. Man is here faced with a decision of faith. Denial of the resurrection is a refusal of faith.

The resurrection accounts in the four gospels have this theme in common. It is true, they do differ in details; [16] the actual utterances seem to be surrounded by mythical motifs; still, as G. Sölingen asserts, the variations are similar to variations in a musical theme. In the modifications of the respective resurrection accounts we have the variations, not the theme. But the theme can be reconstructed, for these variations are rooted in character, not in fantasy; their conformity is therefore transparent. It is, then, no overstatement to say that the *"theme" of the resurrection accounts is the historical reality of the resurrection of Jesus.*

Does this conclusion hold true for all the stories about the life and activity of Jesus? Do they all have as their theme the historical actuality of the accounts contained in them? Or do they claim only to be historical accounts without any intention of teaching historical realities? How about the accounts which at first glance bear a strong mythical imprint, such as, for example, the accounts about driving out evil spirits? In the first place, it would be overhasty and scientifically inadmissible to deny a priori the historical actuality of the accounts. A conscientious method of exegesis must take the texts as they stand and determine what they really intend to say.

For example, when the subject of demons and evil spirits is considered in the New Testament, the first step is to find out what actuality the word "demon" is supposed to stand for. An existential interpretation can state with Bultmann that there comes "into view the knowledge that the world in which man has to live is full of riddles and mysteries . . . ; that the world and human life are founded in, and bounded by, a power which lies beyond everything that can exist in the realm of calculation and control." [17] This otherworldly power the Bible calls Satan or devil. Its reality is beyond question for biblical experience of the world. However, it can be shown that already in the New Testament the demons are "demythed" insofar as the presentation of independent, ghostlike intermediary beings is obsolete; demons are reduced to the destructive force of evil (i.e., of Satan) (Luke 11:14–28), and evil in turn is related to the accountability of man (Matt. 15:16–20).

With this in mind, we see the stories about Jesus' expelling of demons, narrated in historical form, in a new light. For, if "demon" is no longer understood to be a ghostlike intermediary being, but rather a symbolic actuality on the personal level, then a driving-out of demons is historically on a level different from that of plain historicity. It stands, *historically, as an actual exercise of Jesus' power on behalf of man*. But this exercise of Jesus' power *manifests* itself analogically as an expulsion of demons, in terms suitable to the understanding of self and world prevalent at that time, and it is accordingly described in that way and not otherwise. It could be described differently, and would have been if a different era had been testifying to this same manifestation of miraculous power by Jesus. Neither the individual circumstances nor the historical actuality is the "theme"; the theme is the power of Jesus over evil and dark forces insofar as they have taken possession of man. Understanding of the theme of an account is indispensable. All depends upon the *purpose* of a mythological account. [18]

This important distinction is found already in J. Ph. Gabler

(1753–1826): "Regarding the inquiry on whether a myth is historical or not, that is not simply a question of historical presentation and wording; even poetic and philosophical myth may assume a historical garb and give the impression that it is the narration of a historical happening. Most important is the intention to convey a true story; and this, one must seek to determine by a careful scrutiny of the presentation, the wording, and the intrinsic probability of the incident narrated. Unfortunately, in the case of biblical myths, some critics have departed from this rule with unpardonable carelessness . . . and have thereby exposed the entire Bible to ridicule by its enemies, instead of preserving its honor by employing more exact investigations." [19]

To distinguish between historical wording and historical intention in a mythological account, makes it possible to hold as fundamentally probable the relationship to actual happenings of accounts that make historical reality the theme of their statement. The basis for this probability is the law of analogy. But this law lifts all probability out of its own sphere and shows the intrinsic necessity of agreement between account and happening.[20] What the nature of the relationship is and of what the historical actuality really consists—this is the task of the respective text analyses to explain.

In summarizing our consideration of the mythological mode of expression in the New Testament, we can hold to the rule that the mythological element of the New Testament needs interpretation. Actual meaning must be revealed by means of symbols. This may be done, on the one hand, by inquiring into the fundamental understanding of existence, and, on the other hand, by analogical interpretation, which examines the theme of a narrative and sees the meaning of a particular theme in its analogical correspondence to the mythological symbol. This theme may also be the historical reality.

The principles of hermeneutics show the possibility that a

mythological account may influence history. It is, then, the task of analogical interpretation to explain the nature of the relationship of a mythological account to history in such a way as to make a reversion to the naïvely realistic interpretation impossible. This reversion happens at times in particular analyses. Prerequisites and rules for analogical analysis will be presented in the following chapter.

CHAPTER THREE

The Bible's Testimony to Faith

THE NEW TESTAMENT TESTIFIES to faith in Jesus Christ. Anyone who wants to encounter this faith must examine its source, for only there—and always only where the source as source is transmitted firsthand—can the message about Christ be learned in its pure and unabbreviated form. But to understand the apostolic proclamation, one must do more than learn to grasp its content as comprehensively and profoundly as possible; it is crucial that one also master its form. He who seeks to understand the early Christian proclamation will find that its presentation is just as important as the matter presented, since the content becomes clear only when one listens to the language in which it is conveyed. Only he who has learned to evaluate the forms of presentation in the gospels can understand what is meant and with what intention it is said. Only he who makes a discerning examination of the form can appreciate what is being emphasized as important and what is being passed over as nonessential.

Hence it is neither a superfluous project, nor a mere scientific luxury, to attempt to determine the literary classification of a book of the Old or New Testament, the currents of tradition which it may embody, the laws governing the arrangement and unity—or lack of unity—of its individual parts, and whether it belongs to the "primitive rock" or to a later milieu of tradition. In short, one ought to know in what form the apostolic proclamation entered the Bible.

Anyone who reads the gospels carefully and compares the four

47

of them will quickly observe the distinctive way in which each of
them reports the words and deeds of Jesus. He will encounter
difficulties which cannot be solved by a superficial reading of the
Bible. He will see that the expression "belief in" as applied to the
occurrence of certain events in the life of Jesus and in the wording of particular sayings of the Lord, often leads to complications
and contradictions. Perhaps his belief in Christ will be exposed
to doubt and uncertainty occasioned by the Bible itself, but this
may well be the beginning of a deepening of his faith in that
liberty and boldness which is made possible by obedient harken-
ing to apostolic proclamation. The purpose of the considerations
that follow is to show the possibility of this process of the deepening of faith through deepened insight into the uniqueness of the
Bible.

1. One Gospel and Three Synoptics

ANYONE READING the New Testament must at once be struck by the fact that the one "gospel of Jesus Christ" has been handed down in several different literary vehicles. The versions of the so-called synoptics, Mark, Matthew, and Luke, especially, invite comparison, because they agree so extensively that they can be placed side by side in a running synopsis (unified view). One who takes pains to peruse such a synopsis, perhaps the German one by Josef Schmid,[1] will make some startling discoveries. For example, he will notice that although Matthew and Luke each offer twice as much material as Mark,[2] the two later evangelists lean on the earlier one (Mark) with astonishing exactness. Except for a few verses (about thirty) the entire account of Mark is contained in the other two. They even follow the same general arrangement of the material, but then, in certain places, they fill in or regroup on the basis of other sources. Even the manner in which Matthew and Luke work their sources into the prototype set by Mark reveals the peculiarities of the two writers.

We shall direct our attention to the differences between the first three gospels, because an initiation into biblical tradition must above all teach one to interpret and understand the variations correctly. Many a reader who is looking for a vivid picture of Christ in the gospels encounters his first difficulties precisely in the discovery that several different and divergent accounts have been written concerning a given event.

How is it to be understood that each of the three Evangelists records deeds and words of Jesus which the others appear not to know about or, for other reasons, have not incorporated into their accounts? Each of the Evangelists has a private fund, as it were: Mark, only a little; Luke, the most (about a fourth of his work).[3] Thus, for example, we find the well known parable of the seed that sprouts of itself, once sown, only in Mark (4:26–29). The story of Judas' end and of the appearances of the risen Christ to the women and in Galilee occur only in Matthew (27:3–10; 28:9–10; 28:16–20). Luke alone has the narratives about Jesus' bloody sweat in the Garden of Olives (22:43); the women on the way of the cross (23:27–31); the words spoken to the good thief (23:40f.), and those to the disciples on the road to Emmaus (24:13).

Differences also appear in the arrangement of material as well as in the time-and-place succession of events, despite the dependence of Matthew and Luke on Mark; and this could disconcert anyone reading the texts with false expectations. One and the same event may be variously placed, so that one might be tempted to ask about the "correct" sequence. For example, Luke relates the rejection of Jesus by his home town, Nazareth, at the beginning of His public life (4:15–30); Mark and Matthew place it at the close of His activity in Galilee (Mark 6:1–6; Matt. 13:53–58).

Still more notable are the differences within individual accounts and speeches. Let us direct attention to only a few examples: In Matthew, the Our Father contains seven petitions; in Luke, only five, and their wording does not agree exactly with the corresponding turns of expression in Matthew (cf. Matt. 6:9f. and Luke 11:2f.). In the Sermon on the Mount, Matthew begins with his eight beatitudes (5:1–12); Luke has only four, followed by four cries of woe (6:20–26). But much more important than the difference in number of the beatitudes of Luke and Matthew is the content of these differences in the two versions. (We shall treat this problem in a special chapter.) Which of the two gives the "correct" wording of our Lord's words? Again, one would like to ask what "really" happened, when, for example, Mark and Luke speak of *a* possessed man at Gadara, of *a* blind man at Jericho, and of *a* riding animal at the entrance of Jesus into Jerusalem; whereas, Matthew, in recording the same events, mentions *two* possessed men, two blind men, and two riding animals.

What should one hold regarding the traditions which, even in the central passages of the gospel, for example in the accounts of the resurrection, do not agree? [4] In the story of the women on the morning of the resurrection, Mark and Luke each name three, though not the same three, while Matthew speaks of only two and John of only one. According to Mark, the women run away "with trembling and fear," and tell no one (16:8); according to Matthew, they go away, "filled with fear and great joy," in order "to announce" the message of the angel "to His disciples" (28:8). It would be easy to cite more such instances.

As a beginning in independent Bible reading, it will be helpful to learn to distinguish the original from the later version in a synoptic comparison of single passages. As indicated earlier, Matthew and Luke lean heavily on Mark in their presentation. The agreement between Mark and the other two Evangelists is best explained by the fact that Mark's is the oldest Greek gospel and served as a model for the work of the two synoptics, Matthew and Luke. This may be considered the unanimous opinion of synoptic research today. [5]

The relationship of the three synoptics is now explained with the help of a theory which has slowly gained preference among various other attempted explanations. It is the so-called two-source theory. According to this theory, Matthew and Luke are not only literarily dependent on Mark, but they also made use of a second common source—a first written compilation of sayings and speeches of the Lord. This source of sayings, which research designates as "Q," has not been preserved as a literary creation. Still, one may conclude that it must have existed. Only the existence of such a common prototype could explain the frequently verbatim agreements between Matthew and Luke, especially in the parts of their writings which are not dependent on Mark. In view of the fact that Matthew and Luke originated in complete literary independence of each other,[6] and that they nevertheless agree in about 240 verses, we must conclude that they had access to a common source. These are the basic features of the two-source theory.

We have mentioned this theory because the recognition of the relationship of literary dependences among the synoptics is an important step in our initiation. One can, for example, evaluate the individuality and descriptive design of the gospel of St. Luke and thus find out the theologically fertile motifs of early Christian proclamation only if one has closely observed its use and its adaptation of the Mark prototype. The same holds true for Matthew. Only in the intention and in the theological trend of an account about Jesus can one really grasp the meaning of its message. For example, what St. Luke thinks, i.e., under what hypotheses, from what predominant viewpoints and in what sense he wants to present the message of Christ, what he means to emphasize or which misunderstandings he wants to exclude by silence—all these and *only* these considerations can reveal a reliable synoptic comparison. Therefore, a general view is not a superfluous undertaking but a necessary means to arrive at an understanding.

One particularly interesting example will show how necessary and rewarding a comparison can be which deals with Luke's literary dependence on Mark. Many such examples could be selected. This one is outstanding in its clarity.

One who reads carefully the so-called synoptic apocalypse, the description of the events at the "end of the world" as given by

Mark (chapter 13) and Luke (chapter 21), will notice, at second glance, some apparently trifling differences.[7] If one assumes (as the two-source theory does) that Luke is adapting the text as given in the account by Mark, a couple of Luke's dates will appear disconcerting. Whereas in Mark (verse 7) we read the simple statement, "They must come to pass, but the end is not yet," in Luke (verse 9) we have: "These things must *first* come to pass, but the end *will not be at once.*" Evidently Luke, with his insertion of "first" and "will not be at once," wishes to introduce an elastic and not a sharply defined point of time into the series of events. Luke refers more unequivocally to something to come than does Mark with his "not yet."

Also, in verse 12 we find Luke strikingly interested in the time sequence of the events. By his simple observation, "before all these things," he places the persecution of the disciples ahead of the political dissolution. In Mark we read: "For nation will rise against nation, and kingdom against kingdom; and there will be earthquakes in various places, and famines. These things are the beginning of sorrows. . . . For they will deliver you up to councils, and you will be beaten in synagogues, and you will stand before governors and kings for my sake" (verses 8 and 9). Luke first follows this description closely (verse 11), but then continues: "Before all these things they will arrest you and persecute you, delivering you up to the synagogues and prisons, dragging you before kings and governors for My name's sake" (verse 12).

If we now review the entire passage (verses 12 to 19), we recognize in Luke, compared with Mark, a different order in the final occurrences. At the beginning stands the persecution of the disciples (verses 12 to 19), then follows the era of political collapse in wars and revolts (verses 9 and 10), and then the cosmic catastrophe with earthquakes and signs from heaven (verse 11). According to Mark, on the contrary, the disciples are persecuted only in the general crisis of the final era (verses 8 and 9).

Now we ask: Are these shiftings of Luke accidental or do they follow a definite plan of testimony? Is there a fixed plan behind this arrangement?

Anyone who recognizes the individuality of the gospel of Luke will at once conjecture that here the consciously fashioning hand of a writer is at work. And this opinion proves to be true, for already in verse 7, Luke uses an almost tritely historical word to replace a phrase of Mark that bears distinctly redemptive-apocalyptic features. According to Mark's gospel, Peter, James, John, and Andrew ask: "What will be the sign when all these things will begin *to be fulfilled?*" Luke, however, reports that "some" ask: "What will be the sign when that will *happen?*" This change of expression by Luke evidently is intended to remove all eschatological coloring from what was said about the destruction of the Temple at Jerusalem and thus leave open the possibility that the destruction of the Temple could happen even within the normal course of history. What the formulation of the question, "When will that happen?" admits as a possibility is developed further in verses 20 to 24. There again Luke replaces the typically apocalyptic expression, "abomination of desolation," which was used for the profanation of the Temple,[8] by a historical picture, describing the beleaguering and devastation by enemy armies (verse 20) that will crush Jerusalem and carry the Jews into all parts of the world "until the times of the nations shall be fulfilled" (verse 24).

Alongside our first observation, namely, that Luke separates the persecution of the disciples from the apocalyptic epoch, we can place another discovery, namely, that he also divorces the fate of Jerusalem from association with the horrors of the last day and, in contrast to Mark, treats these two themes as being historical to some extent. Further underlining this idea is the form of verse 8, in which Luke records Christ's warning against the prophets who say that "the time" (the *"Kairos"*) is at hand, when in truth it has not yet come. Again, in Luke the call for perseverance is changed from the sense of its intended declaration: Instead of Mark's, "He who perseveres to the end will be saved," we now have, "By your perseverance you will win your soul" (verse 19). Mark's wording, "to the end," is omitted, because for Luke the persecution of the disciples is not yet literally a happening that is to be understood as referring to the end.

To conclude this train of thought, we observe that Luke not only endeavors to separate—to "de-eschatologize," i.e., to remove from the realm of eschatology—the story of eschatological occurrences at the time of Christ's return (Parousia), namely, the persecution of the Christians and the destruction of Jerusalem, but he also makes a corresponding effort to separate the Parousia as far as possible from the course of history. Again and again he cites indefinite intervals of time (verses 9 and 12, 20 to 24; verse 25, the "times of the nations": this is the era in which Luke and his readers are living); he breaks off the connections of Mark's text (verse 19) and now also appropriately introduces the return of the Lord. Instead of, "In those days, after that affliction, the sun will be darkened . . ." (Mark 13:24), in Luke we read simply: "And there will be signs in the sun, moon, and stars." This addition of verse 25 to the passage about the fate of Jerusalem (verses 20 to 24) sharply separates what follows from that passage: The ultimate crisis, which introduces the coming of the Son of Man, begins only now.

By this removal of the Parousia from the realm of history, Luke has taken a decisive step: *He begins to separate the hope of the return of the Lord from the expectation that the arrival of the Lord is imminent.* The question of *when* has become unimportant. Only the fact that the Lord will come is important for the existential situation that Luke wants to make possible for the Church as a consolation in time of persecution and as an appeal for vigilance.[9]

Luke now begins to become conscious of the possibility of an eschatological reality in St. Paul's sense. If we inquire into the historical grounds for Luke's idea, it may be explained that he can write thus because he is writing after the fateful year 70 (when the Temple at Jerusalem was destroyed by the Romans) and because he has reflected on the consequences of a failure of Christ to reappear and can therefore understand the words of Jesus in a sense that had hitherto remained unknown. Theologically speaking, we recognize the historicity of the story of Revelation. The course of history, too, becomes a condition which to Revelation-bearer Luke offers a new possibility of understanding the dealings of God.

This comparison of the texts of Mark and Luke should bring home to us how indispensably necessary a comparative view is for an understanding of the meaning of the New Testament. Only in an encounter with the intention of the author of a text can the wealth, the profusion, and the dignity of the apostolic proclamation be discovered. Of course, this is merely the first step. One who desires to become expert in the reading of biblical texts, who wishes to acquire a more profound grasp of biblical thinking, must take many a further step. Mindful of the question, or better, the temptation to ask: "What did Jesus really say?" one cannot find a satisfactory answer in an introduction to a reading of the synoptics. A comparison of texts will at first demonstrate only the relative individuality of one synoptic writer as compared with another. A full understanding will necessitate, in addition, an inquiry into the relationship of all the gospels to the active proclamation of the faith in the primitive Church, to the contemporary milieu, and—for us—above all, to our modern attitude toward history.

2. The Oral and Written Gospel of Christ

WHAT MATERIALS did the synoptics have at hand when they began to assemble the words and deeds of Jesus? We have already spoken of the written prototype at their disposal (for Matthew and Luke, through Mark: source "Q" and various others). But a glance into the contemporary history of the first century [1] will convince us at the outset that with respect to the gospels we must take into account a much more abundantly flowing source, namely the oral handing-down of the words and deeds of Jesus. First comes the word of mouth, then its commitment to writing. The forms in which the traditional materials appear in the gospels betray their origin at first glance: succinct expressions in the style of a formula, colorful picture-words, simply constructed parables, sharply pointed and at the same time stylized quarrel-dialogues, and adage-like, epigrammatic sayings. Each reveals how the proclamation about Jesus was crystallized into permanent forms, even in its preliterary state. "At the beginning of the history of early primitive Christian literature there stood a tradition of an unliterary nature, consisting of short narratives and striking sayings, which were repeated for practical purposes." [2]

These forms of transmission are the connecting link between Jesus' activity and the written accounts of the synoptic gospels, which in part were set down some thirty to fifty years later. The form of the synoptic gospels can be understood only by studying the previous history of the individual episodes. During that time, these brief stories and sayings "lived," developed, and were given

57

new form in accordance with definite rules. Exegetical science examines these rules with the help of an improved method which has received the name "form criticism" from Martin Dibelius. It assumes that even tradition that is only oral obeys laws that shape its form. "To trace out those laws, to make comprehensible the rise of these little categories, is to write the history of the form of the gospel," says Dibelius.[3] This principle of textual study, already found in J. G. Herder, was more scientifically clarified in the nineteenth century by H. Gunkel (as *Gattungsgeschichte,* or the "history of types," for the Old Testament; cf. below), G. Henrici, J. Wellhausen, E. Norden and, with respect to general literary studies, by J. Burckhardt. The work of these scholars was developed into a method by Dibelius in *From Tradition to Gospel* (*Formgeschichte des Evangeliums,* 1919) and R. Bultmann in his *History of the Synoptic Tradition* (*Geschichte der synoptischen Tradition,* 1921). To the conclusions of form criticism of the gospels we are indebted for our definitive approach to an understanding of the Bible and early Christian tradition. After all, no understanding of the synoptic gospels is possible unless we first know the form and history of their individual episodes.

How, then, does the method of form criticism help us to recognize individual elements of tradition in the gospels, and what clues does this method offer us to see the rules of the development and modification of these elements?[4]

The Elements of Tradition

Anyone who reads the New Testament attentively will notice that specific occurrences, and even the words of Jesus, are fitted into a frame. Very often it is clear that the individual synoptics offer an "editorial frame" of their own, for example, transitional indications of time or place which differ from those of another evangelist.[5]

If one separates the original episodes of tradition from the frame constructed by each biblical author as he collected and edited his material, and compares these episodes with one another, he will recognize definite types in the forms of tradition. Among the words of Jesus (speech material) one recognizes so-called *logien* or words of wisdom (e.g., "Where your treasure is, there also will your heart be," Matt. 6:21 or 6:19–34; 12:34; 24:28); prophetic and apocalyptic words in which Jesus demands conversion and announces the dawn of the reign of God (e.g., Matt. 5:3–9; 11:5f.; 13:16); words of law and rules for community life (e.g., the antitheses of the Sermon on the Mount: "You have heard that it was said to the ancients . . . but I say to you . . . ," Matt. 5:21–36; also, 6:2–18); the "I-words" in which Jesus speaks about His mission and about Himself (e.g., Mark 2:17; 11:25–30), and, finally, the similitudes, which one may distinguish as picture-sentences, parables, comparisons, and real allegories.[6]

The narratives about Jesus (story material) have also been handed down in a number of types. In addition to anecdote-like stories, which were presented as examples (paradigms) in the parish sermon (e.g., the anointing in the house of Simon in Bethania, Mark 14:3–9 or 2:1–12, 23–28; 12:13–17), there are stories that are more complete and have broader applications (e.g., the story of the storm on the lake, Mark 4:35–41 or 5:1–20; 6:35–44).[7] For these stories Dibelius introduced the designation "*Novellen*," which at first seems ambiguous. Another type is the edifying story from the life and activity of Jesus. Dibelius designates this class as "*Legende*." This expression does not mean "untrue story"; it is a concept of form criticism which embraces in its literary family the Last Supper story and the entire account of the Passion.[8] But the concepts "*Novelle*" and "*Legende*" may occasion misunderstanding. They are misleading and should be replaced.

With the help of such classifications, one can now more easily see the structure of the gospels and thus gain a more profound understanding of their individuality and meaning. These categories are not mere conceptions of system-seeking philologists, arrived at by a sort of vivisection; they are genuine aids to comprehension because they show the limits and substance of the forms of tradition. Thus the approach to Bible study exemplified by form criticism will guard, for example, against the danger of linking certain passages of the Bible simply from force of habit or unsuspectingly—passages which in reality do not belong together and which are understood wrongly because they are not viewed as separate entities with definite individuality. And this is a crucial error.

This will become still clearer if one considers the conformity to law with which the individual, written elements of tradition were handed down and changed in form.

The Laws of Form-building

For an understanding of these laws, two means are especially helpful: (1) a study of the variations which Mark's material has undergone as a result of its treatment by Matthew and Luke; (2) a comparison with similar traditions such as the sayings and stories of the Jewish wisdom teachers, Hellenistic narratives and proverbs, and even the Jataka collection of the Buddhist Canon, which R. Bultmann refers to as an "instructive analogy." [9]

These investigations and comparisons show that the forms of tradition of antiquity always had a so-called "seat in life," that is, they corresponded to a definite situation in the life of the circles that preserved and handed them on. The accounts of the life and deeds of Jesus were partly adapted to suit the needs of the community of the preliterary bearers of these messages, and had their "seat in the life of the primitive congregation." This function explains the laws of tradition according to which the accounts were extended and handed on make them useful for instruction, for direction, or for the mission sermon. As an example of extension, our Lord's word in Luke, "He who loses his life will save it" could be handed down in this simple form (17:33) as well as in its expanded form, "He who loses his life *for my sake* will save it" (Luke 9:24). This statement with its elucidating addition also appears twice in Matthew (10:39 and 16:26). In Mark the saying gets a further addition: "for My sake and for the sake of the gospel" (8:35); in John it appears again without any addition (12:25). The fact that a word of our Lord can occur twice in the same work in the same form (Matthew) or in varied form (Luke), goes to show again that the gospels are collections of living pieces of tradition. That kind of doubling (the sayings are called doublets) occurs frequently. The best known example is probably the double report of Christ's feeding of five thousand or four thousand (Mark 6:34–44 and 8:1–10, respectively, and the parallels in Matthew and John), for both versions refer to the same event.[10]

Let us consider two more examples to show that such reshaping also comes under the rules regarding the handing-down of messages.

1. In Luke, we read: "He then spoke to the multitude, saying: 'When you see clouds rising in the West, you say at once that rain is coming; and so it happens. If you notice that the wind is blowing from the South, you say that it is going to become hot; and so it does. You hypocrites, you know how to interpret the appearance of the heavens and of the earth; why can you not interpret these signs? Why can you not of yourselves judge what is right? And when you are going to your superior with your opponent, try to escape from him, lest he drag you before the judge, and the judge turn you over to an officer, and the officer throw you into prison. I say to you that you will not get out before you have paid the last penny'" (Luke 12:54–59). The admonition to make

peace with an opponent at the last minute is, in the context of Luke, an invitation to conversion before the approach of God's judgment. It is a summons to conversion couched in the form of a symbolic statement.

But the equivalent statement in Matthew does not express the same meaning, because the context is different. The text says: "When you therefore bring your gift to the altar and there remember that your brother has something against you, leave your gift at the altar and go and first be reconciled with your brother; then come and offer your gift. Be reconciled with your adversary without delay while you are still on the way with him, so that your adversary will not hand you over and the judge put you in the custody of a court officer and you then be thrown into prison. Truly, I say to you, you will not be released until you have paid the last penny" (Matt. 5:23–26). Here the sense of the Lord's word is altered in consideration of the ecclesiastical community. It is changed into a rule of prudence which counsels reconciliation with an opponent at law. The original style of the passage, its eschatological urgency, has been abandoned. The reason for this is the position of the Church: she needs rules to govern her members.

2. As a second example of the effectiveness of definite rules for reshaping, let us take a well known parable, that of the workers in the vineyard (Matt. 20:1–16). We choose it because it is found only in Matthew. Therefore we are compelled to observe the motives for a transformation in a single text, having no possible basis for comparison other than Matthew's "redaction" and —the original parable.[11]

"For the kingdom of heaven is like the situation of the master of a house who went out as soon as the sun rose, in order to hire workers for his vineyard. And when he had agreed to give the workmen a denarius (the usual day's wages at that time), he sent them into his vineyard. (The agreement was made only with the first laborers.)

"About the third hour [nine o'clock], he went out again and saw others sitting around in the market place. He said to them: 'You may go into my vineyard also and I will give you what is right.' And they went.

"About the sixth and ninth hours [twelve and three o'clock] he went out again and did the same. About the eleventh hour [five o'clock], he went out once more and found still others standing around, and he said to them: 'Why are you standing here idle all day long?' They answered: 'Because no one has hired us.' He said to them: 'You go into my vineyard, too.' And when evening had come, the owner of the vineyard said to his manager: 'Call the workers and pay out the wages, beginning with the last but including the first.'

"And those came who had been hired about the eleventh hour, and they received a denarius each. When the first ones came, they supposed that they would get more. But also they were given a denarius each. When they received it, they murmured against the owner and said: 'These last have worked only one hour and you have put them on a par with us, who have borne the burden of the day and the heat.' He, however, answered one of them: 'Friend, I am not doing you an injustice; did you not agree with me to work for a denarius? Take what you have received and go. It is simply my will to give those who came last the same as you. Am I not permitted to do as I please with what belongs to me? Or are you envious because I am charitable?' " Then follows in Matthew a conclusion that seems to summarize the parable and to reduce it to a formula: "Thus shall the last be first, and the first shall be last" (verse 16a).[12]

What is the meaning of the parable, and how ought one to interpret the closing verse 16? That this verse did not originally belong with the preceding parable, one may gather from the fact that the same sentence (verse 16a) occurs in Mark and Luke in another context (at the end of the dialogue between Jesus and Peter about the reward for following Jesus—Mark 10:31 and parallels) and was probably at first a freely circulating declaration of our Lord.[13] Obviously, Matthew wants the parable to be understood in the sense of the assertion regarding the reversal of the order of precedence on Judgment Day. He must have had in mind the command: Call the workmen and pay their wages and begin with the last down to the first. The parable would then turn out to mean: On Judgment Day, by the will of God, the last are like the first and the first are like the last—there will be no distinction any more. This thought interprets the parable as a lesson of warning for the faithful.

But is this the point of the original parable, too? Indeed, it is stated that at the end all shall receive the same reward—but that is an unemphasized feature in the parable, which, like all parables, has a very definite, pointed meaning. All depends on this point alone; in it lurks the gist of the parable. (It is this that differentiates a parable from an allegory and a metaphor.)

But if we inquire about the meaning of this parable as it stands, without having Matthew's interpretation before us, the medium of comparison will be something altogether different. Our parable has two parts: (1) the hiring of the workers and the instruction of the owner to pay all alike (verses 1–8); (2) the murmuring of the men hired first and their feeling wronged, then the question of the owner of the vineyard: "Are you envious because I am good?" (verses 9–15). Each of these parts contains a climax. This is what we call a two-peak parable, and the emphasis is always on the second peak.[14] The "theological interpretation of the parable must (therefore) proceed from verse 15 and, in general, from the second part (verse 8ff.)."[15] Then we see that everything depends on the payment of the same wages to all, even to those who in no way earned it. *Each* receives a denarius, the existential minimum. The reason for this action is consideration for the poor (verse 15), not ill-humored caprice or self-glorifying generosity. Jesus portrays the magnanimous, charitable act of a man who is deeply concerned about the poor. But in the parable, He speaks of the Father: This is the way God acts; in this way He is good.

W. Pesch expresses this thought very emphatically: "The parable of the kind-hearted master is intended to make clear the fact that God deals with sinners just as the owner did with those hired last, and that the Pharisees are scandalized by God's judgment of sinners as proclaimed by Jesus, just as were the first-hired workers at the action of the owner. Any further interpretation, including that which sees the intention of the parable in the fact that the same pay was given for unequal work, simply does violence to the text. The significant point is not that all received equal wages—this simply serves as the action of the parable. What is meant to stand out is that such a great reward was given to those who came last. The goodness of the master is portrayed by citing the generous wages, which the last group of workers certainly had no claim to. Those who came first, with their argument derived from human juristic thinking, are repulsed by the statement that the master is benevolent and generous. Therefore, the meaning of the parable refers to the primitive religious relationship between God and man." [16]

The original historical setting of the parable therefore contrasts with the prevalent Jewish notion of wages according to which one could "earn heaven." Here the Pharisees and Scribes are told: God is good to those who have not already borne the burden and the heat of the law all day; He is good to the poor and sinners, who have no claim except His goodness.

The shift of accent suggested by verse 16 is evident. The parable of the kind master, originally directed at the Pharisees and Scribes, is recast—for the purpose of instructing the community—

into a parable that suggests a reversal of values on the day of judgment.

We recognize the following rule of reshaping, or transformation. There was a tendency in the primitive Church to express the words of Jesus in terms of the situation of the community and the value of His statements in instructing the faithful. Anyone who wishes to give a responsible explanation of the statements which the community helped to formulate must therefore *first* attempt to ascertain their original form and present their intended meaning. A second step will be to take into account the later application of the parable and its interpretation, which may have come from the preliterary community tradition or only from the gospels themselves. The two together constitute the proclamation of Holy Scripture.

We have now taken a first look at the elements of tradition and considered the most important laws governing its formulation. It has become clear that not only are individual pieces of preliterary tradition essential to the actual understanding of the biblical proclamation, but also their compilation and setting through the "editing" of the biblical author. While the method of form criticism investigates preliterary pieces individually, attention has been concentrated more recently on the "redactional atmosphere" into which the New Testament writer has inserted his own material. The scientific accomplishment of this task, which combines the method of form criticism with other methods, is called "redactional history." [17] Primarily, it is concerned with the complete work; it opposes any "atomizing of material" [18] and can therefore appreciate the Evangelists also as theologians who not only collected the material of tradition but also assimilated it theologically. A good example of this is the theological work of Luke on Mark's version of the parousia passage (Luke 21) and Matthew's interpretation of the parable about the vineyard owner.

If we now look back at our line of thought and our discussion of biblical texts, the following becomes clear: individual pieces of tradition, with their formal individuality and history, not only have determined the written form of the gospels, but also have definitely influenced their *content*. From this it is evident that the sole concern of the biblical message is to give witness to faith. "The Evangelists are not satisfied with merely teaching the reader what the Master taught; they want this teaching to permeate his life. The spirit that animates them in this work is precisely that of the early Church. There tradition was understood as being not simply a mechanically exact repetition of the words of Jesus; it was a question of bearing witness. The words of Jesus are a leaven of life which the early Church hands down, clothed with her own life." [19]

The Law of the Written Copy: The Witness of Faith

"The gospels have their source in early Christian preaching, this word being understood in the comprehensive sense of mission sermon, parish catechizing, coming to an understanding with Jewish environment, all these in turn being at the service of the sermon. This means also that they are documents of faith for the early Christian community." These words of the Munich exegete, J. Schmid,[20] point to the gospel writings as an expression and reflection of scriptural proclamation in general. The law and mainspring of the proclamation of the faith are at once also that of its becoming written. Therefore, we must recall, at least briefly, the individuality of the New Testament proclamation; in particular we will answer the question about the historical accuracy of the reports about the words and deeds of Jesus.

Early Christian proclamation is *address,* a summons to belief in the *redemptive significance* of Jesus of Nazareth in response to the personal testimony and "reliability" of the preacher; it is a proclaiming of the reign of God as the new era of salvation and it includes a call for decision. In the center of this proclamation stands Jesus Christ *as the Risen One* (cf. Peter's sermon in Acts), as exalted Lord at the right hand of the Father, as One who, through His Spirit, remains present in His community. "Gospel of Christ," in the consciousness of the early Church, means the gospel that Christ Himself announces through His representatives, who are aware of being urged by the Spirit of the Lord.

Because Christ is present, the viewpoint of the preachers (and hence also of the Evangelists) is not that of the modern historian. Paul's proclamation of the faith, for example, uses many formulas of belief and preaching taken from current tradition, but he never relates an anecdote about Jesus. Such a thing would be unrealistic and could only convey a "knowledge of Christ according to the flesh" (2 Cor. 5:16). Preachers are not interested in chronology; they see no need to give an eyewitness account of historical happenings, for the Lord Himself is speaking here and now to everyone who hears the message of salvation. This word is a message of salvation as a word already present can be—or else it is not a message of salvation at all. In his book about Jesus, G. Bornkamm, exegete of Heidelberg, explains this peculiarity of early Christian proclamation and tradition: "One can go on to say this: the tradition is not really the repetition and transmission of the word He spoke once upon a time, but rather *is* His word today. In the relating of past history they proclaim who He is, not who He was." [21]

This is the reason for what seems to us today to be the remarkable and surprising combination of conscientious fidelity and ingenuous freedom in presentations of the sayings of the Lord. We find this fidelity and freedom in every comparison of the synoptics. The variations in tradition can ultimately be explained only by a growing lack of interest in historical sequence stemming from the conviction that our Lord is contemporary. This expression may appear to be harsh, but how else than by such a lack of interest due to lively faith can one explain the synoptics' reporting the activity of Jesus in such a way that one cannot with any degree of accuracy say how long Jesus taught and worked in public? [22] The synoptics give us no biographical or psychological information about Him, no portrayal of His character, no chronology of His development, no psychological motivations.

All this *dare* not be important if there is a question of believing in Christ. And this still holds true today. Faith in Jesus Christ is condemned to vagueness if devotional fancy seizes upon it and introduces into the text an interest that is foreign to the gospel. And so the variation of the particular descriptive devices used by the Evangelists is understandable. Since there is no question of the historical sequence of events, words and deeds of the Lord can be assembled according to *objective* viewpoints. Matthew, especially, arranges the material of his message to form compact areas of thought. The Sermon on the Mount, for example, is a thematic compilation of separate sermons of our Lord (Matt. 5–7); other instances are the instructions on the spirit of a disciple (Matt. 18) and the indictments against the Pharisees and Scribes (Matt. 23). Matthew places similar and related ideas together, cyclewise, in recording the deeds of Jesus, for example in presenting the nine accounts of miracles in chapters 8 and 9.

Mark and Luke are also acquainted with this technique (e.g., the five argumentative speeches in Galilee [Mark 2:1–3:6] and the parables about the lost sheep, the lost coin, and the prodigal son [Luke 15:1–32]). Mark, however, is not so severely systematic, and Luke, in the outline of his work, seems to wish to take into account the chronological course of events.[23] Often, one fragment of tradition is joined to another by a key word (key-word arrangement). Thus, for example, in Matthew 5:28 and 29, two statements of our Lord are connected because of the terms "to look at" (28) and "eye" (29).[24] Such a key-word relationship must be recognized if one wishes to avoid seeking or assigning a theological connection where none really exists. This kind of "contextual exegesis" has often led preachers astray, particularly in the average sermon.

Now there still remains the question as to when and in what connection Jesus delivered the various discourses attributed to Him. The crucial concern is with what He said, and whether the New Testament words attributed to Him are actually His words. They are His words. The speeches of Jesus have been handed down with great fidelity and reverence; [25] they always bear the stamp of genuineness, a fact which any apologetic study could easily demonstrate. However, one must "free oneself from the notion" that the speeches of Jesus in the synoptic gospels are "original units and verbatim renderings of what Jesus actually said on a definite occasion." [26] In contrast to apologetics, which must emphasize the historicity of biblical accounts, an initiation is directly concerned with making understandable the character of the Bible *as a witness to faith*.

Anyone who reads a biblical text with no other thought than to ascertain what *happened*, renders a personal understanding impossible. Scripture writers do indeed want to make theological statements, even when they are reporting historical happenings. Theological thinking and speaking based on faith does not "begin with itself" and so "cannot be satisfied with submitting mere tradition"; rather, it is essentially concerned with history and draws its life from a given story.[27] This seems so self-evident that one need not expressly enlarge upon the fact. For understanding, the only important consideration is that the gospels (in fact, the entire New Testament) are not eyewitness accounts, but professions of belief; not reports of once upon a time, but present kerygma, that is, proclamation of religious faith as a challenge that demands belief. The more strange this thought appears to our current thinking, the more necessary it is to familiarize ourselves with the theological individuality of the New Testament.

Since the New Testament writers want to witness faith in Christ, as we pointed out in our preliminary discussion of the Acts of the Apostles, they do not feel it is necessary to create an edifying biography of Jesus or a portrayal of His personality and His character. This fact is significant both for religion and for theology: Anyone who does not wish to throw away his key to understanding (cf. Luke 11:52), must let his interest in Jesus of Nazareth be directed only by what the New Testament says of Him. For example, one who cites the quotation, "Did you not know that I must be about my Father's business?" (Luke 2:49), in order to represent the "noble independence of Jesus' soul" [28] is making a false approach to an understanding of what Luke really wants to say.

This is all the more true if one, because of the absence of definite pronouncements, feels himself justified in making statements like the following: "Never do we hear from His mouth the admission that no other has ever failed to make: 'I have erred.' Never does He betray the slightest trace of surprise which could have disturbed or delayed His judgment. It is true, He did occasionally ask a question, but in such instances, one definitely has the feeling that He asked for the sake of others, not for His own."

By following such a method one can naturally paint an edifying picture (just as did those apocryphal gospels which were rejected by the Church of the second century). One can describe Jesus' exterior manner of life; one can speak about His "creative power and breadth of spirit," the acuteness and speed of His judgment," the "profundity and compass, the originality and independence of His knowledge," His strength of will and His "tender inner life," or of His fixity of purpose (proof: the twelve-year-old in the Temple), His self-possession, His moderation in thinking and willing (proof: the Son of God has not come to destroy souls but to save them [Luke 9:55ff.]), and His "concord and many-sidedness." But this method places us outside the realm in which the message of Jesus Christ can be perceived as it is intended to be heard, i.e., as a demand for conversion and a call to faith. One cannot be too insistent in warning against this sort of flight into the fictitious.

Another example: The expression, "I am the truth" (John 14:6), referring to the truthfulness of Jesus, is claimed to point to "perhaps the most conspicuous trait in the character of the Saviour." Enthusiasm for the veracity and the "inner life of Jesus" even leads to an interpretation of His death: "And while Pilate asks the cynical question, 'What is truth?' (John 18:38), Jesus allows Himself to be condemned to death, lest He betray a lack of confidence in the truth; He sacrifices His blood and life as a martyr for truth." Such romantic accounts of the life of Jesus are well meant, but they are astoundingly lacking in respect and good taste, and they mislead some who are seeking the genuine truth about Christ. One finds presentations of the life of Jesus which emphasize the fact that (unfortunately) no authentic portrait of the physical appearance of Jesus can be offered, that one can only resort to conjecture. But usually there follows a product of such conjecture as this: Whatever His human exterior may have been, He made an overpoweringly impressive appearance. An indescribable abundance of charm and mildness, of benevolence and love, of strength and discretion, of seriousness and majesty, of winning sympathy and royal dignity streamed forth from His person." Well, one could tolerate such meditations, but when, as an argument in favor of this "spontaneous effect of the appearance of Jesus," the reaction of Philip (John 1:45) is adduced: "Him about whom Moses in the law, as well as the prophets, wrote—we have found Him," then not only is the individuality of John's gospel unrecognized (cf. below), but the way to the Christ of faith has been barred, too.

The gospels are religious writings—that is the decisive insight for an "initiation." The mystery of Christ reveals itself in the historical fact of His human reality.[29] The testimony of the gospels concerning the story of Christ views events in the light of the end; it sees the life of the Lord in the light of Easter faith and therefore it is able to perceive the mystery of Christ as already operative in the wonderful deeds of Jesus. This thought will become more intelligible in what follows.

3. Proclamation and Prophecy

The Fourth Gospel

THAT WHICH MAKES the synoptic gospels testimonials of faith and theological writings, comes to light even more clearly in the fourth gospel. Here the consciousness of the fact that in proclamation the exalted and present Lord is speaking has reached its final result. In John it is fully evident that Christian proclamation and, above all, theological thought view the story of Jesus from the standpoint of its ending, that is, of death and resurrection. If there is a question of comparing John with the synoptic gospels, even a superficial view will make it evident that there is an entirely different style of presentation. In place of the loosely juxtaposed, separate pieces (pericopes) and sayings of the Master (*Logien*), there are here long and coherent speeches and dialogues. One clearly perceives the consciously shaping hand of a literary writer. The style of Jesus' discourses is different—no longer the popular, picturesque style of the Jewish teacher of the people, but the didactic guidance of thought of an intellectual; no longer the freshness of the spontaneous religious address but the maturity of theological contemplation.

This situation can be explained in a naïve way by saying that in the synoptics Jesus was speaking to simple folk, while in John He was dealing with learned men and politicians. But this explanation proves to be false even if one stays on the same plane as the naïve biblicist. In the gospel of John, Jesus speaks to the crowd

74

of common people (cf. 6:26f.; 7:37f.; 12:23f.) as well as to individuals of this class (4:7f.) in the same fashion. Also, the other
persons, the Baptist for example, speak in the same way.

On the other hand, if one knows how to read a text as text, one
will recognize in the different style of the fourth gospel a different *literary type*. Not only is the atmosphere of the utterance
different, but likewise also the point of view from which Christ
and the work of salvation are contemplated. "One receives the
impression that the Evangelist, as prophetic spokesman of the
exalted Lord, ought to pronounce before the assembly of his communities the revelatory announcements resounding from his
Master's very being, in such a way that through the word once
spoken, the present Lord might now announce and reveal Himself before His disciples and before the world entrusted to Him,
to the end that people should see Him and submit to His dominion." [1] Tradition about Jesus is still considered, but only in
separate passages; [2] relationship of the mystery of Christ to the
Christ-event rests on a phenomenology which contemplates the
mystery of the "incarnate Word" *as a whole*. It is true that John's
gospel also contains important historical data, for example, the
duration of Jesus' activity; but the historical happening *before* the
death on the cross and the actual fact *after* the resurrection are
projected into each other in such a way that one can no longer
say in the case of a certain expression that John puts into the
mouth of Jesus, that he means to report it as a "historical" word
of God.

The great thematic discourses of John's gospel, the so-called
"revelation discourses," may be understood as proclamation which
permits the exalted Lord to speak in the manner of theological
reflections. One might read, as a case in point, the conversation
between Jesus and the Samaritan woman at the well (John 4).
Here it becomes clear that there is no question of John's re-
producing a conversation verbatim; we can see that he is present-

ing in dialogue form a literary statement of the salvific significance of Christ and of the appearance (epiphany) of God in Christ.

"Why is it [the gospel of John] so obviously distinct from its three predecessors? Like them, it is a narrative of words and doings which testify that Jesus was the Son of God. But it is almost impossible to avoid the critical conclusion that, although the Fourth Evangelist depends upon and has made use of records of the words and actions of Jesus known to us from the synoptic gospels . . . he has refashioned everything that he has chosen to record in a consistent, literary form. Far from being composed, for instance, like the synoptic gospels, of short sayings and incidents, the fourth gospel takes the form of an almost continuous argument, which passes quite imperceptibly from narration to explanation, so that it is impossible, at times, to be sure whether the author is recording words of Jesus or commenting upon them. But this results in a new picture of Christ's ministry. Where are the short epigrammatic sayings, the semi-poetic aphorisms, the parables suddenly thrown out after the manner of the rabbis?" [3] Witness is being given to what Jesus is, not to what He said.

Just as His discourses present Jesus in symbolic image as the revealer of God, so also are His miracles, in a special sense, "signs." They represent the Word of God Himself in symbolic form: Jesus the light-bearer (in healing the man born blind), the dispenser of the true bread of life (in feeding the four thousand), the conqueror of death and giver of eternal life (in raising Lazarus). John consciously associates these miracles with the words that interpret them and point to the symbolic meaning of these occurrences (9:5; 6:26–58; 11:25f.). In all this it is evident that "the Evangelist has impressed upon the words of Jesus the stamp of *His* spirit and *His* speech." [4]

In John, *also the form* of presentation is determined by the knowledge already in evidence in the synoptic gospels without, however, having become effective as an element of literary style, viz., that the living Lord, the Kyrios, is the active subject of proclamation. The fourth gospel, as the form of its prologue (1:1–14) clearly shows,[5] is a unique kind of liturgical poetry. The proclamation of the Church "has reached that point on the level of Johannine proclamation at which proclamation changes into prophecy." [6] Therefore, it would be emphatically and theologically incorrect to characterize the form of John's gospel by saying that he puts his own theological thoughts into the mouth of the historical Jesus. It can rather be said that John knows himself to be the spokesman of the living Christ. Through him passes the word of Him who has gone out from the Father and come into the world and who now is again with the Father while still remaining with His own for all time.

Anyone who has once learned to appreciate the individuality of this prophetic picture language will have access to an understanding of the religious world of John. He will everywhere find contact with the mystery of the superhistorical Lord *in* the literary frame of the fourth gospel. This mystery can be penetrated only by means of prayerful pondering—an "initiation" must cease where reality begins. It can only sharpen the attention and inspire study. This study must first seek to comprehend the differences between John and the synoptics: the difference in their *material,* the changed *outline* of the message, and, above all, the new *style* of expression. In this form, the *content,* in its theological individuality, then becomes visible: the self-revelation of the Son of God, His universal redemptive significance, and, at the same time, the decisive character of faith in Him.

The Apocalypse

The New Testament message, from proclamation to prophecy, reaches its climax in the Revelation of John. If the prophecy of the Johannine gospel was still bound in the "frame" of the historical Christ-event, here the seer declares the "revelation of Jesus Christ which God has given him" (Apoc. 1:1) in the rare atmosphere of vision. In place of an intimate combination of proclamation and prophecy we now find pure prophecy. In spiritual apparitions, John the Apocalyptic receives the interpretation of salvation history.

But it is interpretation veiled in symbol which itself requires explanation. The mystery of Christ and of the divine plan of salvation is symbolized in images and allegories, in codes of mysterious numbers, colors, constellations, and animals. A true understanding of this mysterious book must be based on the interpretation of these symbols. Although the symbols themselves are not the subject of the revelation, the *apokalypsis* explains itself by means of these signs. Thus, the symbolism of the frequently recurring number seven would have to be explained, or that of the seven horns or the seven eyes of the Lamb (5:6), or again, the long garment (1:13) or the two-edged sword protruding from the mouth of Christ (2:12; 19:5).

Commentaries on the Apocalypse mention various interpretations. The basic mythological symbols of mankind, as they are found in Babylonian, Iranian, and Mandaean myths, in Hellenistic astrology, and particularly in Jewish apocalyptic writings about religious history—all these are sources from which explanations are properly drawn. Nowhere are the images exhaustively explained. But more recent research has been able to correct the most glaring misunderstandings of the past and to offer basic direction for interpretation. Accordingly, the medieval interpretation [7] based on Alexander of Bremen (about 1250) and Nikolaus of Lyra's book of sermons (1321) is an especially disastrous error that is still today of considerable consequence in some sects.

According to this interpretation, the Apocalypse proposes to foretell in allegorical pictures the actual course of history to its end. The epochs of world and Church history, even their leading figures, are supposed to be designated in the Apocalypse, cryptically, but still decipherably. It is held that the seven circular letters signify the seven epochs of Church history. It is plain that this type of allegorical exegesis misunderstands the text. For what the prophecy of the Apocalypse says about the end of this era and the dawn of the new age cannot be made to fit into the scheme of the historical passage of time. What is represented as a time sequence is rather the explanation of the eschatological salvific event unfolding in concentric circles around *one* central point. From a constantly changing viewpoint, a happening is described which, according to the existential time-notion of the Bible,[8] can be understood only as a personal event and can be described only by existential categories.

Only such an approach to the interpretation—let us call it the existential-eschatological approach—makes possible a true understanding of this book while at the *same time* adapting itself to the story of the author *and* to the eschatological future.[9] (The seven Churches of the Apocalypse are, in the first place, the actual communities at Ephesus, Laodicea, etc., of the first and second centuries, and only then vicarious symbols of the Church.) What was said about the existential interpretation of the mythological symbols in the New Testament holds true especially for understanding the Apocalypse, because here the prophetically affected being, in response to a call from God, becomes a witness to faith.

Whether the author of the Apocalypse, who calls himself John (1:1), is the beloved disciple John, or, more likely, John the presbyter of Ephesus, is unimportant for the *understanding* of the Apocalypse. The most ancient Christian tradition is not unanimous on this point.[10] On the other hand, there is no disagreement about this book's belonging to the canon of "holy" writings.[11] The effort to become personally engaged in its interpretation of the event of salvation and in the prophetic mood of its world of thought and symbol will mean for everyone a deepening and enrichment of his religious understanding.

4. Proclamation and History

Acts of the Apostles

IN THIS BOOK we find a new kind of vehicle for conveying God's word. It is unique in the New Testament and different from anything in ancient literature. The Acts of the Apostles is attributed traditionally to Luke, author of the third gospel, and, unlike the gospels, it is a genuine literary work. In this book Luke is no longer satisfied to set the separate fragments of tradition in their proper milieu and to connect them in such a way that the specific theological concept harmonizes with the material of tradition. He acts not only as editor but also as author in the full sense of the word.[1] His plan itself, to write a history of the time following the Ascension of Jesus, is without precedent.[2] Luke's accomplishment appears in the clearest light when one takes into account the variety and comprehensiveness of the source material that had to be assimilated.[3] He worked the various traditions about the discourses and deeds of the Apostles into a unified whole so successfully that modern research finds it almost impossible to identify the separate sources.[4] It seems probable that his tangible, written source was simply a list of the stations which Paul visited on his journeys—a so-called itinerary.[5] All other sources are completely fused into the new literary product.

If one wishes to grasp the individuality of this kind of presentation, one must call to mind Luke's literary design. Only then will a clear picture of the literary genre of the Acts of the Apostles emerge. Luke proposes to trace the route over which the gospel traveled from Jerusalem "unto the ends of the earth" (Acts 1:8).[6] He does not do this by writing a history of the apostolic Church, consistently noting all occurrences. It is evident that he saw no value in completeness of content or in precise chronology. He does not even recount the activity of all twelve Apostles. Outstanding in his story are Peter and Paul. Their success exemplified the triumphant spread of the gospel of Christ.

However, the "golden thread" in his narrative is not the labors of the Apostles but the propagation of the message of salvation through the operation of the Holy Spirit.[7] This shows that although Luke wants to present a historical account and gives his attention in the first place to recording events, his real design is not historical but theological. For him, historical events are worth recording only insofar as God's salvific activity and Christ's presence in history become apparent in them. It is of first importance for an understanding of the Acts of the Apostles to be aware of this fact, for it is the theological purpose of the book that renders understandable Luke's usual practice of not only reporting historical events but of previously interpreting them. He wants to show that things happen according to spiritual laws.

Thus, for example, it is quite likely that Luke (16:6f.) interprets the events of St. Paul's second missionary journey in accordance with his own "mission theology" and accounts for the route of the Apostle by assuming a direct intervention of the "Spirit of Jesus" (16:7). The Holy Spirit hinders Paul and his companions from following their plan of "announcing the Word in Asia" (16:6); the Spirit of Jesus also thwarts their attempt to go to Bithynia, compelling them finally to "pass by Mysia and land at Troas" (16:8). By means of these allusions, Luke renders not simply a historical account, but to some extent a theological interpretation of history.[8] As in Luke's gospel, so also in the Acts of the Apostles, one must always be prepared to find a theological concept consistently carried through. All problems of interpretation as well as the question of whether Acts is a source of history [9] are to be settled on this basis. All difficulties in understanding this book will have to be attacked with the thought in mind that in Acts, historical information and theological interpretation of history are combined to produce a unique piece of literature.

An Old Testament Example

It may seem arbitrary or even irrelevant, in an initiation into the New Testament, to refer back to the Old Testament. Yet the New Testament grows out of the environment of the Old; hence it makes sense to present the ground structure of biblical statements as *statements of faith* by means of an example from the Old Testament. We have recognized witnessing to the faith in the gospels as the law for writing them—as the motive and fundamental principle for that writing. This law is based on the very individuality of the Old Testament. The Old Testament books, too, even the "historical" books of Israel, are witnesses to the experiencing of God in faith, and they receive their literary and objective theological individuality from it. Here also is the foundation of the uniformity of the Old and New Testament way of thinking. This very uniformity justifies us in speaking about *biblical* thinking in the sense of a historical and objectively new kind of potentiality in religious thinking—a potentiality without which, even today, Christianity cannot be understood.

In the "model" from the Old Testament, particular attention must be paid to the relationship between the assertions of faith and history, respectively. As an example, we have chosen the accounts about Elias from the Third Book of Kings (chapters 17 to 19 and 21). They take us into the time of King Achab, that is, to the earlier half of the ninth century before Christ.[10]

The figure of Elias plays an important role in Old Testament and in Jewish post-biblical thinking. In the New Testament, along with Moses, Abraham, and David, he is one of the most frequently named Old Testament figures.[11] In addition, there are many popular tales and sagas, as well as three "apocalypses" from the third and fourth centuries after Christ, that deal with Elias. The reason for this active interest in him may be the tradition about his being taken up to heaven (4 Kings 2:11),[12] and the later prediction of his return (Mal. 3:23; Septuagint 4:4). But what are the biblical accounts to which such a rich tradition owes its origin? And upon what historical happenings do the accounts of the books of Kings rest?

These two questions are really *two*. Remembering the history of the New Testament structure, one will find this self-evident; for in Old Testament texts more than in the New Testament, one has to presume that the written form of an account comes only at the end of a long-existent tradition, and that this tradition survives and is handed on in definite, more or less fixed forms and literary types. The time interval between the happening and the final formation of the currents of tradition by the Old Testament writer is greater than in the New Testament domain. The Elias accounts, for example, appear in their final redaction [13] only after an interval of three hundred years from the events reported, despite the fact that the development and organization of the Elias tradition began soon after the occurrences, and in the books of Kings written sources were already prepared.[14]

But such a process of handing-down always includes reshaping and expansion, since the reproduction is motivated by a definite intention. What became apparent in the case of the history of tradition-forms in the New Testament will show up here, too. The intention that determined the form of the Elias tradition is of a *theological* nature. It is necessary to understand this "theology of the Elias accounts," and therefore the religious significance of the prophet-figure, in its actual historicity. For this endeavor we

must again pose the questions that are fundamental to all interpretation: How are the statements meant; what realities do they
signify; from what style of thinking do they stem, and why are
they so formulated, and not otherwise?

The text first tells about the famine, the altercation between
Elias, messenger of Jahweh, and the servants of the Canaanite
deity of vegetation, Baal, and God's judgment on Mount Carmel.
This thread of the narrative is advanced by the account of the
end of the drought: Elias, praying, awaits the beginning of the
rain but is then seized by the Spirit of God and runs ahead of
the chariot of the king in ecstatic jubilation. For Jahweh is again
Lord over Israel and now blesses her anew.

Into this lucidly developed composition several "anecdotes"
or "scenes" are inserted: the feeding of the prophet by ravens
(3 Kings 17:2–7), his miracle of oil and flour for the widow of
Sarephta (17:8–16), and the raising to life of her son (17:17–
24). The meeting with Abdias, house minister of the king
(18:7–16), and the appearance of Elias before the king (18:17–
19) are other separate anecdote-like pieces of tradition. A second
complete composition is given in chapter 19: the encounter of
Elias with God on Mount Horeb. The account of the judicial
murder of Naboth in chapter 21 is again a complete piece of
tradition paralleling the actual course of the narrative.

If we next ask about the relationship of the accounts to historically ascertainable events, our stories agree in several important
details with historical accounts from other sources. Not only 3
Kings 17:1, but also Flavius Josephus records a great drought at
the time in question. This Jewish historian of the first century of
our era, in his work, *Antiquitates Judaicae* (VIII, 13:2), refers
to Menander of Ephesus, a historian of the second half of the
third century before Christ. Menander wrote a history of Phoenicia, using the original documents in the archives of Tyre.
Therefore he is cited quite often by Josephus as witness to the

historical correctness of biblical accounts. According to the testimony of Menander, a one-year drought [15] had devastated the land in Phoenicia at the time of King Ittobaal of Tyre. One may assume that this refers to the same drought as that found in 3 Kings 17. For in addition to historical, there is also in our case literary evidence which proves 3 Kings 17:1 to be a statement of a genuine historical background for the events touching Elias.[16]

Similarly, the historical background of the story about the decision on Carmel (18:19–40) can be proved: [17] The region around Carmel had fallen to the double kingdom of Juda-Israel after David's victory over the Philistines. Originally, Canaanites inhabited the territory. The Israelites who settled there under David and Solomon apparently erected the altar to Jahweh which, according to 3 Kings 18:30, was later destroyed. Since the list of countries in 3 Kings 4:7f. no longer mentions Carmel, this region had most likely already become the property of the city-state of Tyre, which later relinquished it to Achab. More and more, the Israelites living there were exposed to the Phoenician Baal-cult and "finally turned in both directions" (3 Kings 18:21), which means that they worshiped Jahweh and Baal at the same time. The decisive conflict involving the prophet Elias begins here. Whoever is in possession of the sanctuary on Carmel determines the "official" religion and therefore also the government of the land with its mixture of Canaanite and Israelite inhabitants. King Achab submits to the demand for a "war of gods" and acts very prudently in the affair, because he had to be king over both nationalities. The outcome of the "war of gods" is a constitutionally valid decision.

A third historically available element of the Elias accounts ought to be mentioned. In 3 Kings 21, King Achab attempts to acquire a piece of land from his subject Naboth by means of an exchange. But Naboth hesitates to give up the vineyard he has inherited. So the king has someone slander Naboth and then incites the crowd to stone him. This story agrees in all details with the one that is known from contemporary history. Israelitic agrarian law forbids the sale or exchange of family property;[18] the claim of the king, on the other hand, derives from Canaanite law and would extend the absolute kingship of the Orient over Israel also.[19] The accusation of blasphemy gives the king the chance to have the crowd stone Naboth, thereby disposing of him with legal sanction. Naboth's property goes to the state treasury, as provided by law. It is from this legal murder, the scriptural account of which agrees exactly with the historical tenor of the law, that the story of the prophet's interference and his religious mission takes its origin.

Now then, do the biblical accounts of Elias agree with history? This question may now be asked, for, even if more numerous and more exact historical data were available, it would still be clear that the text is not at all intended to present "history." The text clearly indicates that it is to be understood "theologically," since it is designed to speak about God and about Him alone. Therefore, to read an Old Testament text correctly, one must first and always inquire into its "theology." The theology of the Elias accounts can be recognized chiefly from the literary setting in which they are handed down. The author of the books of Kings fashions the "annals" of the various kings according to a fixed pattern of criticism. The crucial question is whether or not the king tolerated heathen cults. For the theology of history in the books of Kings determines the weal or woe of Israel by the attitude of her king toward God: whether his heart is with Jahweh or not.[20]

Achab too is judged from this viewpoint. As a result, he appears in a much less favorable light than history would justify.[21] His figure within the historico-theological pattern of the books of Kings is in some measure overshadowed by the power of the Elias accounts, which, as independent pieces of tradition with their own dynamism, are enclosed in a setting that is foreign to them and there go beyond their limits. For the religious self-consciousness of Israel, Elias is the man of God who, in a critical hour of history, rescues and propagates belief in Jahweh. To emphasize this, Achab and the entire plan of the author must give way.

To grasp the "theology of the Elias stories," one must first of all take into account the "setting"; but then, as a second step, one must try to understand the character of Elias himself, as well as the purpose for which these reports and tales about him were written. In the various parts of this narrative, it becomes clear that Elias is the prototype of the man of God in traditional religious thought. He is the one who, like Moses, asserts Jahweh's claim to sovereign authority in Israel. The portraits of all later prophets are modeled on this archetype. Elias teaches not only a "theoretical monotheism"; he makes this belief in Jahweh effective in the everyday life of Israel. He is, as G. Fohrer says, the representative of a "practical monotheism." [22] He does not discuss and deny the existence of Baal; he is fighting to establish the worship of Jahweh instead of Baal. The triumph of faith in Jahweh over the worship of the Canaanite god of nature, Baal, is *the* great theological theme of *all* fragments of the Elias tradition, particularly the stories of the drought and the bountiful rain, of God's judgment on Carmel, and the interrogation of the oracle of Achasia.

The actual prophetic statements about Jahweh serve the same theological end. It is a new trait in Israelitic thinking that is manifested when drought and rain are attributed to the intervention of Jahweh. Theology before Elias considers God as the master of nature only in extraordinary manifestations of power, such as the annihilation of the enemy and the preservation of His chosen people: He sends locusts and blood upon Egypt and feeds the Israelites with manna and quail. Thus, Elias teaches Israel to see the hand of God in affairs that were formerly understood to be subject to the deity of vegetation, Baal. Now, Jahweh and only

He sends or withholds rain and sunshine. In this way the concept of God was broadened and enriched so much that it served as an effective counterpoise to the worship of Baal.

Moreover, the account about the appearance of God on Mount Horeb brings new features into the picture of Jahweh. It is plainly the intention of this story to complete that of the visible manifestation (theophany) of God in Exodus 19; Israel was to see God under new symbols of experience. In Exodus 19, He was seen under the "veil" of storm, fire, and earthquake; here, the symbol is that of a gentle breeze. Elias tones down the features of the vision of Moses. The God who bursts forth in a storm becomes a calm dispenser of blessings upon the earth. Again, this new portrayal of God's self-communication makes it possible to establish anew Jahweh's claim to dominion and thus to maintain, active and strong, the faith of the fathers.

After one has recognized this fundamental trait as the real reason behind a passage, one will find an approach from the whole to the separate parts of the Elias tradition. The key to understanding, here as in the forms of the New Testament tradition, is the literary genre. If, for example, it is the *theme* of the preliterary tradition and of the literary setting of the matter to be transmitted to establish belief in Jahweh, then the accounts about Elias are to be classified as *theological writings* and *not as historical accounts*.

We have seen the relationship between what is recorded in a text and what is known about events from available, historical data. To understand the Bible, however, it is much more important to observe the theological peculiarity and purpose of the accounts and thus, before all else, to recognize their divergence from history writing in the modern sense. The significance of the figure of Elias can be explained only in theological categories. But what are the "theological categories" of our accounts? By what means is the "intrinsic truth" of the prophet-portrait shown?

What potentialities and what liberties does religious thinking possess in representing as he truly is, a prophet called by God?

Israel produced a great number of literary types to express its witnessing to the living God. There are *epigrams* (sayings that refer to worship or law; proverbs and riddles); there are *songs* (working and drinking songs; love and wedding songs; lampoons; dirges; war and victory songs; finally, the great religious hymns). Besides these, there are many prose types: speeches, prayers, records, annals, and the poetic narratives such as fairy tales, fables, short stories, sagas, and legends. All these are expressions of a culture that has developed through the centuries, and many of them belong to the best of world literature.

One who wishes to read and interpret them has to be able to understand the language of all these different types. He must learn to listen; he must have a sympathetic understanding of a strange and historically distant culture. Annals of the Old Testament, for example, belong under historical accounts, but follow the rules of ancient Oriental history-writing, which are different from those governing the modern presentation of historical facts. One who was not willing to consider this fact—one who, for example, wanted to interpret the so-called historical books of the Old Testament as precise, eyewitness accounts—would not only explain them unhistorically, and therefore unrealistically, but would also not be taking Holy Writ seriously.

In his *Atlas of the Bible* Grollenberg makes this observation about scriptural history-writing: "When . . . a number of books of the Bible were listed as historical, the inevitable result was that readers now judged their contents by the standards of modern notions about history. Besides, belief in their divine origin helped to create the view that the Holy Books complied with the demand for objectivity and historical reliability to a far greater degree than any other book. The starting point for evaluating Scripture was the idea that the various biblical accounts dealt

only with historical events—with naked, solid facts . . . Thus
arose the type of literature called Bible history. Through this
literature, in the context of the historical books, history from the
beginning of the world till the death of John the Evangelist was
finally understood in the same way that the history of Rome, for
example, would be understood in any profane book. Only gradually did the realization dawn that this way of understanding biblical accounts was in error." [23]

To comprehend Scripture as its authors meant it to be understood, all depends on whether one agrees that the Bible speaks
about God and His dealings with men. However, on this plane of
religious testimony, all the potentialities of human speech are
utilized to draw attention to the mystery of the relationship between God and man. But this mystery goes beyond the limits of
what appears as an *external* historical fact. Hence the religious
thinking of the Old Testament had to find a path that would lead
toward the *intrinsic* truth of an event. This way was, above all,
the saga, the classical means of the most ancient biblical strata of
tradition for reflecting and holding fast the religious experience
of God's dealings with man.

In the saga, the religious truth of an event expresses itself. As
in the case of annals, the saga arises from a happening.[24] It is related to history, just as Old Testament faith is essentially related
to historical time. "The forces which formed the saga are in
essence identical with those which reigned supreme in history." [25]
The Israelitic saga is the record of a nation's encounter with God,
and as such it is "genuine, historical material" (Buber). Being
closer to reality than the so-called historical account, the saga is
able to express the essence of faith and history. "Accordingly, it is
not a question of belief or disbelief, but simply a question of more
penetrating knowledge . . . whether one will understand a traditional tale of the Old Testament as saga or as history. And the
anxious worry that the Old Testament would lose by the accept-

ance of such sagas is also totally unfounded," says H. Gunkel, the originator of the so-called history of types.[26]

After these reflections, let us take another look at the stories about Elias. We recalled the historical background of the events involving him; we deduced the theological purpose of the Elias tradition from the text. In answer to the question of the form which the ancient Oriental world usually employed to present the inner truth about a religious figure, we found that it was the saga. On the basis of these findings, the possibility now arises of advancing our understanding of the books of the Old Testament by penetrating more deeply into them, especially the accounts about Elias. In these stories there are some so-called "motifs" which also appear in the presentation of other stories. Most noticeable is the relationship of the Elias stories to the Moses tradition. The parallel is carried through, even to individual features: the forty days and nights, the cave of Elias and Moses' cleft in a rock, and, most telling of all, the use of the same word for the passing by of Jahweh in both narratives. This parallel construction brings out even more strikingly the contrast between the two appearances of God—as fire, cloud, and lightning on the one hand, and as a gentle breeze on the other.

Also, besides the two encounters with God on Horeb, we find that the Elias and the Moses traditions share a historical motif.[27] The competition of the prophets on Mount Carmel reveals the features of the contest which Moses carries on with the Egyptian sorcerers (3 Kings 18:20–40 and Exod. 7:8–13, 20–22; 8:2–28), and the information (3 Kings, 17:6) that Elias receives bread in the morning and meat in the evening conforms to the same motif-pattern by which the Israelites in the desert were fed with manna (bread) in the morning, with quail (meat) in the evening.[28]

From these parallel motifs, we see that the two men of God, Elias and Moses, are considered and represented from the same point of view, and always with an eye to religious experience, which never loses sight of the partnership between God and man, even when it pretends to be recounting historical details. The same thing is true when we compare the stories about the prophet Eliseus with those about Elias. The same "motifs" are applied to both of these men of God, in order to illustrate their religious significance. The story that is told about Elias and the widow of Sarephta is also applied to Eliseus (4 Kings 4:1–7). Also in their resuscitations of the dead (3 Kings 17:17–24 and 4 Kings 4:18–37), one cannot fail to recognize the parallels. From this it may be deduced that in these anecdotes or, also, sagas, there is no intention of communicating isolated historical events. The purpose is, rather, to show that a specific prophet, here Elias or Eliseus, is understood and presented as the bearer of a theological message.

Research into the history of types points the way to an insight into this theological aim of communication. This course can lead us not only to a deeper knowledge of the historical restrictions to which the Revelation of God has submitted; it will, above all, render faith free to acquire a more profound, matter-of-fact, ingenuous attitude because, finally, the Revelation of thousands of years is beginning to speak directly.

CHAPTER FOUR

Interpretation and Penetration

The Letters of St. Paul

WE NOW TURN OUR ATTENTION again to the New Testament and consider a new form of proclamation: the letter. More than a third of the New Testament consists of letters, of the actual correspondence of one man directed to a particular individual or to a group of people. The ancients were familiar with fictitious letters, too. These are devices of clever literary men to lend the colorful vividness of a personal letter to a narrative, a report, or even a treatise. The New Testament epistles, however, are completely unliterary communications not even remotely intended as exercises for sharpwitted theologians who might turn and twist every word in an effort to distill a doctrine from them. They are a kind of address, every thought of which has reference to a definite occasion, a specific person, or a particular community; every word has grown from the circumstances and conditions that arise in human association and speech. Anyone who desires to understand an epistle fully must keep in mind the origin and the milieu of the writer and his style of thinking and expressing himself, as well as the living conditions and the individuality of those whom he is addressing. One must never try to understand and explain a passage "in isolation," nor separate the "what" of a statement from the "how" of it. The "how," the "why," and the "wherefore" figure so strongly in the inner law of form governing words and thoughts that this law not only produces the message and then, separated from it, is contemplable; it also is the essence and innate dynamism of the message.

One who knows how to read an epistle of St. Paul as a letter, as a witness of faith, of the experiencing of God, and of Christian theology—such a one will also be in a position to evaluate the other New Testament epistles. Therefore, we shall consider the letters of St. Paul as exemplary witnesses to New Testament letters in general. The justification for this choice of a model lies simply in the plan of our initiation; in addition, however, there is the uniqueness of the Pauline writings, which may be characterized as theologically the most significant, humanly the most fascinating, and historically the most instructive letters of the New Testament. Moreover, they constitute the oldest parts of the New Testament as a whole, for the first epistle of Paul to the community in Thessalonica, modern Salonica, was written in its present form only some eighteen years after the death of Jesus.

1. The Influence of Writer and Receiver on the Form of an Epistle

WHAT KIND OF PERSON is it who is writing this letter? Which currents of tradition does he draw from? What is the nature of his thinking and feeling? Who are the people to whom he is writing? Why is he writing to them? Most important, why is it helpful to ask these questions if one wishes to read his letters with understanding, joy, and profit?

We have to understand the character of this man who, as no other Apostle, has influenced the lives and thoughts of Christians down to the present day. But to understand him means to know how he understood himself before God and before the community of the believers in Christ. Paul likes to call himself a "slave of Christ" and he sees in Christ his Master; but *this* relationship of service is unique, since he never knew the earthly Jesus personally. Nevertheless, he considers himself as an *apostle*, as the last of the "Twelve" to be chosen, as having the right and duty to claim equal authority with those "who were in our company along with the Lord Jesus" (Acts 1:21). The hour of his selection occurs in his experience with Christ on the way to Damascus (Gal. 1:15–21; Acts 9:1–9), when the Lord appeared to him also (1 Cor. 15:8), forced him to the ground, and made him His "chosen instrument for the heathen nations." Grasping the meaning of this incident and accepting its consequences are henceforth the basic preoccupations of Paul's life.

The thoughts of this learned theologian now center on the powerful Lord who is able to divest Himself of divine transcendence and take the fate of a man in hand, requiring obedience. Slowly, Paul grasps the truth: He whom he has encountered is endowed with that power which Israel of old recognized as the "becoming-present" of God: He is endowed with the Holy Spirit of God. By the symbolic word "breath" or "breath of wind," biblical thought grasps the greatest mystery of religious existence, viz., that God, who is above and outside history, communicates Himself and becomes experienceable in the innermost heart of man. This, for Paul, is the solution of the old problem of religious history of how man might come into contact with God. He has learned by experience that "the love of God is poured into our hearts by the Holy Spirit" (Rom. 5:5).

And this power of the divine "becoming-present," which Paul calls *pneuma*—breath, or spirit—he sees being transferred to the risen Lord, Jesus Christ, who has been lifted up to the super-historical plane of God Himself. Christ has power to impart the Spirit. That is why communication between Him and man is possible. Therefore, Paul's experience with Christ at Damascus is as real as his own being.

For this reason too, the most significant declaration, existentially speaking, that Paul can make about Christ is contained in that famous and oft-misunderstood sentence in his second letter to the Corinthians: "The Lord is spirit; and where the Spirit of the Lord is, there is freedom" (3:17). In this sentence is expressed Paul's way of comprehending how the Kyrios, Christ, is able to intervene in human destiny and make it serve God's purpose: Such a thing is possible because Christ has power, as Spirit of God, to make Himself accessible to the experience of man. What the believer experiences in himself as effective power, what, as a driving power, tends toward God (Rom. 8:26)—this is to be attributed neither to a potentiality of man nor to a spontaneous, superhuman demoniacal power. It is Jesus Christ. " 'The Lord is spirit' means that in Christ, God comes to man in a manner that lays hold of him profoundly, that liberates, opens, creates, converts, re-creates—in a word, Christ comes as grace." [1]

We began to examine the religious life of St. Paul in order to be able to understand and evaluate his letters. It has turned out that in this process we have begun almost imperceptibly to talk about Christ. One has to speak about Christ in order to understand Paul. For Paul's understanding of himself is completely dependent on his understanding of his Lord. The fundamental law for a life based on Christ also holds true here. A person who says of himself, "No longer is it I who live, but Christ lives in me," cannot be characterized in any other way than by describing him in his relationship to Christ. Paul's relationship to his *Kyrios* grows out of his experience of Christ's power over the Spirit, for it is this alone that makes such a relationship possible.

This thought already constitutes the first step of our initiation into the epistles of St. Paul. If one constantly bears in mind that Paul is conscious of a habitual, direct exchange of life with his Lord and Master, thanks to the divine power of the spirit, one will gain a better understanding of the central thought patterns of the Apostle according to Scripture. The meaning of the spiritual development of the community, of unity in the Church, of the presence of Christ in His Church and in her proclamation and tradition; the meaning of freedom from sin, law, and death, and finally, the meaning of resurrection from the dead—none of these can be made understandable except through Paul's conception of the *pneuma* of Christ.[2]

It is true that Paul understands the spirit, the *pneuma*, in a manner that will astound many a reader. Upon hearing the word "spirit," one person may think of "the spiritual" as distinguished from the physical and material; another may think of the third divine Person as represented in systematic theology and in the dogma of the triune God. But neither of these interpretations agrees with Paul's way of thinking; both are foreign to him. *Why* his thoughts and opinions are different from those of current philosophical and dogmatic language, and *what* basic rules will enable us to ascertain what he wanted to say—these questions can engage our attention only in another connection.

He who wishes to speak about Paul must speak about Christ. But equally necessary is a second consideration: Whoever wants to understand Paul must appreciate his relationship with his churches. True, it is not the business of an initiation into biblical thinking to describe the concrete parish conditions of the Pauline churches. That belongs to the classical "Introduction to the New Testament." Still, anyone who attempts to plumb the depths of Paul's unique being must recall that in the life of the Apostle, not only is *Christ* living in him, but in a sense the *rest of mankind* is also. The welfare of his churches is his constant concern. The "care of all the churches" (2 Cor. 11:28) is with him always.

It lies in the very nature of this man of dialogue that he admits his fellow-being completely into his own existence. And anyone to whom Paul has once opened his heart will never let him go. How moving is his love for his people Israel (cf. Rom. 9–11)! Ever and again, the fate of this nation tortures him (Rom. 10:1): a blinding "veil covers their face" (2 Cor. 3:15); they no longer experience their Lord; and their piety (Rom. 10:2), because it is mere legal worship (Gal. 3; Rom. 9), is a useless beating of the air. In Romans, Paul has written a sentence which, as no other, reveals the range of his spirit and the profound devotion of his heart: "I speak the truth in Christ, I lie not, and my conscience testifies in the Holy Spirit that I am bearing great distress and unceasing pain in my heart. Indeed, I would even wish to be anathema from Christ for the sake of my brethren, my kinsmen according to the flesh" (Rom. 9:1–3).

The same passion for giving himself to others binds him to his churches: "Gladly will I offer myself and even be entirely consumed for your souls" (2 Cor. 12:15; cf. Phil. 2:17). To the Philippians, "his longed-for brethren, his joy and his crown" (Phil. 4:1), whom he carries "in his heart" (1:7), he writes: "God is my witness that I long for all of you sincerely in the love of Jesus Christ" (1:8). In writing to the Galatians, he expresses both personal and apostolic concern: "I should like to be with you; I am suffering distress regarding you" (4:20).

In the first letter to the Thessalonians, there is a bold and beautiful image: "As a mother presses her children to her heart, thus did we feel toward you and wanted to let you share not only in the gospel but also in our inmost selves, for we had learned to love you" (1 Thess. 2:7f.). The sentiment that here bursts forth longs for reciprocation; his dialogue-inviting admission begs a reply: "It would be a consolation for me to know that I am being supported by the zeal of your love, not only while I am with you" (Gal. 4:18). "If I love you so extravagantly, shall I then find a more meager return of love?" (2 Cor. 12:15).

But this is not all. If one wishes to understand the relationship of Paul to his churches, it is necessary to consider the further fact that Paul knows himself to be an apostle of Jesus Christ, and that he, like "the Twelve" (1 Cor. 15:5ff.–8; Gal. 2:7ff.; I Cor. 9:1ff.), has from Christ full authority to preach. Only by keeping this fact in mind, can one understand the peculiarity and justification of some of his statements. Thus Paul says: "*I command* you through the grace that has been given to me . . ." (Rom. 12:3). This *grace* is the apostolic authority by which Paul *must* speak (1 Cor. 9:16) and from which he knows: "My speaking and proclaiming did not consist of persuasive, epigrammatic sayings but of demonstration of the Spirit and of power . . ." (1 Cor. 2:4). Yes, he can even say: "We come as ambassadors in the place of

Christ, since indeed God admonishes through us. We beg you in Christ's name: Be reconciled to God" (2 Cor. 5:20).

What self-understanding stands back of those words? What picture of God's salvation message is before Paul's eyes? At the end of his letter to the Romans (15:19), he says that he has brought "the gospel of Christ to completion from Jerusalem all the way around to Illyricum." Bringing the gospel to completion means not simply that Paul has announced the content of the Christian message completely, without being silent about anything. Rather, an understanding of the "gospel of Christ" is operative here which, though unfamiliar to us, is self-evident to Paul. The "gospel of Christ" is a redemptive act of God that will be realized in man at the hour when the ambassador of God announces and proclaims it. In the procedure of announcing, the truth announced will become reality. Concretely: Wherever the dawning of God's dominion is proclaimed, this dawning will become actual—"a power for salvation to everyone who believes" (Rom. 1:16). Thus, the "gospel" is not simply in the first place a report about past happy occurrences—in the way that perhaps many understand the expression "good news." Rather, it becomes the accomplished salvation message about things to come, and men can assimilate it existentially into their lives through faith.

To "bring the gospel to completion" means, then, to actualize it, to make it a power in one's life—a creative occurrence—to allow it to come into its own in that one proclaims it. This understanding of the "gospel of Christ" is founded in the Old Testament. It is only through Hebraic thinking that Paul's conception of himself as apostle and authorized announcer "in Christ's place" can be explained. Only in the circle of biblical thinking is this existential concept of a message of joy and salvation possible.[3] The existential category, "for me," is known only to biblical thought, since this thought alone is constantly concerned with the personal dialogue between God and man. The salvific act of God can be realized and the result of what is proclaimed can be brought about, only when and insofar as the word of the proclamation goes forth and takes effect within the horizon of the existential "for me." When Paul employs the formula, "for everyone who believes," this is what he means. Let us consider the relation of Hebraic-biblical thinking to *time*. For precisely what we understand by "time" makes it difficult to appreciate the primitive Christian gospel as address and creative occurrence.

For us, the gospel is the written proclamation of the faith composed at a definite and ascertainable point in history. In this context the time of the proclaiming and writing, and the year 1965, are two points on one time level, representing two points of view that are separated from each other by a constantly growing space of time. We speak of the great *space* of time which lies between ourselves and the Apostles, and we think of a long *interval* of time as lying behind us. Our representation of time is spatial and therefore governed by quantity. As especially E. v. Dobschütz [4] and T. Boman [5] have demonstrated, this is a Greek heritage. The Hebrew thinks in a different pattern. For him, the mere passage of time considered as quantity plays no role. For him, time is identical with what has happened or is happening in it. He looks upon the *content* of the event, and therefore thinks of the quality of the respective time.[6] Time is not a chronological process and hence a mechanical passage; it is rather a happening that becomes occurrence in rhythmic condensations: "A time for weeping and a time for laughing; a time for complaining and a time for dancing; a time for being silent and a time for speaking; a time for loving and a time for hating; a time for war and a time for peace; a time to be born and a time to die" (cf. Eccl. 3:2–8).

This happening must not be thought of as an "event in itself." Rather, it is entirely and absolutely dependent on the bearer of the action or suffering, or, with particular reference to mankind, the speaker at any given time. For Hebrew thinking, there is no such thing as "time in itself"; there can be only "my time" or "his time"; there is no absolute time—only relative time. "The consciousness of the speaker is the fixed point." [7] In this way, history becomes a rhythmic interplay of time *contents*, a dynamic union of completed and uncompleted. But the still uncompleted may become simultaneous with the completed if the contents of both times should come to coincide. "Strict simultaneity is therefore the same as psychological identity, since two spiritual contents converge." [8]

Our attempt to initiate ourselves into the manner of thinking which underlies the biblical concept of a creative occurrence of the salvation message (and which, moreover, also furnishes the key to an understanding of biblical eschatology) here arrives at its salient point: The "time of the gospel" can "for me" become occurrence, since this "time" is not to be thought of as a distant *space* of time or *interval* of time or a *point* of time, but as a happening which is able to develop its dynamism in such a way that for me its content becomes simultaneous. In other words: The "at-that-time" of the message of redemption can for me become a "now"—the past can become present—if I "realize" the proclamation, if I cause the rhythm of my being to coincide with the message of redemption.

This explains how Paul can speak "in Christ's place" and present his proclamation as the present salvific act *of God*. In doing this he is not trying to raise the value of his activity by means of solemn exaggerations; he is simply ingenuously adhering to his nation's rule of thought as a foregone conclusion, that is, to the Hebrew concept of time. Against this spiritual background he also writes his epistles, so that we can recognize the following stipulations as the intrinsic laws of their form: first, the peculiar relationship of Paul as the "latest called" workman, to his *Kyrios*; then, the significance of his encounter with Christ at Damascus

and his constant experience of the Spirit; then, his human attach-
ment to his congregations, and, above all, his conviction that he is
an apostle and a preacher of God's salvation message, "in Christ's
place."

2. Didactic Writing or Epistolary Address?

THE UNIQUENESS of the circumstances which determine the range of ideas in a Pauline epistle makes it understandable that a particular passage should not be understood today in terms of itself in isolation from other considerations, since it was written into a letter and was therefore a message to someone. For example, in the seventh chapter of the first epistle to the church at Corinth, there appear statements that are, it is true, formulated as general truths and which at first sight one could misunderstand if one wished to make out of them a "Christian doctrine about marriage and virginity."

At the beginning of the chapter, Paul says, in reply to inquiries from the congregation: "It is good for a man not to touch a woman." Now, when one considers the reality, one finds it difficult to understand this statement—all the more so in view of the account of creation (Gen. 2:18; cf. Tob. 8:6): "It is not good for man to be alone." And the sentence: "But if you marry you commit no sin" (verse 28)—doesn't this impress one as being a provoking concession of a rigorous ascetic? Likewise, verses 3 to 5 indeed refer to the "duty" of the conjugal debt but at once add that this "duty" is mentioned only as a concession, not as a law. The passages cited, in fact the entire seventh chapter of First Corinthians, would produce an almost grotesque picture of the Pauline-Christian theory of marriage if one expected to find literal "doctrine" here. (In fact, it has often been asserted that for Paul, marriage is nothing but legitimized incontinence.)

105

However, if one reads chapter 7 as an instruction in letter form, one gains radically different impressions. *Who* is dictating the letter to *whom* and under *what* circumstances? These are questions that must first be considered. Only then will it become clear what is *meant* and what *content* the form of the letter and its several statements designate. At what situation are Paul's words directed? In the case of the Corinthians, to whom, notoriously, no vice was unknown, Paul condemns unchastity with such severity (1 Cor. 5:1-13; 6:12-20) but the question might well arise as to whether every kind of sex relation were not forbidden to a Christian. W. Schmithals formulates the question of the community as follows: "If relations with a prostitute are denied us, does that mean that, even in marriage, we should abstain from sex relations as much as possible, or even that we must either dissolve the marriage or, if unmarried, remain celibate?" [1]

Against such radical ideas, Paul expressly maintains that married people have a right to the body of their spouses (verse 3f.), and he exhorts them not to deprive each other, unless by mutual agreement they wish to devote themselves wholly to prayer. Even so, he tells the Corinthian married people, it must be only for a time, "lest Satan tempt you." Thus, Paul keeps his feet firmly on the ground of high regard for marriage, in accordance with Jewish, Old Testament ideas. It is clear to him that everyone should so live as the Lord has directed and God has called him (verse 17). For each is fitted out with the gift of grace allotted to him (verse 7b), the one for the married state, the other to remain single.

Some might now object that in verse 2 Paul betrays the full measure of scorn for matrimony: It is only to escape the evil of incontinence that anyone should marry at all. But this interpretation of the verse is again much too abstractly systematic. In reality, the sentence, "Because of unchastity, let every man have a wife and every woman a husband" (verse 2), was addressed to the church of Corinth. But if that is the case, then the sentence expresses neither a wearily resigned admission nor the universally valid assignment of a purpose for marriage; rather, it is a recommendation: Because of the danger of unchastity (in view of the prostitution nuisance in Corinth), every Corinthian man ought to have *his* wife and every woman in Corinth *her* husband. If it were a general rule of Christian life, the demand would be absurd in another way also: in the sense of St. Paul, there could be no such thing as an unmarried state for a Christian; but Paul himself offers the strongest arguments against such a view.

Also in this regard, the fact remains that Paul's thinking about men and matrimony is sober. Still, he is not filled with that rejection or condescending toleration of matrimony which might grow out of an ascetic philosophy of life. This becomes evident when one considers his attitude toward virginity, how he justifies it and why he recommends it. We just recalled his dictum that it is better for a man not to touch a woman, and we said that this thought, taken as a general truth, is not understood in a manner consonant with Paul's intention in uttering it. What is his intention? Are there other thoughts expressed in chapter 7 which point in the same direction?

In verse 8 he advises the unmarried and widows to remain like himself, even if it be only on condition that they not "fall into difficulty." In this case, Paul would concede that it is better to marry than to burn (verse 9). Verses 26 and 40 also would discourage marriage, and in verses 32 to 34 we read the misleading sentences: "The unmarried man is concerned with the Lord's affairs—how he can serve the Lord.[2] The married man is concerned with things of the world—how he can be of service to his wife—and he is divided. The unmarried woman or the virgin devotes herself to the Lord's interests, so that she may be holy in body and mind. The married woman thinks about the world—how she can serve her husband." Again, these words "in themselves" place marriage and "living for the Lord" in an opposition which would admit of only two possibilities: either they "are not to be taken so exactly" or marriage should be rejected completely.

Now, to ascertain the meaning of the situation, one must allow it to speak for itself. This situation is to be understood only "historically." Paul himself characterizes it with the sentence: "The time is short" (verse 29); and again: "The form of this world is already past" (verse 31). This is the key to an understanding of the entire chapter. What Paul thinks about marriage and non-marriage is expressed with a view to the parousia of the Lord, the moment when He comes in glory after the course of this world has come to an end, when the prince of this world will have to disappear and God will hand over to His Christ the government of the world. In other words, everything is said with a view to the time when the ancient promises of a new heaven and a new earth will be fulfilled.

Paul sees this moment as very near at hand. Of the two Greek words for time, "chronos" denotes the mechanical passage of time and "kairos," on the other hand, refers to a space of time that is limited and characterized by particular circumstances, such as, in this instance, the interval still remaining before the parousia.[3] And this period is "condensed." Things to come are already the law of the present hour. Therefore, it is wise not to "establish" oneself any more in the world nor to arrange one's affairs according to its pattern. (And here lies the Archimedean point from which the thoughts of St. Paul about marriage and virginity can be explained.)

For the world is already at an end, and Paul feels justified in advising everyone to "remain as he is" and not to marry at all. In a certain sense, it will not pay to do so any more. He who is married should remain so; he who is engaged should not marry; he who is still free should not seek a bond. But why will it not pay any more? Because the parousia, which Paul believes is immediately at hand, is bound up with the terrible crisis of this era. This crisis will bring "tribulation of the flesh" (verse 28) for the married man; since he is united with another, he will experience the final affliction as double distress. He worries about the world, and *he must do so*—the sentence in verse 33 is not meant disparagingly—since he must be at the service of his wife and is responsible for her, too (verses 4, 5, 33).

Paul thus describes very simply the order of this world: Thus it is and thus must it be. But since the married man has to support his partner, Paul, considering anticipation of the final crisis easier to bear in the single state, wishes the Christian of the last times to be free, to be spared the "tribulation of the flesh," and to be "free from worry" (verse 32), so that he can await the Lord with independent and undivided mind. Undivided attention and spiritual vigilance seem to be the decisive factors. For Paul, as for Jesus, the advice in favor of remaining unmarried is not an ascetical summons; it is his personal advice. In verse 25, the Apostle states expressly that he has no command from the Lord about this matter. Still, it is a recommendation made against the background of imminent expectation, which makes it understandable. Furthermore, in view of the crisis before which the message of the Lord's return has placed all earthly, human existence, the advice is meaningful and will remain so as long as the Church is waiting for the Lord.

It has now become apparent how decisively the historical and existential situation of the writer affects the thought content of a letter. The real meaning of the seventh chapter of First Corinthians will not be found except by way of an interpretation that constantly takes into account the historical situation of St. Paul and his understanding of his role in salvation history. This also means that the letters of the New Testament require "existential interpretation." Only after feeling one's way into the writer's religious convictions will one be able to see through his message.

Any attempted explanation that passes up this "detour" will miss its mark. One can never fit the movement of thought from a New Testament epistle directly into a system by naïvely proclaiming a passage to be the "word of God." One must first consider the historical milieu and the human flavor of this word as a key to understanding. Remember, the letter is an address; it is not direct doctrine. It is the address of a definite person to definite partners. And even when, in a letter, a "lesson" is formally imparted or an item of doctrine is simply conveyed, that is done with a definite motive: to substantiate, to prove, or to appeal.

The theology of St. Paul is one man's explanation and penetration of Christ's salvation message. It becomes the standard of all theology from the fact that it belongs to that understanding of the message of Christ which is still within the body of apostolic tradition.

Here, too, the rule holds: Not only *what* is said is significant, but *how* it is stated is also so important that it demands attention for all time. Historical interpretation, then, is the basis for every objectively systematic deliberation.

CHAPTER FIVE

Present and Future: A Key Concept

ANYONE WHO HAS FOLLOWED our initiation thus far may perhaps be disheartened. Is it actually so difficult to understand the Bible? Does one really have to be so concerned about the time in which the New Testament came into existence? Is not the Bible applicable to all ages and therefore also fundamentally intelligible to every age? Is it not sufficient for an understanding of it to apply sound human intelligence in a spirit of devout reverence for Holy Writ? And the Catholic will ask: Is it not enough—indeed, must it not suffice—to understand Holy Scripture according to the criteria of spiritual awareness possessed by the average member of the Church, and thereby to read the various passages, let us say, in the same spirit that one would listen to a Sunday sermon? Are there really still new aspects?

An answer to the last question would take us beyond the limits of our initiation. Only the future, only prolonged labor in the field of biblical theology, will answer this question. With respect to the other questions, let us propose the following thesis for discussion: There can be no adequate knowledge of what the Bible wants to tell us until we have inquired into the original historical meaning of a given statement, that is, until we have sought out the literal sense of the Bible. Hence, no serious study of Scripture can dispense with the method of historical criticism. In order to prove this thesis, we shall again discuss a central thought of the New Testament.

In the terse sobriety of the oldest gospel text, the beginning of

111

Jesus' public activity in Galilee is described in the single sentence: "When John had been delivered up, Jesus went to Galilee and proclaimed God's message of salvation: 'The time has come and the kingdom of God is at hand; be converted and believe in the message of salvation'" (Mark 1:14-15). This sentence makes known all that Jesus would do; it epitomizes all He would say, and indicates who He is. That the blind will see, the lame walk, lepers be healed, and the deaf hear; that the dead will rise, and— odd in this list—salvation will be preached to the poor (Matt. 11:5); that Jesus will speak in parables (Mark 4:33); that He will dare to use the powerful expression, "but I say to you," in his Sermon on the Mount; that He will finally climb the road to the cross—this is all based on the Good News: The reign of God is near.

Every sentence of the New Testament is set against the background of hope that God will rule over the world. No matter how one understands or judges this belief, the New Testament cannot be understood, even as a testimony of the history of religion, unless one takes into account the intended force of the expression "Kingdom of God." Anyone who wishes to read the New Testament, even if only for the sake of information—anyone, above all, who wants to grasp its contents will necessarily have to keep in mind the watchword, "regal rule of God." Present and future, God and history are so dialectically bound together in this key phrase that neither the picture of God (theology) nor the picture of man (anthropology) nor the interpretation of history as found in the Bible can prove meaningful without it.

An initiation into the New Testament must devote much attention to the biblical representation of the kingdom of God. We shall not do that here in the style of biblical theology, which assembles and presents, if possible, all the declarations of the New Testament according to historical and methodical points of view.[1] Instead, we shall try to show, using a single text as model, how n like manner they have persecuted the prophets before you' (Matt. 5:1–12).

St. Luke's version of the beatitudes will surprise many a reader: "But He looked at His disciples and said: 'Blessed are you poor people, for the kingdom of God belongs to you. Blessed are you who now go hungry, for you shall be filled. Blessed are you who are now weeping, for you shall laugh. Blessed are you when men hate you, reject you, insult you, or rob you of your good name on account of the Son of Man. Rejoice on that day and be glad, for you are assured of a great reward in heaven. Your fathers treated the prophets in the same way. On the other hand, woe to you who are rich, for you have already received your consolation. Woe to you who now eat well, for you shall have to go hungry. Woe to you who are now laughing, for you shall find cause for lamenting and weeping. Woe to you when everybody flatters you. Your fathers acted in that same way toward the prophets'" (Luke 6:20–26).

The differences between these two versions strike one at once: Matthew records eight beatitudes, Luke only four; but Luke compensates by adding four antithetical laments, which Matthew does not have. Matthew has Jesus speak in third person ("Blessed are the poor in spirit"), thus creating a disparity between the speaker and the listeners. It is evident that he is thinking less of the first audience of Jesus and more of his own, for whom his writing is intended. In Luke, however, Jesus speaks directly to the readers of this gospel: Blessed are you poor. These two observations in themselves permit us to assume that Luke has preserved the form that is closer to the original.[4] For terseness and directness may generally serve as characteristics of the more original version of the text.[5]

Still, let us consider not only the form but also the content of the words. Blessed are the poor in spirit—this certainly is a word of consolation for the destitute, who have neither

the proclamation of God's dominion pervades
As our example, we have selected the beatitude
on the Mount. These will lead us toward the cent
mation of Jesus, and they are at the same time part
to our contemporary way of thinking.[2]

In no other passage of the New Testament doe
clearly, so simply, and so paradoxically revealed that
a message of salvation. Proclaimed blessed are the po
gry, the sorrowful, the despised—and these words st
beginning of that collection of our Lord's discourses tl
sternly and without compromise the conditions for adm
the Kingdom of God. To whom are the beatitudes a
Here again, one cannot pave the way to understandin
by a comparison of the forms in which the passages ha
handed down to us.[3] In a discussion of the beatitudes, such
parison leads very far and is at the same time a valuabl
toward an initiation into synoptic reading.

The text of Matthew is familiar: "But when He saw the c
of people, He went up the mountain. After He had seated F
self, His disciples approached Him. Then He opened His mo
and taught them as follows: 'Blessed are the poor in spirit,
theirs is the kingdom of heaven. Blessed are the sorrowing, f
they shall be comforted. Blessed are the meek, for they sha
possess the land. Blessed are those who hunger and thirst fo
righteousness, for they shall be satisfied. Blessed are the merciful,
for they shall obtain mercy. Blessed are those who have a pure
heart, for they shall behold God. Blessed are the peacemakers, for
they shall be called the children of God. Blessed are those who
suffer persecution for the sake of justice, for theirs is the kingdom
of heaven. Blessed are you when people despise and persecute
you and falsely accuse you of all manner of evil on account of Me.
Be glad and rejoice, for your reward in heaven will be great. For

money, nor property, nor power, nor even influence over their own fate. Nevertheless, "Blessed are the poor in spirit," says Matthew. Whatever may be the exact meaning of this statement, this much is evident: Matthew's text appends something that detracts from the social tone of the original setting. Can those who are materially rich still be "poor," according to Matthew? The second beatitude of Matthew also takes a more spiritualized and expanded form. It is not the poor who are hungry, who are addressed; rather, it is all those who hunger and thirst for righteousness. This not only adds a new thought; it alters the tone of the whole. What Luke offers as a word of comfort has here become a "catalogue of virtues" (J. Schmid) or a short catechism (G. Bornkamm).

But what significance is to be attached to these divergences between Matthew and Luke? Let us attempt to answer the question in several steps. First, we are concerned with the sense of the original presentation, in this case that of Luke. Only then can we proceed to the text of Matthew. Finally, the two forms of the statement should be compared on the basis of their common meaning. Therefore, the questions are: What does Luke say? what does Matthew say? and, lastly, what does the New Testament say?

According to Luke, Jesus looks at His disciples and exclaims: Blessed are you poor, for the kingdom of heaven is yours. He is speaking not only to the Twelve, the inner circle of trusted friends, nor yet to the great crowd before Him; it is to those who have already followed Him in a spirit of faith that He now speaks. This fact is important because it forbids our applying the demands of the Sermon on the Mount only to a small circle of chosen ones; but it also indicates that only those who have already bound themselves to the Lord by faith will be able to understand. To whom, then, does the word "poor" apply? Is it to those who possess no means and no power? Yes! The text here requires us to change our thinking so as to accustom ourselves to a basic trait of biblical thinking, viz., that God stands on the side of the poor. The salvation that Jesus is proclaiming is a prophetic message from the Holy God, who comforts the poor by lifting them out of the dust and dirt of their existence (Ps. 113:7) and cheers them by "establishing His throne" among them, the downtrodden and the abased (Isa. 57:15; cf. 49:13).

This concern of God for the poor can be observed throughout the entire Old Testament. One who wishes to enter intimately into the biblical conception of God will have to learn to bear with the severity that lurks in the thought of this partiality of God for one particular class of people. Some have attempted to understand the poor (*anawim*) to be the pious (*chassidim*) and in this way to dissociate the salvation promised to the poor from external circumstances of the life of those thus favored. So much is true: the poor are declared blessed, not *because* they are destitute but because in their need they have been looking for deliverance by the hand of God. But they can expect everything from God only because they can expect nothing from the world. Their behavior before God is bound to their situation in the world.

Thus, in the beatitudes of Luke, it is actually the destitute and therefore the despised who are meant. It is to the "little people," the oppressed, the humiliated, the wronged and despised who do not observe the "law" and are therefore rated as inferior and third-class; [6] it is to those who have no connections, no assurances for their life—it is to all of these that the words are spoken: The kingdom of God is yours. To these people on the dark side of life the Messiah is sent. "The Spirit of the Lord rested upon me because He has anointed me; He has sent Me to bring the salvation message to the poor, to proclaim liberation to the captive and eyesight to the blind; to release the oppressed, to announce the Lord's year of grace." Luke places this word of the prophet (Isa. 61:1–2) as a program at the beginning of Jesus' public activity (4:17f.), and the fulfilling of this word runs like a leitmotif through the entire gospel.[7]

"Enlightened" religiosity, which looks upon the relationship between God and man as purely a disposition of mind, is frightened by the biblical notion that God takes cognizance of the social position of a person. Anyone who interests himself in the biblical world of ideas must become accustomed to the fact that the relationship of man to God is based entirely on the indivisible being of man. In the Bible this is not meant in an abstract, moral sense; it is something concrete in the sphere of Jewish Old Testament revelation, viz., that God as a matter of course takes a different attitude toward the poor than the one He assumes toward the rich, simply because "poor" and "rich" are not accidental, ultimately unimportant, merely external circumstances of life—as, for example, a Platonist might well believe. Rather, poverty and riches are conditions of our human existence in which a definite degree of receptivity for God is already included. For biblical thought, "poor" and "rich" are realities that bear direct significance for salvation.

This is not the place to discuss Jesus' stand with respect to wealth.[8] We shall simply cite a few of His expressions: It were easier for a camel to pass through the eye of a needle . . . ; one cannot serve God and mammon; the laments of the Sermon on the Mount. The severity of these expressions of our Lord shows clearly that it would be wrong to try to water down the beatitude regarding the poor by alleging "spiritualization" (neither does Matthew do this, as we shall see). This severity above all shows how completely the whole life of man on earth is dependent on God.

This interrelationship of "life in the world" and "life with God," this "worldliness" of the Christian message belongs to those elements which determine the individuality of biblical accounts and also to some extent the manner of their presentation. Unless one keeps in mind this tendency to express ideas concretely, one will often not even know what the author is talking about.

In this connection, what is the meaning of the promise which Jesus appends to the beatitude: "For the kingdom of God is yours"? Has not many a reader suspected that the beatitude in favor of the materially destitute was meant to comfort the poor, as it were, with a promise of future beatitude? If they have been shortchanged in this life, they may at least nourish the hope that their lot in the "life after death" will be happier. This suspicion can easily arise from religious thought of a general, static character. The unbiblical pairing of "here" and "hereafter," which are understood to designate two timeless levels, one above the other, distorts the meaning of what the beatitude of the poor promises and also makes more difficult an understanding of what the Bible intends to say in the expression "kingdom of God."

The original Greek phrase does not signify something in the sense of "hereafter" as though it were not already always on the way toward men. Moreover, the corresponding Hebraized expression of Matthew, "kingdom of heaven," does not indicate a "kingdom that is or will be in heaven," but rather the "reign of Him who is in heaven. It is something otherworldly in its origin and not simply because of the place where it will be established." [9] Closely allied to this conception is the biblical idea that the reign of God began with the proclamation of it by Jesus, though it still continues to be a future otherworldly kingdom. The parables of the self-sprouting seed (Mark 4:26–29), of the mustard seed (Mark 4:30–32), and of the weeds among the wheat (Matt. 13:24–30) show that for the New Testament concept of the history of salvation the seed of what is to come has already been dropped into the ground and is growing to produce a harvest. This dialectical structure of the reign of God, in which the present is present only because it is related to its opposite, the future, and only the two as simultaneously "planted" can establish the full actuality—this is the "mystery" which only the believer "to whom it is given" (Mark 4:10-12) will be able to grasp.

Our endeavor to offer an initiation into the Bible has now reached a decisive point.[10] The entire New Testament, and in particular the beatitude of the poor, will not be understood unless this double character of the reign of God is seen as background.

We have already mentioned the tendency of Hebraic thinking to perceive present and future as dynamically intertwined. Applied to the representation of God's kingdom and to the clause, "for yours is the kingdom of God," this means: The new situation of salvation in history, which becomes actual with its proclamation by Jesus, since God will establish His final dominion over *this* world and will be "all in all" (1 Cor. 15:28), can already be "laid hold of" by those to whom it is given.[11] But it is given above all to the poor, whose hearts are so empty that they have room for something new. It is because of this emptiness that they are declared blessed and capable of that joy which streams into the heart of the believer as soon as he abandons himself to God. The "kingly reign of God" is indeed at the same time future and present actuality for the New Testament: future because it will not be completed until the end of this present world; present because Jesus has already announced His message and because man, by the conversion of his heart and his turning to Jesus, can gain a share in the powers of the One to come (2 Cor. 5:17).

Since it is true that a man can lay hold of the coming dominion of God over the world as a potentiality of his present being-in-the-world, the beatitude concerning the poor is not an attempt to console on the strength of the hereafter. Since the poor man and the one rejected by the "vast world" can incipiently admit into their interior life the joy of the final wedding (joy that can be described only as spiritual), precisely because they are poor and empty, the kingdom of God as God's eschatological activity means for them a reality by which their concrete being is determined just as substantially as by their need.

Also, for the believer in Christ the dominion of God is a reality and just as much a condition of his existence as the condition of "poor" or "rich." That, however, two worlds—the realm of the power of God and the concrete, earthly circumstances of man's life—far removed from each other as they may be according to our way of thinking, can still become "existential" for Christian self-understanding, is a kind of concretizing and a "making worldly" of otherworldly actualities; and this is unmistakably possible within the dynamic thinking of the Bible.

Only within biblical thinking is it possible to put "salvation" and the "kingdom of God" on equal footing.[12] The rule of God as something in the future is already present and active as a new potentiality of one's being-in-the-world; for this reason it can be "my salvation." For the believer, salvation is not the fruit of the immanent potentialities of his self-understanding. Rather, salvation is given to him by spiritual generation (cf. Jas. 1:18: "begotten by the Father of lights through the word of truth") as a new source that cannot be traced back to himself. Since the transcendent rule of God can become salvation, the Christian need not put his hope for the salvation of his being in historical progress or any other exercise of self-redemption.[13] Therefore, the demand of the Sermon on the Mount to expect *everything* from God is not an extravagant absurdity.

One word more regarding Matthew's beatitude in favor of the poor. What does he mean—and what does he not mean—when he refers to those who are "poor in spirit"? The average person might understand the Evangelist to mean either those who are "poor in the Holy Spirit," that is, those inspired by the Holy Spirit to be undemanding, or those who are "poor of spirit" (more specifically, weak of mind), that is, obtuse.[14] Matthew means something else. Apparently he wishes to obviate a misunderstanding to which this original form of the Lord's words, "blessed are the poor," could lead, namely, that the poor are simply proclaimed blessed because they are poor, regardless of their attitude toward their plight. We have seen that in Luke, too, such an interpretation of the first beatitude is impossible. Moreover, for Luke all depends on whether a man sees his need as a reason for expecting salvation from God, whether in his heart he submits, and whether he calmly accepts poverty as his lot.

The meaning of Matthew's phrase, "in spirit," is exactly what we deduced from Luke's version of our Lord's words in the context of his whole gospel, and from the meaning of the Hebrew word for poor (*anaw*). We might say: Blessed are those who are poor in their heart, in their inmost soul. One who is poor in his heart; one who regards himself as the poor man who expects nothing from the world and nothing from himself, but expects all things from God; one who possesses not only the purse but also the soul of a poor and humbled man—to such a one is promised a share in the dominion of God, that is, in a word, salvation.[15] Therefore also, the expression "blessed are the poor in spirit" says the same as Luke's wording about those who in any situation of their lives have to endure actual want or real danger to life. Hence, too, the next verse speaks simply of "those who mourn." [16]

The fundamental religious behavior which the addition of "in spirit" demands is of such a nature that it can be realized only on the basis of actual distress. That misery and want, and riches, too, are not exclusively financial conditions is taken for granted in biblical thinking. The word "poor" may be applied to everyone who has been demoted, defrauded, or is unsatisfied; to everyone whose life is scarred by disillusionment and privation of love, recognition, or freedom. But to all of these many aspects of poverty, it is common that they bespeak actual misery so real that it changes the life of the person, prejudices it, or even, perhaps, strikes at its vital core.

Matthew's version of the Lord's words, then, in no way detracts from their eschatological significance and prophetic dynamism. In the proclamation of salvation, this dynamism refers precisely to the poor,[17] in that God turns toward those who are truly abandoned and promises them the joy of His kingdom. What kind of doctrine would follow if one wished to interpret the sentence about the poor in spirit in a "spiritualized" form? Matthew would be saying: It is unimportant whether one is poor or rich, in want or well filled; the only important thing is the conviction that one is a beggar in the sight of God. Such an interpretation would take all the force out of his beatitude. It would then be nothing more than one item of a universally applicable table of Christian virtues.

One must become accustomed to the thought that the beatitude of the poor really applies only to those who are living in misery and want, be it from lack of material goods or a lack of love. This does not mean that one who is rich, whether in property or in the high esteem of men, cannot be a Christian; but *this* beatitude is not directed to him.[18] Any kind of moral judgment that ascribes certain merits to one and denies them to another is completely foreign to the beatitudes.[19] This prophetic passage is intended for no other purpose than to comfort (Luke) and to appeal to men to allow themselves to be comforted (Matthew). This is apparent in Luke but also evident in Matthew as a basic intention. And its prophetic power rests heavily on the fact that its promise applies to the poor man without any question whatsoever of an equivalent achievement in return.

So much for the beatitudes. We have not attempted an explanation of the text as a whole,[20] but have touched only those questions whose clarification might be particularly valuable for a more profound encounter with the New Testament. This representation of God's dominion would not fit any other historical picture, whether religious or political, not even that of Jewish future expectation. Here, in the New Testament, it proves to be a key to understanding.[21]

"All the beatitudes are directed toward the coming kingdom of God and are embraced in one idea, that God wills to be present with us and will be with us all, in as manifold and individual a way as our needs are manifold and individual. With special clarity, therefore, these very words of Jesus show that the kingdom of God cannot be described as can an earthly thing or a distant wonderland—every attempt to 'define' it can thus only come to grief—for it is a happening, an event, the gracious action of God." [22]

CONCLUSION

A Pressing Question

AFTER WHAT HAS BEEN SAID, there still remains a pressing question which we cannot easily evade. It is the question of whether the Bible is the "word of God." Is not the nature of Holy Scripture misunderstood if we speak of the various utterances of the Lord as having been compiled by an editor, introduced and supplemented by means of transitional passages, and even, very possibly, changed? Is not the inspiration of the Holy Spirit denied by conceding such great significance to the "theology" of the community or of an individual author? Does not this sort of biblical theology confuse the faith of the Christian? Does it not surrender the final bastion of Christianity when by synoptic and historical comparisons, by source analysis, literary criticism, and existential interpretation, it at least apparently calls in question the unity of Holy Writ as revelation inspired by the Holy Spirit?

All these questions are combined and at the same time aggravated by the question of the relationship between the Church and the Bible. This is, in the first place, a historical question: To what extent does the historical birth of the Bible belong to the realm of the community of the faithful of the first century? But this is also a problem of the present: To what extent is the correct understanding of the Bible—today and always—dependent upon the right understanding of the Church? The answer to the present-day question may be gathered from history. A glance at history shows that one cannot speak of the Bible without thinking of the Church, for it was the Church that produced the Bible.

This is most clearly recognized by the more recent exegetical research, which very definitely maintains that there was a living tradition *before* there was any definite form in writing, that is, that there existed a "gospel before the gospels," as it were. Anyone who has entered into the New Testament can easily realize that the Bible without an actively believing community is just as unthinkable as a child without parents. The so-called canon-formation substantiates this statement. In the course of the second century, there grew in the Church the realization that she was obliged to accept a certain list of writings while others, the so-called Apocrypha, she did not consider obligatory. By this decision of great theological consequence, the Church bound herself to maintain an unalterable criterion which from then on stands above her (though not outside her). This criterion is the so-called Canon of Scripture. It was possible for the Church to formulate a Canon by her own authority only because she is conscious of a superior vital continuity which has already, on its own authority, produced the writings giving testimony to Jesus; because she knows that she herself has grown out of the environment of apostolic proclamation and that this proclamation is guaranteed against error by the living Lord.[1]

This intimate connection of Scripture and the Church justifies the conclusion that the *Church* provides the milieu in which the individual can enter into the message of the New Testament and experience its significance for salvation. Membership in an assembly of believers is a necessary condition for understanding the New Testament as witness to Christ; but it also provides the prospect of understanding this witness intimately.

The Church, which, as the original Church, issued the Scriptures and by the establishment of a fixed Canon bound herself in such a way to her origin that any post-apostolic church could be a church only insofar as it was united with the original Church and transmitted this origin as origin—this Church rightly possesses a consciousness that the Holy Scriptures are "inspired" and that they have God as their author.[2]

The traditional explanation of inspiration can no longer assimilate the conclusions of modern exegesis and church history. However, in 1958 Karl Rahner proposed an explanation of inspiration[3] that not only exposed the absurdities of the traditional view,[4] but also offered a new approach. His concept of inspiration provides an answer to the questions of historians that is so revolutionary that it might well meet with universal approval. Hence, in the following we are expressly following K. Rahner.[5]

To invoke the thesis he develops in detail, we will begin by saying that for Rahner inspiration is assured by the simple fact that God established the Church. God is the author of the Scriptures by virtue of the fact that He wills the Church to be such that she produces the Scriptures out of her own being, as witness to the consciousness of her faith—a witness growing out of the creative power of her life. "The inspiration of the Scriptures . . . is but simply the causality of God in regard to the Church, inasmuch as it refers to that constitutive element of the Apostolic Church, which is the Bible" (pp. 50–51).

To understand how the Church could come to know which books had God as their author, we must take a look at the primitive Church. Of course, God's will to save men gave her a unique, unrepeatable mission to fulfill. Not only does the primitive Church represent the temporal beginning of the Church, but also, as the historically tangible realm in which revelation still occurs, she represents that time in which God acts in a manner in which He will never again act, even to the end of time. The primitive Church is the time of the first generation—the time when the Church is yet to come into existence. (Naturally, when theology says that revelation ceased at the death of the last Apostle, it means this time, not a calendar date.) The primitive Church is the Church in the process of being born (cf. pp. 44–46). "God, then, as the founder of the Church, has a unique, qualitatively not transmissible relationship to the first generation of the Church, which He has not in the same sense to other periods (or, rather, which he has to these only through the first)" (p. 44).

But this Church, whose birth process continues for a definite time—so we may conclude with Rahner—is, in all her really essential acts, originally and expressly launched and steered by God precisely because she is an evolving Church. (We say "essential acts" to exclude those which do not belong to the perfection of her being, such as conflicts and disagreements.) She is, "therefore, in a unique and eminent sense the work of God: *Deum habet auctorem*" (p. 45). Hence she is also the "permanent ground and norm for everything that is to come. It is the law according to which the whole course of the Church is being steered" (p. 45).

Consequently, the era of ecclesiastical tradition begins only *afterwards,* growing under the assistance ("*sub assistentia*") but not under the inspiration of the Holy Spirit ("*sub inspiratione Spiritus Sancti*"). It is "*norma normata,*" not "*norma normans.*" With Möhler, Geiselmann, and Söhngen, we may assert that the apostolic proclamation is a "plenteous source" to which nothing can be added.[6] Everything that follows receives its right of existence and its dignity exclusively from this source.

The development of Scripture belongs, then, to the life functions of the primitive Church which were willed by God in a unique manner. Scripture comes into being as a result of the vital process of the early Church. It is the deposit of her faith, her preachings, her written word. This has a twofold meaning: Because Scripture is an expression of the life of the *primitive Church*, it shares her individuality and binding power, that is, her canonicity. Because Scripture came into being as an authentic *expression of the life* of the primitive Church, the criterion is thereby given for recognizing which books have God as their author. And, indeed, this is a standard which is not concerned with the qualities present in the writings, which, in the opinion of the theologians, could not have led to a safe judgment about inspiration (pp. 24–25). By what right could one, for example, exclude the letters of Ignatius of Antioch? [7]

It is true that in the nature of things (since God is the author) a certain knowledge about actual inspiration is made possible only by divine revelation. A revelation from God, which is always a historical transmittal of redemption, cannot simply be understood as an explicit statement; it is possible rather, as "fact presenting itself" (p. 66), that is, as an intervention of God. As applied to our question, this means that revelation of the fact that a certain writing is inspired "is simply given by the fact that the relevant writing emerges as a genuine self-expression of the primitive Church" (p. 65). Therefore, one does not have to take refuge in historically unlikely hypotheses, for example, that the individual Apostle received the revelation (but how?); that his letter was inspired; that he then communicated this fact, and that this communication was handed down in the Church. The factual history of the Canon, with its long period of uncertainty concerning the judging of individual writings, shows how unfounded such an assumption is (e.g., the epistle of Barnabas of the "Pastor of Hermas") (pp. 64f.). The historical report and the theological inquiry into the "how" of revelation therefore opens up a historically tangible space of time for the writing to come into existence, and for the slow development of the consciousness that this particular writing is an authentic fruit of the self-realization of the primitive Church, in other words, that it is inspired.

For anyone who is seeking in the Bible the authentic testimony of Jesus Christ, this understanding of the words "primitive Church," "Canon," and "inspiration" will show the mutual relationship of Bible and Church. Therefore, it is still true today that Bible and Church are the two signposts that mark the path to Jesus of Nazareth.

Notes

Introduction

[1] J. W. Goethe, *Poetry and Truth from My Own Life* (Public Affairs Press, 1949).

[2] K. Rahner, "Current Problems in Christology," *Theological Investigations* (Helicon, 1961), I, p. 154.

[3] Evangelicals agree with this view: "All schism has its root in a difference of theology," writes P. Häberlin in *Das Evangelium und die Theologie* (1956), p. 12.

[4] Pope John XXIII, Address of January 30, 1959, *The Pope Speaks*, vol. 5, p. 274.

[5] For the Catholic interpretation of Scripture and tradition to be applied here, cf. the end of this book: "A Pressing Question."

Chapter One

[1] Cf. the last chapter on Church, Scripture, and inspiration.

[2] K. Girgensohn, *Die Inspiration der Heiligen Schrift* (1926), p. 46.

[3] W. Dilthey, *Die Entstehung der Hermeneutik, Gesammelte Schriften* (1926), p. 46.

[4] For the distinction between true and substitute symbol, cf. K. Rahner, "Zur Theologie des Symbols" in *Cor Jesu* (Rome, 1959), p. 467: "We would arrive at merely secondary aspects of the nature of symbols if our point of departure were that two realities, which were presupposed both to be already existing in themselves in their nature and to be intelligible in themselves, were like one another in some way, and this similarity could offer the possibility that each of the two realities might point to the other, might draw attention to the other, might be used by us precisely as a likeness of, as a symbol for the other; in this way symbols differ from one another (and so can be distinguished) only according to the degree and the more or less exact mode of the two realities' superficial similarity. Since each reality has some sort of similarity with all others, this approach toward an understanding of symbols would offer no possibility by which one

could distinguish genuine symbols ('real' symbols) from merely arbitrarily determined signs, signals and numerals ('representative' symbols)."

5 E. Cassirer, *The Philosophy of Symbolic Forms* (Yale, 1953), I, p. 106.

6 *Ibid.*, p. 108.

7 Concerning these general rules of interpretation, followed since the time of Aristotle, cf. R. Bultmann, "Problem der Hermeneutik" in *Glauben und Verstehen*, II, p. 50, under the reference to W. Dilthey.

8 J. W. Goethe, *Farbenlehre*.

9 Explicitly, for example, in 2 Cor. 5:7 that we live by faith and not by visible form. *Eidos* may not be translated actively as vision. Cf. G. Kittel, *Th. W.*, II, p. 372. Also, the biblical representation of εἰκων, ὅμοιος (ὁμοίωμα) and μορφή shows this understanding. For the ideas mentioned, cf. *Th. W.*, II, pp. 378ff.; IV, pp. 750–62; V, pp. 186–88, 191–97.

10 Augustine: "Let neither of us say that he has already found truth. Let us seek it as though it were unknown to both of us. For then we shall be able to seek conscientiously and harmoniously if neither of us arrogantly presumes to assert that he has already found it" ("Contra epistulam quam vocant Fundamenti," *C. S. E. L.*, 25, p. 195).

11 Thomas Aquinas: cf. Dominican transl. of *Summa Theol.*, I, p. 14.

12 "Between the creator and the creature so great a likeness cannot be noted without the necessity of noting a greater dissimilarity between them." Denzinger, *The Sources of Catholic Dogma* (B. Herder, 1957), p. 171.

13 H. Schürmann, *Aufbau und Struktur der neutestamentlichen Verkündigung* (1949), p. 52.

Chapter Two (Part 1)

1 Cf. especially the peculiarity of biblical parables, pp. 62–66.

2 W. F. Otto, "Gesetz, Urbild und Mythos" in *Die Gestalt und das Sein. Gesammelte Abhandlungen über den Mythos und seine Bedeutung für die Menschheit* (1955), pp. 66–90. Cf., by the same author, "Theophania" in *Rowohlts deutsche Enzyklopädie*, 15 (1956), pp. 22–27.

3 P. Tillich, *R. G. G.*, IV, p. 364.

4 M. Dibelius, *From Tradition to Gospel* (Scribner, 1935).

5 R. Bultmann, "New Testament and Mythology," *Kerygma and Myth*, ed. H. W. Bartsch (Macmillan, 1953), I, p. 10.

6 Cf. *L. Th. K.*, VII, p. 412 (Simon).

7 Otto, "Gesetz, Urbild und Mythos," p. 75.

8 Cassirer, *The Philosophy of Symbolic Forms* (Yale, 1955), II, p. 50. Cf. also Otto, "Gesetz, Urbild und Mythos," pp. 66–75.

[9] H. Fries, "Mythos und Offenbarung" in *Fragen der Theologie heute* (1957), p. 12.

[10] H. Schlier, "Das Neue Testament und der Mythos" in *Hochland*, 48 (February, 1956), p. 208.

[11] *Ibid.*

[12] E. Schick, "Formgeschichte und Synoptikerexegese," *Ntl. Abhdl.* (1940), 18, pp. 122–28.

[13] Schlier, *op. cit.*, p. 240.

[14] Schlier speaks of myths "which have largely deposited the mythical into patterns and have thus become sign language, which have ultimately at some time formalized themselves into formal categories of thinking and viewing for the comprehension and presentation of salvation events" (*op. cit.*, p. 204).

[15] Cf. Schlier, *op. cit.*, and R. Bultmann, "Zum Problem der Entmythologisierung," in *Kerygma und Mythos*, II.

[16] Cassirer, *Philosophy of Symbolic Forms*, II, p. 239.

[17] *Ibid.*, p. 239.

[18] This distinction is particularly stressed in H. Fries, *L. Th. K.*, III, p. 902: "While myth and mythological discourse are well adapted to each other, they are just as strongly differentiated. Mythological language may be separated from myth as religion. A mythological expression can be given for a matter placed in opposition to myth." Cf. also R. Schnackenburg, "Von der Formgeschichte zur Entmythologisierung" in *Kerygma und Mythos*, V, p. 93.

[19] G. Bornkamm, *Jesus of Nazareth* (Harper, 1960), p. 23.

[20] J. Bernhart, *Bibel und Mythos* (1954), p. 45.

[21] Cf. Schlier, *op. cit.*, p. 211. Thomas Aquinas expresses a similar opinion when he says: "In Scripture divine things are presented to us in the manner which is in common use among men." (Cf. Pius XII in *Divino Afflante Spiritu*, N. C. W. C. translation, p. 19, note 30.)

[22] Cf. Schlier, *op. cit.*, p. 212.

[23] Bernhart, *op. cit.*, p. 37.

Chapter Two (Part 2)

[1] Cf. Fries, *L. Th. K.*, III, p. 903: "The problem of demythologizing is really the old problem of the inevitable oneness and divergence between concept and presentation."

[2] E. v. Dobschütz, in *Von Auslegen des Neuen Testaments* (1927), observes that from 1720 till 1820 a biblical hermeneutic appeared almost every year, while in succeeding years only a few have been published.

[3] An easily accessible survey of the subject may be found in *L. Th. K.*,

III, pp. 898–904, in the article "Entmythologisierung" (Vögtle, Fries), and in the literature cited there. Cf. especially also Fries, *Mythos und Offenbarung*, pp. 11–43, and R. Marlé, *Bultmann et l'interprétation du Nouveau Testament* (1956).

4 In this sense, cf. also Schnackenburg, *Kerygma und Mythos*, V, p. 85.

5 Bultmann, "Zum Problem," p. 184.

6 Fries also calls attention to this in *L. Th. K.*, III, pp. 903ff.

7 Bultmann, *Kerygma und Mythos*, II, p. 187.

8 *Ibid.*, pp. 184, 186: "The customary talk about mythical concepts and representations as pictures and symbols suggests the question of what may be the meaning of these images and symbols. Surely an evident meaning must be expressed in them. Is this meaning to be formulated again in mythical language so that the meaning of the language would in turn have to be explained—and so on, ad infinitum? That is clearly absurd; actually, even the representatives of the symbol theory (to be specific) are accustomed to give explanations in unmythological language."

9 Cf. A. Vögtle, *L. Th. K.*, III, p. 899.

10 For this concept of the historical, cf. Vögtle, *L. Th. K.*, III, pp. 899ff.

11 Evangelical theologians are also opposed to using the existential interpretation as the only hermeneutic method, e.g., Gloege and Althaus. P. Althaus, in *Fact and Faith in the Kerygma of Today* (Muhlenberg Press, Philadelphia, 1959; also published under the title, *The So-called Kerygma and the Historical Jesus* [Oliver and Boyd, London, 1959]), says: "Under no circumstances is it legitimate to decree that what cannot be existentially interpreted, i.e., what cannot at the same time be interpreted as an utterance about my own existence, is 'mythological' " (p. 89).

12 Cf. the articles "Anthropologie" and especially "Angelologie" by K. Rahner in *L. Th. K.*, I, as also the discussion on Christology and the doctrine of the Trinity in K. Rahner generally (*Theological Investigations* [Helicon Press], I and II).

That this anthropological reduction does not involve a contentual limitation on man or on the "Christ for me" (therefore, not a narrowing of Christology to soteriology) need not be further emphasized; it can be sufficiently recognized in Rahner's theology as well as in the fact that his concept of existence differs from that of Bultmann; the two theologians can be compared *only* from a formal standpoint. Cf. also K. Barth's criticism of Bultmann in *Church Dogmatics*, III, 2, 47. Here a transcendental reduction is meant—one which considers man not as a subject for contemplation but as a condition for knowledge of the world. Cf. K. Rahner, "Current Problems in Christology," *Theological Investigations*, I, p. 249.

13 This contentual consequence of Bultmann's assessment also proceeds from hypotheses of philosophy and reform theology. Since we are not concerned with Bultmann's program, but with understanding biblical texts,

we may forego an explanation of these hypotheses. Cf. the Catholic argument with Bultmann in *Kerygma und Mythos,* V.

[14] R. Bultmann, "Christologie des Neuen Testaments" in *Glauben und Verstehen,* I, p. 265. This is also stressed today in profane history.

[15] E.g., S. Moser, "Der Begriff des Gesetzes in den Wissenschaften" in *Alpach-Jahrbuch* (1948), p. 38: "History is therefore in any case not a reproduction of actuality nor a photograph of a given past. Only tradition is given. But history is proposed to us as always providing significantly repetitive connection by sense and word with the past. One can interpret such a connection only by assuming a perspective, by utilizing categories, e.g., of such opposite natures as power and right, personality and mass, order and freedom." This holds true even more decidedly for reports that give testimony of religious experience (cf. chapter 1, pp. 23f.).

[16] A good introduction to the difficulty concerning the resurrection accounts is given by J. Schmid in his treatise, "Die Geschichtlichkeit der Auferstehung Jesu" in his commentary on Matthew in R. N. T., I, pp. 383–89.

[17] Bultmann, *Kerygma und Mythos,* II, p. 183.

[18] This distinction goes back to the important classification of myths as historical or philosophical, introduced into biblical science by archaeologist Christian Gottlob Heyne (1729–1812) and further developed by Eichhorn and Gabler. Historical myths are founded on historical events (such as the founding of a city or the deeds of great men of antiquity). Philosophical myths present explanations and speculations about gods, the world, etc. (theogony, cosmogony). Cf. C. Harlich and W. Sachs, *Der Ursprung des Mythosbegriffs in der modernen Bibelwissenschaft* (1952). We consider the distinction practical and fruitful. The "victory" over it by D. F. Strauss was not fortunate and as a consequence the work of Hartlich-Sachs (pp. 148–64) was not justified.

[19] J. P. Gabler, *Urgeschichte,* II; cited by Hartlich-Sachs, *Mythosbegriff,* p. 32.

[20] Cf. A. Vögtle, "Die Entmythologisierung des NT als Forderung einer zeitgemässen Theologie und Verkündigung," *Freiburger Dies Universitatis* (1955–56), IV, p. 38. "The principle of the analogical application of our notions about God and His activity makes it possible for theology really to emphasize the truthful character of our statements while at the same time looking at them with a critical eye."

Chapter Three (Part 1)

[1] Josef Schmid, *Synopse der drei ersten Evangelien* (1956).

[2] Mark has 661 verses, Matthew 1068, Luke 1149.

[3] J. Schmid, "Das Evangelium nach Matthäus," R. N. T., I, pp. 13–20;

A. Wikenhauser, *New Testament Introduction* (Herder and Herder, 1958), §26.

4 Cf. Schmid, "Matthäus," *R. N. T.*, I, p. 385: "Die Geschichtlichkeit der Auferstehung Jesu."

5 Cf. Schmid, "Matthäus," *R. N. T.*, I, pp. 17–20; Wikenhauser, *Introduction*, p. 250; G. Bornkamm, *Jesus of Nazareth*, Appendix I, p. 215f. The theory that Mark could not have been the youngest of the three authors rests on the following observations:

1. It would be hard to see why Mark took a passage from Matthew and Luke and omitted so many important passages (e.g., the childhood stories and the Sermon on the Mount).

2. In all parts which agree with Matthew and Luke, Mark gives the most original presentation: Linguistically, he is more clumsy; he is popular in his bent for irrelevancies; he is theologically more singular and pays less attention to community needs (e.g., he portrays the weaknesses of the apostles and disciples more dispassionately than Matthew and Luke).

6 This also can no longer be contested, since J. Schmid, *Matthäus und Lukas* (1930). Cf. Wikenhauser, *Introduction*, p. 210f.

7 Cf. for the following: R. Bultmann, *History of the Synoptic Tradition* (Harper, 1963); H. Conzelmann, *Theology of St. Luke* (Harper, 1961; Faber, 1960); C. H. Dodd, "The Fall of Jerusalem" in *Journal of Roman Studies*, 37 (1947), pp. 47–54; K. Grobel, *Formgeschichte und synoptische Quellenanalyse* (1937); P. Volz, *Jüdische Eschatologie* (1934), and the commentaries on Matthew and Luke by Schmid, Lagrange, Plummer, Hauck, Klostermann, Rengstorf.

8 Cf. Klostermann.

9 Thus there appears clearly in Luke what was already evident in Mark, viz., a gradual comprehension that the Parousia is delayed. Cf. Mark 13:10 and 13:7.

Chapter Three (Part 2)

1 Cf. P. Wendland, *Die urchristlichen Literaturformen* (1912), pp. 258–390.

2 Dibelius, *From Tradition to Gospel*, p. 287.

3 *Ibid.*, p. 4.

4 Wikenhauser gives a good, brief description and evaluation of form criticism in *Introduction*, pp. 253–77. Also, Schmid, "Matthäus," *R. N. T.*, I, pp. 5–13. For detailed statements, cf. E. Fascher, "Die Formgeschichtliche Methode" (Beiheft 2 of *Zeitschrift für neutestamentliche Wissenschaft*, 1924), for the Protestant viewpoint, and E. Schick, "Formgeschichte und Synoptikerexegese," *Neutestamentliche Abhandlung*, 18, for the Catholic view.

5 The critical work of K. L. Schmidt, *Der Rahmen der Geschichte Jesu* (1919), especially pp. 1–17, provides a good insight into this phenomenon.

6 The classification of the material and the designation of the individual types is according to Bultmann. It is considered correct by Catholic exegetes. Cf. Wikenhauser, *Introduction*, p. 274.

7 In Dibelius the classification of material is more moderate than in Bultmann, who tries to combine form criticism with historical criticism and hence declares wonder stories and legends to be conceptually "unhistorical."

8 The Passion story is, however, of a separate class insofar as it has been, from the beginning, a more coherent and complete account and because it belongs in the center of salvation preaching.

9 *History of the Synoptic Tradition*, p. 7.

10 This is proved above all by John 6:26f. and by the fact that John and Luke know of only one feeding.

11 Cf. for what follows, J. Jeremias, *The Parables of Jesus* (Scribner, 1955); Schmid, "Matthäus," *R. N. T.*, I, on this point, and W. Pesch, *Der Lohngedanke in der Lehre Jesu* (1955).

12 That Matthew really views the parable in the light of these words and does not, as is sometimes asserted, try to place the parable simply into formal connection with what preceded it as shown by οὕτως. Thus he included verse 16 as well as having the parable conform to the equivalent sentence in 19:30; Matthew takes the parable as confirmation and illustration of the words: Many who are first will be last; but the last will be first (19:30).

13 Bultmann, *History of the Synoptic Tradition*, p. 177.

14 Cf. J. Jeremias, *Gleichnisse*, p. 23.

15 Schmid, "Matthäus," *R. N. T.*, I, p. 286.

16 Pesch, *Lohngedanke*, pp. 11f.

17 The definitive work on this method is W. Marxsen, *Der Evangelist Markus. Studium zur Redaktionsgeschichte des Evangeliums* (1956): cf. especially the introduction, pp. 7–16.

18 *Ibid.*, p. 12.

19 J. Dupont, *Les Béatitudes* (1958), I, p. 204. Cf. R. Schnackenburg, "Jesusforschung und Christusglaube" in *Catholica*, 13 (1959), pp. 1, 1–16.

20 "Matthäus," *R. N. T.*, I, p. 8.

21 Bornkamm, *Jesus of Nazareth*, p. 17.

22 "Matthäus," *R. N. T.*, I, p. 6; Wikenhauser, *Introduction*, pp. 292–93.

23 Conzelmann and Marxsen even say that Luke intended to write a "life" of Jesus but did not succeed.

24 Cf. "Matthäus," *R. N. T.*, I, p. 101.

25 Cf. *ibid.*, p. 11.

26 *Idem.*

27 Cf. Bornkamm, *Jesus of Nazareth*, pp. 23 and 13–26.

28 The following citations are taken from narratives about the life of Jesus that are still being printed. The names of the authors are not important. We do not mention them lest our practical purpose be mistaken for polemics.

29 Cf. Bornkamm, *Jesus of Nazareth*.

Chapter Three (Part 3)

1 H. Kahlefeld, "Die Wiederentdeckung des Kultes" in *Die Welt in neuer Sicht* (1959), p. 68; cf. especially also: H. Kahlefeld, *Die Epiphanie des Erlösers im Johannesevangelium* (Rothenfelser Reihe).

2 Thus, e.g., 2:19; 4:44; 12:25; 13:16, 20; 15:20. The miracle accounts also stem from a written prototype. Cf. R. Bultmann, *Theology of the New Testament* (Scribner, 1955), II.

3 Hoyskyns-Davey, *Riddle of the New Testament* (Faber and Faber, 1936), pp. 185–86.

4 A. Wikenhauser, "Evangelium nach Johannes," *R. N. T.* (1957), p. 23.

5 Cf. R. Bultmann, *Das Evangelium des Johannes* (1952), p. 2.

6 H. Schürmann, *Aufbau und Struktur*, p. 33.

7 Wikenhauser, *Introduction*, p. 558.

8 Cf. chapters 4 and 5.

9 The final-historical, the contemporary-historical and the tradition-historical forms of interpretation (cf. Wikenhauser, *Introduction*, pp. 559–62) could well find a fitting relationship only in the existential-eschatological interpretation here indicated.

10 Cf. Wikenhauser, *Introduction*, pp. 547–53.

11 *Ibid.*, pp. 562 f.

Chapter Three (Part 4)

1 Cf. M. Dibelius, "Style-Critique of Acts" in *Studies in the Acts of the Apostles* (Scribner, 1956).

2 *Ibid.*, E. Haenchen, *Die Apostelgeschichte* (1956), p. 86.

3 Dibelius, *op. cit.*

4 Wikenhauser, *Introduction*, pp. 327 f.

5 For this theory, cf. especially the already mentioned treatise of Dibel-

ius and the commentaries of O. Bauernfeind (1939) and Haenchen (1956).

⁶ Cf. the introductions of the commentaries by Wikenhauser and Haenchen; also Dibelius, *Studies.*

⁷ This is distinctly in evidence in the story of Cornelius (Acts 10:1–11). Cf. Dibelius, "The Conversion of Cornelius" in *Studies.*

⁸ The intention—to interpret—is apparent in the repetition of the motif, "It is God who is doing this," in verses 6 and 7, because the motif runs through the entire Acts of the Apostles. Cf. on the Cornelius story, E. Haenchen, *Apostelgeschichte*, p. 100. Explanation of the meaning of the story, 16:6ff., is clear not only when Luke, as writer, simply manipulates his itinerary, shortening and interpreting (cf. Haenchen, *ibid.*, pp. 93, 429f.), but also when he speaks as a companion of St. Paul and therefore as an eyewitness. On this problem, cf. Wikenhauser, *Die Apostelgeschichte* (1951), and *Introduction*, p. 328.

⁹ Cf. A. Wikenhauser, "Die Apostelgeschichte und ihr Geschichtswert," *Ntl. Abhdl.* (1921), VIII, pp. 3–5.

¹⁰ Our presentation is based on the following: G. Fohrer, *Elia* (1957); O. Eissfeldt, *Einleitung in das AT* (1956); C. Gordon, *Geschichtliche Grundlagen des Alten Testaments* (1956); J. Steinmann, "La geste d'Elie dans l'Ancien Testament" in *Elie le prophete, Sammelband der Etude Carmelitaines* (1956), I; G. v. Rad, *Old Testament Theology* (Harper, 1962); A. Jeremias, *Das Alte Testament im Licht des alten Orients;* R. Kittel, *Geschichte des Volkes Israel.*

¹¹ For Elias in the New Testament, cf. *L. Th. K.*, s. v. Elias (J. Schmid) and *Th. W.*, II, pp. 930 f. (J. Jeremias).

¹² Cf. also Sir. 48:10, Radermacher and Charles, "Ethiopic Text," 89:52; 93:8, and Josephus, *Antiquitates*, 9:28.

¹³ With v. Rad, *Theology*, pp. 334 f. we assume that the books of Kings are the work of the same deuteronomist who wrote the Book of Judges. Cf. also Eissfeldt, *Einleitung*, p. 342.

¹⁴ Cf. Fohrer, *Elia*, pp. 45f., and R. Kittel, *Bücher der Könige*, pp. 159–61.

¹⁵ It has often been stressed that the report in 3 Kings 18:1 ("in the third year the word of the Lord went out to Elias . . .") does not contradict this estimate of time (duration of drought, one year). Cf. G. Fohrer, *Elia*, p. 57. Israelitic reckoning of time can understand, e.g., the fourteenth month as already the "third year," since the adjacent months of the previous and the following years are counted as full years.

¹⁶ Cf. Fohrer, *Elia*, p. 58, and C. Gordon, *Grundlagen*, pp. 295 ff., on the combining of historical notes and epic as proof of the genuineness and antiquity of ancient Oriental narratives.

¹⁷ Cf. for what follows, Fohrer, *Elia*, pp. 59 and 70 f.

[18] Gordon, *Grundlagen*, p. 198; Fohrer, *Elia*, pp. 72–74.

[19] Fohrer, *Elia*, p. 72.

[20] Cf. Eissfeldt, *Einleitung*, p. 341; v. Rad, *Old Testament Theology* (Harper, 1962), pp. 334–40.

[21] Cf. Fohrer, *Elia*, pp. 65f. and 76.

[22] *Ibid.*, p. 80.

[23] Grollenberg, *Atlas of the Bible* (Nelson, 1956).

[24] E. Herzfeld, *Mythos und Geschichte*, cited by M. Buber, *Moses: The Revelation* (Harper, 1958), p. 14.

[25] Buber, *Moses: The Revelation*, p. 19.

[26] R. G. G., V, 49. The history of types is the form criticism of the Old Testament. It examines the literary types in the Old Testament and their preliterary tradition-forms. The method of form criticism derives from Gunkel's beginning.

[27] In general, the Moses tradition strongly affected the deuteronomic historical work. Cf. v. Rad, *Old Testament Theology*, p. 339.

[28] Cf. Fohrer, *Elia*, p. 48.

Chapter Four (Part 1)

[1] R. Guardini, *Das Bild von Jesus dem Christus* (1953), p. 44.

[2] Cf. for this, *Kyrios und Pneuma* (1961).

[3] The Greek concept εὐαγγέλιον lacks this notion entirely. It is unprofitable for the understanding of Paul. Cf. Friedrich, *Th. W.*, II, pp. 705 ff.; R. Asting, *Die Verkundigung des Wortes im Urchristentum* (1939), p. 308; for the Old Testament understanding of "good news," cf. Isa. 40:9; 41:27; 52:7, and rabbinic sources in Billerbeck, III, pp. 4–11. For the entire field, also E. Molland, *Das paulinische εὐαγγέλιον* (1934).

[4] "Zeit und Raum im Denken des Urchristentums," in *Journal of Biblical Literature* (1922), pp. 212 ff.

[5] *Das hebräische Denken im Vergleich mit dem Griechischen* (1956), pp. 104–33.

[6] Cf. T. Boman, *Hebräisches Denken*, pp. 120 ff.

[7] *Ibid.*, p. 125.

[8] *Ibid.*, p. 128.

Chapter Four (Part 2)

[1] W. Schmithals, *Die Gnosis in Korinth*, p. 198.

[2] On translating ἀρέσκειν as "serving," cf. Foerster, *Th. W.*, I, p. 455.

[3] Cf. J. Weiss in his *Kommentar zum I. Korintherbrief*, p. 197.

Chapter Five

1 Very good basic notions about these questions may be found in K. Rahner, "Current Problems in Christology" in *Theological Investigations,* I, pp. 150–57.

2 Brief, more easily accessible presentations are: K. L. Schmidt, the article "βασιλεία" in *Th. W.,* I, pp. 579–95; J. Schmid, "Reich Gottes," *R. N. T.,* II, pp. 31–39; Bornkamm, *Jesus of Nazareth,* pp. 64–95; R. Schnackenburg, *Gottes Herrschaft und Reich* (1958).

3 Naturally, no complete interpretation of the beatitudes is given here. That is the task of commentaries on the New Testament. We restrict our comments strictly to the points of this passage which seem to be particularly suitable for an initiation.

4 That is today the opinion of nearly all exegetes. Cf. J. Schmid, "Lukas," *R. N. T.,* II, pp. 132 f., "Matthäus," *R. N. T.,* I, pp. 75 f. and J. Dupont, *Les Béatitudes* (1954), pp. 79 ff. All authors, pro and con, are given there.

5 In the more recent literature, T. Soiron, in *Die Bergpredigt Jesu* (1941), pp. 142 f., seems to be the only author who does not recognize this principle and, e.g., considers the addition, "in spirit," in Matthew (5:3) to be the original.

6 Cf. Billerbeck, *Kommentar zum Neuen Testament aus Talmud und Midrasch,* II, p. 494.

7 Cf. H. Windisch, *Meaning of the Sermon on the Mount* (Westminster, Philadelphia, 1951), p. 175.

8 Cf. exposition in J. Schmid, "Das theologische Problem der Bergpredigt," *R. N. T.,* I, pp. 154–60, and "Jesu Stellung zum Reichtum," *R. N. T.,* II, pp. 194–96.

9 Schmid, "Markus," *R. N. T.,* II, p. 32.

10 Cf. Billerbeck, *Kommentar zum Neuen Testament,* I, pp. 172–84.

11 Schmid, "Das Theologische," *R. N. T.,* I, p. 156.

12 Cf. Windisch, *Sermon on the Mount,* p. 199.

13 This is not meant ethically (as the self-deifying of man on the one hand and humility before God on the other), but in view of the premoral "psychological" potentialities of human existence.

14 Cf. Schmid, "Matthäus," *R. N. T.,* I, p. 75f.; Soiron, *Bergpredigt,* p. 145.

15 Most Church Fathers explain the "poor in spirit" as the "humble," esp. Augustine (*De sermone Domini in monte,* I, 1, 4).

16 Cf. Schmid, "Matthäus," *R. N. T.,* I, p. 79.

17 This is all too often forgotten with respect to the interpretation of the

differences between Luke and Matthew, e.g., also by M. Dibelius, "Die Bergpredigt" in: *Botschaft und Geschichte*, I, pp. 120 and 148; cf. p. 143, too.

[18] This follows also from the emphatic expressions αὐτῶν and αὐτοί. In Greek, they are superfluous unless they are meant to stress. The blow is naturally directed against the Pharisees and Scribes (Matt. 5:20) and the hypocrites (Matt. 6:20); cf. in this sense, also, Windisch, *Sermon on the Mount*, pp. 26–27, and K. Bornhäuser, *Die Bergpredigt* (1923), p. 25.

[19] "Nulle question de piété ou de vertu chez les pauvres, de culpabilité ou d'oppression chez les riches," says J. Dupont, *Les Béatitudes*, p. 214, and interprets the beatitudes well, even if wrongly, as prophetic "principe de la compensation" (*Les Béatitudes*, pp. 213–15), like the account (Luke 16:25f.) about the rich man and Lazarus.

[20] Anyone interested will easily find appropriate literature. I call attention especially to the cited works by Dibelius and Schmid and to the passages in R. Guardini: *The Lord* (Regnery, 1954).

[21] With this key, one could now easily approach further texts, e.g., the parables about the kingdom of God. Dibelius, too, calls the "kingdom of God" the key which can solve all problems concerning the Sermon on the Mount (*Bergpredgt*, p. 145).

[22] Bornkamm, *Jesus of Nazareth*, p. 77.

Conclusion

[1] For confirmation and discussion of this theology of tradition, cf. P. Neuenzeit, *Das Herrenmahl* (1960).

[2] Denzinger, 1787; cf. 783.

[3] Concerning the inspiration of Scripture, cf. *Quaestiones Disputatae*, I (1958).

[4] K. Rahner, *Inspiration in the Bible* (Herder and Herder, 1961), pp. 12–38.

[5] The figures in parentheses indicate page numbers in Rahner's *Inspiration*.

[6] Cf. G. Söhngen, "Überliefenung und apostolische Verkündigung" in *Einheit in der Theologie*, pp. 203–324, especially 318 ff.

[7] The example of the letters of St. Ignatius, which are so close to Scripture, shows clearly that a writing has to be not only an essentially accurate expression of the life of the early Church but the fruition of that life, i.e., it must belong to the first generation, thereby being apostolic.